AIN'T
NO
MAKIN'
IT

About the Book and Author

"I ain't goin' to college. Who wants to go to college? I'd just end up gettin' a shitty job anyway." So says Freddie Piniella, an intelligent boy from Clarendon Heights, a low-income housing development in a northeastern city. How is it that in contemporary America, a nation of dreams and opportunities, a boy of eleven can feel trapped in a position of inherited poverty?

Ain't No Makin' It is the story of how American life looks from the bottom, of anticipated immobility rather than mobility. In telling this story, author Jay MacLeod addresses one of the most important questions in modern social theory and policy: How is social class inequality reproduced from one generation to the next?

MacLeod draws upon his experience living in a low-income housing project where he gained the trust of its young male inhabitants. He records the vivid accounts of their friendships and families, their work and school experiences—all in an effort to understand the forces that either shape their aspirations or leave them with no aspirations at all.

The two neighborhood gangs—one called the Hallway Hangers and the other the Brothers—are very different. The low ambitions of one group ensure that they will remain at the bottom of the social structure. The other boys, however, take the achievement ideology to heart. This divergence is especially surprising because the Brothers, who aspire to middle-class respectability, are composed almost exclusively of black members while the discouraged Hangers are predominantly white. In comparing the characteristics of the two groups, the author develops a powerful argument that demonstrates how the structure of class inequality is reproduced from one generation to the next.

Jay MacLeod examines the main currents of thought in social reproduction theory, adding to that literature a new analysis and offering policy recommendations. Perhaps the greatest virtue of *Ain't No Makin' It*, however, is the ethnography. MacLeod's book represents the first comprehensive insider's account that demonstrates the influence of work, family, and school on lower-class youths. The boys' statements resonate with an honesty seldom captured by scholarly studies. After meeting Frankie, Craig, and the other youths from Clarendon Heights, the reader will come away with a clearer understanding of what it means to be poor and without hope in America.

Jay MacLeod is a Rhodes scholar studying theology at Pembroke College, Oxford University.

*For Preston Ela,
1907–1983,
and Norm Charpentier,
1941–1987*

AIN'T
NO
MAKIN'
IT

Leveled Aspirations
in a Low-Income Neighborhood

JAY MACLEOD

Westview Press / Boulder, Colorado

Published in 1987 in the United States of America by Westview Press, Inc.; Frederick A. Praeger, Publisher; 5500 Central Avenue, Boulder, Colorado 80301

Library of Congress Cataloging-in-Publication Data
MacLeod, Jay.
  Ain't no makin' it.
  Bibliography: p.
  Includes index.
  1. Urban poor—United States—Case studies.
2. Socially handicapped youth—United States—Case
studies.   3. Social mobility—United States—Case
studies.   4. Equality—United States—Case studies.
I. Title.
HV4045.M33   1987   305.5'69'0973   87-2215
ISBN 0-8133-7164-3
ISBN 0-8133-7163-5 (pbk.)

Printed and bound in the United States of America

 The paper used in this publication meets the requirements of the American National Standard for Permanence of Paper for Printed Library Materials Z39.48-1984.

10   9   8   7   6   5   4   3

CONTENTS

ACKNOWLEDGMENTS

This book has not been a solo undertaking. There is hardly an idea contained herein that is not the product of friendly debate with Katherine McClelland, my thesis adviser. Her commitment to this project has been unwavering, and her sensitivity as teacher made every minute spent with her valuable time indeed. Other people have made major contributions to the book as well. Stephen Cornell's advice on fieldwork, theory, and the appendix has been invaluable. Without the help and encouragement of John Womack the book never would have been submitted for publication. Thanks also are due to Paul Willis for his example and for reading and commenting on a draft of the book. Peter Bearman, Debra Satz, Michael Quirk, Doug Taylor, Rob Malley, and John Dickie also read the manuscript and provided useful advice and suggestions. I appreciate David Karen's thorough reviews of the book, especially his penetrating comments on the theoretical sections.

Dan Porterfield took time out from Shakespeare, Eliot, Dickens, and his own work to pore over the book and bring his pen to bear on nearly every page in a desperate attempt to minimize my "butchering of the English language, like all sociologists." He and Sally Asher clarified my thinking on a number of issues and kept me laughing during the fourteen months of revision, much as Jane Rosegrant, Greg Johnson, and John Stern did during the writing of the initial draft. Thanks also to the following for their boundless support and help transcribing interviews, editing, and typing: Valerie Barton, David Finegold, Karen Herrling, Betsy Kirkland, Kate Porterfield, Shelly Taylor, Hugh Thompson, Tina Tricarichi, and Sue Vivian. I am grateful to Dr. John Platt and Bishop Kallistos Ware of Pembroke College, Oxford, for letting my academic work slide as I strove to finish the book. Dean Birkenkamp and his colleagues at Westview Press have been helpful with the manuscript and patient with my complete ignorance of the publishing process. Finally, thanks to the residents of Clarendon Heights, especially the Brothers and Hallway Hangers; they made the study possible.

Jay MacLeod

1

SOCIAL IMMOBILITY IN THE LAND OF OPPORTUNITY

"Any child can grow up to be president." So maintains the dominant ideology in the United States. This perspective characterizes American society as an open one in which barriers to success are mainly personal rather than social. In this meritocratic view, education ensures equality of opportunity for all individuals, and economic inequalities result from differences in natural qualities and in one's motivation and will to work. Success is based on achievement rather than ascription. Individuals do not inherit their social status—they attain it on their own. Because schooling mitigates gender, class, and racial barriers to success, the ladder of social mobility is there for all to climb. A favorite Hollywood theme, the rags-to-riches story resonates in the psyche of the American people. We never tire of hearing about Andrew Carnegie, for his experience validates much that we hold dear about America, the land of opportunity. Horatio Alger's accounts of the spectacular mobility achieved by men of humble origins through their own unremitting efforts occupy a treasured place in our national folklore. The American Dream is held out as a genuine prospect for anyone with the drive to achieve it.

"I ain't goin' to college. Who wants to go to college? I'd just end up gettin' a shitty job anyway." So says Freddie Piniella,[1] an intelligent eleven-year-old boy from Clarendon Heights, a low-income housing development in a northeastern city. This statement, pronounced with certitude and feeling, completely contradicts our achievement ideology. Freddie is pessimistic about his prospects for social mobility and disputes schooling's capacity to "deliver the goods." Such a view offends our sensibilities and seems a rationalization. But Freddie has a point. What of Carnegie's grammar school classmates, the great bulk of whom no doubt were left behind to occupy positions in the class structure not much different from those held by their parents? What about the static, nearly permanent element in the working class, whose members consider

1

the chances for mobility remote and thus despair of all hope? These people are shunned, hidden, forgotten—and for good reason—because just as the self-made man is a testament to certain American ideals, so the very existence of an "underclass" in American society is a living contradiction to those ideals.

Utter hopelessness is the most striking aspect of Freddie's outlook. Erik H. Erikson writes that hope is the basic ingredient of all vitality;[2] stripped of hope, there is little left to lose. How is it that in contemporary America a boy of eleven can feel bereft of a future worth embracing? This is not what the United States is supposed to be. The United States is the nation of hopes and dreams and opportunity. As Ronald Reagan remarked in his 1985 State of the Union Address, citing the accomplishments of a young Vietnamese immigrant, "Anything is possible in America if we have the faith, the will, and the heart."[3] But to Freddie Piniella and many other Clarendon Heights young people who grow up in households where their parents and older siblings are unemployed, undereducated, or imprisoned, Reagan's words ring hollow. For them the American Dream, far from being a genuine prospect, is not even a dream. It is a hallucination.

I first met Freddie Piniella in the summer of 1981 when as a student at a nearby university I worked as a counselor in a youth enrichment program in Clarendon Heights. For ten weeks I lived a few blocks from the housing project and worked intensively with nine boys, aged eleven to thirteen. While engaging them in recreational and educational activities, I was surprised by the modesty of their aspirations. The world of middle-class work was entirely alien to them; they spoke about employment in construction, factories, the armed forces, or, predictably, professional athletics. In an ostensibly open society, they were a group of boys whose occupational aspirations did not even cut across class lines.

The depressed aspirations of Clarendon Heights youngsters are very telling. There is a strong relationship between aspirations and occupational outcomes; if individuals do not even aspire to middle-class jobs, then they are unlikely to achieve them. In effect, such individuals disqualify themselves from attaining the American definition of success—the achievement of a prestigious, highly remunerative occupation—before embarking on the quest. The existence of this disqualifying mechanism suggests that people of working-class origin encounter significant obstacles to social mobility.

Several decades of quantitative sociological research have demonstrated that the social class into which one is born has a major influence on where one will end up. Although mobility between classes does take place, the overall structure of class relations from one generation to the next remains largely unchanged. Quantitative mobility studies can establish the extent of this pattern of social reproduction, but they have difficulty demonstrating *how* the pattern comes into being or is sustained. This is an issue of immense complexity and difficulty, and an enduring one in the field of sociology, but it seems to me that we can learn a great deal about this pattern from youngsters like Freddie. Leveled aspirations are a powerful mechanism by which class inequality is reproduced from one generation to the next.

In many ways, the world of these youths is defined by the physical boundaries of the housing development. Like most old "projects" (as low-income public housing developments are known to their residents), Clarendon Heights is architecturally a world unto itself. Although smaller and less dilapidated than many urban housing developments, its plain brick buildings testify that cost efficiency was the overriding consideration in its construction. Walking through Clarendon Heights for the first time in spring 1981, I was struck by the contrast between the project and the sprawling lawns and elegant buildings of the college quadrangle I had left only a half hour earlier. It is little more than a mile from the university to Clarendon Heights, but the transformation that occurs in the course of this mile is startling. Large oak trees, green yards, and impressive family homes give way to ramshackle tenement buildings and closely packed, triple decker, wooden frame dwellings; the ice cream parlors and bookshops are replaced gradually by pawn shops and liquor stores; book-toting students and businesspeople with briefcases in hand are supplanted by tired, middle-aged women lugging bags of laundry and clusters of elderly, immigrant men loitering on street corners. Even within this typical working-class neighborhood, however, Clarendon Heights is physically and socially set off by itself.

Bordered on two sides by residential neighborhoods and on the other two by a shoe factory, a junkyard, and a large plot of industrial wasteland, Clarendon Heights consists of six large, squat, three-story buildings and one high rise. The architecture is imposing and severe; only the five chimneys atop each building break the harsh symmetry of the structures. Three mornings a week the incinerators in each of the twenty-two entryways burn, spewing thick smoke and ash out of the chimneys. The smoke envelops the stained brick buildings, ash falling on the black macadam that serves as communal front yard, backyard, and courtyard for the project's two hundred families. (A subsequent landscaping effort did result in the planting of grass and trees, the erection of little wire fences to protect the greenery, and the appearance of flower boxes lodged under windows.) Before its renovation, a condemned high-rise building, its doors and windows boarded up, invested the entire project with an ambience of decay and neglect.

Even at its worst, however, Clarendon Heights is not a bad place to live compared to many inner-city housing developments. This relatively small development, set in a working-class neighborhood, should not be confused with the massive, scarred projects of the nation's largest cities. Nevertheless, the social fabric of Clarendon Heights is marked by problems generally associated with low-income housing developments. Approximately 65 percent of Clarendon Heights' residents are white,

25 percent are black, and 10 percent are other minorities. Few adult males live in Clarendon Heights; approximately 85 percent of the families are headed by single women. Although no precise figures are available, it is acknowledged by the City Housing Authority that significant numbers of tenants are second- and third-generation public housing residents. Social workers estimate that almost 70 percent of the families are on some additional form of public assistance. Overcrowding, unemployment, alcoholism, drug abuse, crime, and racism plague the community.

Clarendon Heights is well known to the city's inhabitants. The site of two riots in the early and mid-1970s and most recently of a gunfight in which two policemen and their assailant were shot, the project is considered a no-go area by most of the public. Even residents of the surrounding Italian and Portuguese neighborhoods tend to shun Clarendon Heights. Social workers consider it a notoriously difficult place in which to work; state and county prison officials are familiar with the project as a source for a disproportionately high number of their inmates. Indeed, considering its relatively small size, Clarendon Heights has acquired quite a reputation.

This notoriety is not entirely deserved, but it is keenly felt by the project's tenants. Subject to the stigma associated with residence in public housing, they are particularly sensitive to the image Clarendon Heights conjures up in the minds of outsiders. When Clarendon Heights residents are asked for their address at a bank, store, or office, their reply often is met with a quick glance of curiosity, pity, superiority, suspicion, or fear. In an achievement-oriented society, residence in public housing is often an emblem of failure, shame, and humiliation.

To many outsiders, Freddie's depressed aspirations are either an indication of laziness or a realistic assessment of his natural assets and attributes (or both). A more sympathetic or penetrating observer would cite the insularity of the project and the limited horizons of its youth as reasons for Freddie's outlook. But to an insider, one who has come of age in Clarendon Heights or at least has access to the thoughts and feelings of those who have, the situation is not so simple. This book, very simply, attempts to understand the aspirations of older boys[4] from Clarendon Heights. It introduces the reader not to modern-day Andrew Carnegies, but to Freddie Piniella's role models, teenage boys from the neighborhood whose stories are less often told and much less heard. These boys provide a poignant account of what the social structure looks like from the bottom. If we let them speak to us and strive to understand them on their own terms, the story that we hear is deeply disturbing. We shall come to see Freddie's outlook not as incomprehensible self-defeatism, but as a perceptive response to the plight in which he finds himself.

Although the general picture that emerges is dreary, its texture is richly varied. The male teenage world of Clarendon Heights is populated by two divergent peer groups. The first group, dubbed the Hallway

Hangers because of the group's propensity for "hanging" in a particular hallway in the project, consists predominantly of white boys. Their characteristics and attitudes stand in marked contrast to the second group, which is composed almost exclusively of black youths who call themselves the Brothers. Surprisingly, the Brothers speak with relative optimism about their futures, while the Hallway Hangers are despondent about their prospects for social mobility. This dichotomy is illustrated graphically by the responses of Juan (a Brother) and Frankie (a Hallway Hanger) to my query about what their lives will be like in twenty years.

JUAN: I'll have a regular house, y'know, with a yard and everything. I'll have a steady job, a good job. I'll be living the good life, the easy life.

FRANKIE: I don't fucking know. Twenty years. I may be fucking dead. I live a day at a time. I'll probably be in the fucking pen.

Because aspirations mediate what an individual desires and what society can offer, the hopes of these boys are linked inextricably with their assessment of the opportunities available to them. The Hallway Hangers, for example, seem to view equality of opportunity in much the same light as did R. H. Tawney in 1938—that is, as "a heartless jest . . . the impertinent courtesy of an invitation offered to unwelcome guests, in the certainty that circumstances will prevent them from accepting it."[5]

SLICK: Out here, there's not the opportunity to make money. That's how you get into stealin' and all that shit. . . . All right, to get a job, first of all, this is a handicap, out here. If you say you're from the projects or anywhere in this area, that can hurt you. Right off the bat: reputation.

The Brothers, in contrast, consistently affirm the actuality of equality of opportunity.

DEREK: If you put your mind to it, if you want to make a future for yourself, there's no reason why you can't. It's a question of attitude.

The optimism of the Brothers and the pessimism of the Hallway Hangers stem, at least in part, from their different appraisals of the openness of American society. Slick's belief that "the younger kids have nothing to hope for" obviously influences his own aspirations. Conversely, some of the Brothers aspire to middle-class occupations partly because they do not see significant societal barriers to upward mobility.

To understand the occupational hopes of the Brothers and the Hallway Hangers—and the divergence between them—we must first gauge the forces against which lower-class individuals must struggle in their pursuit of economic and social advancement. Toward this end, the next chapter considers social reproduction theory, which is a tradition of sociological literature that strives to illuminate the specific mechanisms and processes that contribute to the intergenerational transmission of social inequality. Put simply, reproduction theory attempts to show how and why the United States can be depicted more accurately as the place where "the rich get richer and the poor stay poor" than "the land of opportunity." Social reproduction theory identifies the barriers to social mobility, barriers that constrain without completely blocking lower- and working-class individuals' efforts to break into the upper reaches of the class structure.

Once we have familiarized ourselves with this academic viewpoint, we shall switch perspectives abruptly to the streets in order to consider how the Brothers and Hallway Hangers understand their social circumstances. How do they view their prospects for social upgrading, and how does this estimation affect their aspirations? What unseen social and economic forces daily influence these boys? How do they make sense of and act upon the complex and often contradictory messages emanating from their family, peer group, workplace, and school? In examining this terrain, we shall touch upon many theoretical issues: the role of education in the perpetuation of class inequality; the influence of ethnicity on the meanings individuals attach to their experiences; the relationship between structural determinants (e.g., the local job market) and cultural practices (e.g., rejection of school); the degree of autonomy individuals exercise at the cultural level; the destabilizing roles of nonconformity and resistance in the process of social reproduction; the functions of ideology; and the subtlety of various modes of class domination. Our emphasis throughout, however, will be on the occupational aspirations of the Brothers and the Hallway Hangers, how these aspirations are formed, and their significance for the reproduction of social inequality.

Such an agenda can be addressed most thoroughly by a methodology of intensive participant observation. To do justice to the complexity and richness of the human side of the story requires a level of understanding and distinction that questionnaire surveys are incapable of providing. The field methods employed in this study are not unlike those of most sociological ethnographies in which the researcher attempts to understand a culture from the insider's point of view. But my methods are unique in some ways because of my previous involvement with the community (see the appendix for a detailed account of the fieldwork). Having worked and lived in the neighborhood for three summers directing a youth program, I was already close friends with many Clarendon Heights residents prior to the beginning of my research. Without this entree into the community, as a college student from rural New Hampshire I would have faced massive problems gaining the trust and respect of my subjects. As it was, acceptance was slow, piecemeal, and fraught with complications. But with the hurdle of entree partially overcome, I was able to gather a large amount of sensitive data, most of it during a twelve-month period of participant observation in 1983 when I lived in the community.

This study concentrates not on Freddie Piniella and the other boys in the youth enrichment program, but on their high-school-age role models whose aspirations are better developed. Only Mike, my oldest charge in the first summer of the youth program, later became a member of the Brothers and thus is included in the study. Nevertheless, my roles as community worker and researcher were never entirely distinct, and the dependence of the latter on the former is clearly illustrated by my first "interview," which was undertaken, strangely enough, not in Clarendon Heights but in my college dormitory.

One evening in late February 1983, Mike, with whom I had maintained a steady relationship since his graduation from the youth program a year and a half earlier, phoned my room. I had been down at the Heights that day and had stopped by his apartment, but Mike had not been home. His mother and grandmother had lamented to me about his poor performance in school, and I had offered to help in any way I could. On the telephone Mike gradually turned the conversation to school. He said he was doing fairly well, but he had failed English. I said I would help him prepare for tests, at which point he mentioned a report on Albert Einstein due in a few days. He had not had much luck researching the topic and hoped I could help. We arranged to meet the next day near the university. After reading an *Encyclopedia Britannica* article on Einstein and photocopying it, we got something to eat in the college dining hall and went up to my room. While I did some reading, Mike worked on his paper at my desk.

Before I knew what was happening my first unstructured interview was under way. Mike suddenly began talking about his future, about, in fact, his occupational and educational goals and expectations. The ensuing conversation lasted an hour and a half and touched on many subjects, but in that time Mike described the high school's curricula, spoke of his own experience in the Occupational Education Program, expressed his desire to work in the computer field, and graphically communicated the role of the achievement ideology in the school. His computer teacher, Mike mentioned, assured the class that a well-paid programming job could be secured easily upon graduation. When I asked Mike about all the unemployed teenagers in Clarendon Heights, his response betrayed his own internalization of the achievement ideology: "Well, you can't just be fooling around all the time. Those guys, they was always fucking off in class. You gotta want it. But if you work hard, really put your mind to it, you can do it."

Thus began my formal research, which was to involve me deeply with the community during the next year. The data focus on the fifteen teenage boys who constitute the Brothers and the Hallway Hangers. Much time was spent with these peer groups during all four seasons and at all hours of the day and night. The simultaneous study of both groups was a difficult undertaking because of the animosity that exists between them and the consequent aspersions that often were cast upon me by members of one group when I associated with the other. In the end, however, the effort was well worth the trouble, as the comparative material that I managed to gather is of great importance to the study.

Field notes, a record of informal discussions, and transcripts of taped, semistructured interviews with each boy (individually and, on occasion, in groups) make up the main body of the data. In the few instances where interviews were not taped, the dialogue is not verbatim. Rather, it is my best rendering of what was said, which was recorded as soon after the discussion as possible. To round out the research, discussions with some of the boys' parents and interviews with teachers, guidance counselors, and career counselors also were undertaken.

This ethnographic account provides an intricate picture of how poverty circumscribes the horizons of young people and how, at the societal level, the class structure is reproduced. Before turning to the boys of Clarendon Heights and their families, friends, workplaces, and school, however, we must review the work of a number of social theorists who have tackled the problem of social reproduction. If we are to understand what we see on the streets, if we are to make sense of the forces that act upon these boys, and if we are to generalize from their experiences in any meaningful way, we must situate our work in a broader theoretical framework by letting theory inform our data and, ultimately, by allowing our data to inform theory.

NOTES

1. All names of neighborhoods and individuals have been changed to protect the anonymity of the study's subjects.

2. Erik H. Erikson, *Gandhi's Truth* (New York: Norton, 1969), p. 154.

3. Ronald Reagan, "State of the Union Address to Congress," *New York Times*, 6 February 1985, p. 17.

4. I am reluctant to contribute to the imbalance between studies of boys and girls, but the exigencies of participant observation made it difficult for a person with my previous involvement in the neighborhood to consider females.

5. R. H. Tawney, *Equality* (London: Allen and Unwin, 1938), p. 110.

2

SOCIAL REPRODUCTION IN THEORETICAL PERSPECTIVE

Why is there a strong tendency for working-class children to end up in working-class jobs? It is this question, a perennial one in the field of sociology, that social reproduction theorists have addressed during the past fifteen years. Although reproduction theorists draw on the work of Max Weber and Emile Durkheim, their greatest intellectual debt is to Karl Marx. Marx writes in *Capital*, "The capitalist process of production . . . produces not only commodities, not only surplus-value, but it also produces and reproduces the capitalist-relation itself; on the one hand the capitalist, on the other the wage-labourer."[1] In the most general terms, social reproduction theory explains how societal institutions perpetuate (or reproduce) the social relationships and attitudes needed to sustain the existing relations of production in a capitalist society. Reproduction theorists attempt to unravel how and why individuals of modest social origins are at a decided disadvantage in the struggle for lucrative and prestigious jobs. These theorists share a common interest in uncovering how status or class position is transmitted. But in doing so, they follow somewhat different approaches.

On one end of the spectrum are theorists who advocate deterministic models of reproduction; on the other end are those who put forth models that allow for the relative autonomy of individuals in their own cultural settings. Deterministic theories take as their starting point the structural requirements of the capitalist economic system and attempt to demonstrate how individuals are obliged to fulfill predefined roles that ensure the successful accumulation of capital and the perpetuation of a class society. Culturally attuned models begin with the experiences of individuals, and only after understanding people on their own terms do these models attempt to connect those experiences with the demands of capitalist social relations. In this review of reproduction theory, I shall begin with Samuel Bowles and Herbert Gintis, who represent the economic determinist end of the spectrum, progress through the works of Pierre Bourdieu and Basil Bernstein, and finally consider Paul Willis and Henry Giroux on the other end of the continuum.

THE ECONOMIC DETERMINISM OF BOWLES AND GINTIS

As Marxists, Bowles and Gintis begin their analysis with the forces and relations of production. In reviewing the American educational system, they point out the ways in which it is subordinated to and reflective of the production process and structure of class relations in the United States. Thus, they suggest that "the major aspects of the structure of schooling can be understood in terms of the systemic needs for producing reserve armies of skilled labor, legitimating the technocratic-meritocratic perspective, reinforcing the fragmentation of groups of workers into stratified status groups, and accustoming youth to the social relationships of dominance and subordinancy in the economic system."[2] Although their analysis takes the role of the family into consideration, they give the family little autonomy and insist that it, too, is largely dependent on the social relations of the production process.

Bowles and Gintis emphasize their "correspondence principle," which highlights the similarity between the social relations of production and personal interaction in the schools. "Specifically, the relationships of authority and control between administrators and teachers, teachers and students, students and students, and students and their work replicates the division of labor which dominates the work place."[3] Bowles and Gintis argue that strong structural similarities can be seen in (1) the organization of power and authority in the school and in the workplace; (2) the student's lack of control of curriculum and the worker's lack of control of the content of his/her job; (3) the role of grades and other rewards in the school and the role of wages in the workplace as extrinsic motivational systems; and (4) competition among students and the specialization of academic subjects and competition among workers and the fragmented nature of jobs.[4] In short, the social relations of the school reflect those of the capitalist mode of production; through its institutional relationships, the system of education in the United States "tailors the self-concepts, aspirations, and social class identifications of individuals to the requirements of the social division of labor."[5]

Insofar as these conditions apply to all students, however, their influence cannot explain the reproduction of class relations. An effective explanation must indicate the ways in which the educational system treats students differently depending on their social origins. In taking up this task, Bowles and Gintis elaborate the factors that contribute to class-based differences in socialization. They begin by demonstrating that there are major structural differences among schools. Schools serving working-class neighborhoods are more regimented and emphasize and behavioral control. In contrast, suburban schools offer more open classrooms that "favor greater student participation, less direct supervision, more student electives, and, in general, a value system stressing internalized standards of control."[6]

These variations reflect the different expectations of teachers, administrators, and parents for children of different class backgrounds. Working-class parents, for example, know from their own job experiences that submission to authority is an important value for success in the workplace; they will insist that the schools inculcate this value. Middle-class parents, reflecting their position in the social division of labor, will expect more open schools for their children.[7] Even within the same school, argue Bowles and Gintis, educational tracks, which cater to different classes of students, emphasize different values.

Although Bowles and Gintis stand diametrically opposed to the mainstream functionalist tradition of sociology with its emphasis on social consensus and integration, their characterization of the correspondence between the needs of the capitalist system and the effects of the educational system draws on functionalist arguments. As Karabel and Halsey point out, the basic difference between the two perspectives is that functionalists view the functions of the system of education "as serving the general interests of society as a whole whereas the Marxist views them as serving the particular interests of the capitalist class."[8] By postulating a tight fit between schooling and the larger social order, both traditions imply a static equilibrium that has difficulty accommodating historical change.

The fairly rigid structural correspondence Bowles and Gintis posit between the educational and economic systems leads to other theoretical problems. As Henry A. Giroux points out, this theory of social reproduction is too simplistic and overdetermined. Human subjects are viewed as passive role bearers shaped by the demands of capital. Student nonconformity and oppositional behavior are not acknowledged. "What is disregarded in the notion of 'correspondence' is not only the issue of resistance, but also any attempt to delineate the complex ways in which working-class subjectivities are constituted. . . . We are presented with a homogeneous image of working-class life fashioned solely by the logic of domination."[9] Although Bowles and Gintis break important ground by examining how the process of schooling reinforces relations of dominance and inequality among classes, their theory ultimately is too crudely deterministic to capture the complexity of social reproduction.

CULTURAL CAPITAL AND HABITUS: BOURDIEU'S THEORY OF REPRODUCTION

Pierre Bourdieu, a prominent French reproduction theorist, is more indebted to Weber and Durkheim than to Marx, yet Bourdieu also is influenced by the French structuralist movement, which seeks to delve beneath the surface of observed cultural forms to find the "deep" principles and logic according to which empirical reality functions. Drawing on these perspectives, Bourdieu forges an original theory in which class structure plays a more nuanced role, but one that does not preclude deterministic elements.

Bourdieu's most important contribution to reproduction theory is the concept of cultural capital, which he defines as the general cultural background, knowledge, disposition, and skills that are passed from one generation to the next. Cultural capital is the centerpiece of Bourdieu's theory of cultural reproduction. Children of upper-class origin, according to Bourdieu, inherit substantially different cultural capital than do working-class children. By embodying class interests and ideologies, schools reward the cultural capital of the dominant classes and systematically devalue that of the lower classes. Upper-class students, by virtue of a certain linguistic and cultural competence acquired through family upbringing, are provided with the means of appropriation for success in school. Children who read books, visit museums, attend concerts, and go to the theater and cinema (or simply grow up in families where these practices are prevalent) acquire a familiarity with the dominant culture that the educational system implicitly requires of its students for academic attainment. As Giroux contends, "Students whose families have a tenuous connection to forms of cultural capital highly valued by the dominant society are at a decided disadvantage."[10] Hence, the school serves as the trading post where socially valued cultural capital is parleyed into superior academic performance. Academic performance is then turned back into economic capital by the acquisition of superior jobs. The school reproduces social inequality, but by dealing in the currency of academic credentials the school legitimates the entire process.

There are four main points in Bourdieu's theory. First, distinctive cultural capital is transmitted by each social class. Second, the school systematically valorizes upper-class cultural capital and depreciates the cultural capital of the lower classes. Third, differential academic achievement is retranslated back into economic wealth—the job market remunerates the superior academic credentials earned mainly by the upper classes. Finally, the school legitimates this process "by making social hierarchies and the reproduction of those hierarchies appear to be based upon the hierarchy of 'gifts,' merits, or skills established and ratified by its sanctions, or, in a word, by converting social hierarchies into academic hierarchies."[11]

Bourdieu's model is not quite that simple, however. He recognizes, for instance, that the conversion of economic capital into cultural capital is not a precise one and thus that "the structure of distribution of cultural capital is not exactly the same as the structure of economic capital."[12] Moreover, in the upper reaches of the class structure, despite the decline of the family firm, economic capital is still passed on directly to the next generation, and the importance of educational attainment and cultural capital is correspondingly lower. Bourdieu also argues that "children's academic performance is more strongly related to parents' educational history than to parents' occupational status"[13] and contends that class-based differences in cultural capital tend to have a decreasing importance as one ascends the educational ladder. For Bourdieu, "social class background is mediated through a complex set of factors that interact in different ways at different levels of schooling."[14]

But throughout his theoretical discussion, Bourdieu concentrates on the upper half of the class structure; here he specifies most precisely the mechanisms by which schooling reinforces differences in cultural capital and translates them into labor market rewards. In distinguishing among different status groups in the middle and upper classes, Bourdieu analyzes each group's strategy in maintaining its position in the French educational system. As David Swartz points out in his review of Bourdieu's work, however, "it is doubtful whether the same model applies as well to lower-class groups that do not hold much capital and do not reproduce themselves through a rational [educational] investment strategy."[15]

In addition to cultural capital, Bourdieu employs the concept of habitus, which he defines as "a system of lasting, transposable dispositions which, integrating past experiences, functions at every moment as a matrix of perceptions, appreciations, and actions."[16] The habitus "could be considered as a subjective but not individual system of internalized structures, schemes of perception, conception, and action common to all members of the same group or class."[17] Put simply, the habitus is composed of the attitudes, beliefs, and experiences of those inhabiting one's social world. This conglomeration of deeply internalized values defines an individual's attitudes toward, for example, schooling. The structure of schooling, with its high regard for the cultural capital of the upper classes, promotes a belief among working-class students that they are unlikely to achieve academic success. Thus, there is a correlation between objective probabilities and subjective aspirations, between institutional structures and cultural practices.[18]

Aspirations reflect an individual's view of his or her own chances for getting ahead and are an internalization of objective probabilities. But aspirations are not the product of a rational analysis; rather, they are acquired in the habitus of the individual. A lower-class child growing up in an environment where success is rare is much less likely to develop strong ambitions than is a middle-class boy or girl growing up in a social world peopled by those who have "made it" and where the connection between effort and reward is taken for granted. "The habitus is the universalizing mediation which causes an individual agent's practices, without either explicit reason or signifying intent, to be none the less 'sensible' and 'reasonable.'"[19]

The habitus engenders attitudes and conduct that enable objective social structures to succeed in reproducing themselves. The educational and job opportunity structures are such that individuals of lower-class origin have a very reduced chance of securing professional or managerial jobs. This fact filters down to the lower-class boy (for a girl the outlook is much bleaker) situated in his habitus from the experiences and attitudes of those close to him. Responding to the objective structures, the boy loses interest in school and resigns himself to a low-level job, thereby reinforcing the objective structures. Whereas the theory of Bowles and Gintis relies on economic determinism, Bourdieu's determinism is a result of the circular relationship he posits between structures and practices, in which "objective structures tend to produce structured subjective dispositions that produce structured actions which, in turn, tend to reproduce objective structure."[20]

Bourdieu insists that the relationship between structure and habitus is dialectical, but his mechanistic language nevertheless reflects an emphasis on structural determinants. Human agency is not absent in Bourdieu's system, but, as Giroux contends, the scope for reflexive thought and individual action is circumscribed severely. Opposition, challenge, delegitimation, diversity, and nonconformity have no place in Bourdieu's theory. "Every established order tends to produce the naturalization of its own arbitrariness."[21] The mechanisms of cultural and social reproduction remain hidden because the social practices that safeguard the political and economic interests of the dominant classes go unrecognized; instead, they are considered the only natural, rational, or possible ones. In Bourdieu's view, there seems to be no escaping this symbolic order. His is a radical critique of a situation that is essentially immutable.

Bourdieu postulates no strict correspondence between the educational system and the economic system; although he believes that the educational system can be understood only with reference to the larger social structure of which it is a part, he insists on that system's relative autonomy. Giroux captures the essence of Bourdieu's argument when he contends that "rather than being directly linked to the power of an economic elite, schools are seen as part of a larger social universe of symbolic institutions that, rather than impose docility and oppression, reproduce existing power relations subtly via the production and distribution of a dominant culture that tacitly confirms what it means to be educated."[22] Bourdieu's subtle mind produces an elegant, sophisticated theory of cultural and social reproduction. But although his arguments are rich in logic, "many of his most interesting insights and theoretical formulations," Swartz reminds us, "are presented without empirical backing or specification of appropriate empirical tests."[23]

BERNSTEIN'S THEORY OF LANGUAGE CODIFICATION

Basil Bernstein, an innovative British social theorist, gives serious consideration to the interactional level of social life (the motives, relationships, and actions of individual social actors) and treats the cultural sphere as an object of critical inquiry in its own right, thereby avoiding the tendency to see cultural forms and practices largely as the reflection of structural forces conceptualized at the societal level. Through his theory of language codification and its relationship to social class on the one hand and schooling on the other, Bernstein links micro- and macro-sociological issues. Influenced by Durkheim and the French structuralist movement, Bernstein, in some respects, goes well beyond Bourdieu in terms of methodological rigor by analyzing both structures and practices and actually demonstrating their relationship. Nevertheless, for all its distinctiveness, Bernstein's work is understood most easily in the context of Bourdieu's theory of cultural capital.

Bourdieu argues that schools require cultural resources with which only specific students are endowed; Bernstein looks specifically at the educational ramifications of divergent linguistic patterns among children of different social strata. Bernstein begins by tracing the implications of social class for language use. In a highly complex argument, he contends that class membership generates distinctive forms of speech patterns through family socialization. Working-class children are oriented to "restricted" linguistic codes, while middle-class children use "elaborated" codes. By linguistic code, Bernstein does not mean the surface manifestations of language such as vocabulary or dialect, but rather the underlying regulative principles that govern the selection and combination of different syntactic and lexical constructions.[24]

Linguistic codes, which ultimately are rooted in the social division of labor, derive from the social relations and roles within families. While rejecting an outright correlation between social class and linguistic code, Bernstein claims that working-class children generally grow up in homes where common circumstances, knowledge, and values give rise to speech patterns in which meanings remain implicit and dependent on their context (a restricted code). Middle-class families, in contrast, use elaborated codes to express the unique perspective and experience of the speaker; meanings are less tied to a local relationship and local social structure and consequently are made linguistically explicit.[25] In their introductory essay to *Power and Ideology in Education*, Karabel and Halsey explain how distinct class-specific forms of communication are engendered.

> Participation in working-class family and community life, in which social relations are based upon shared identifications, expectations, and assumptions, tends to generate a 'restricted code,' for the speaker who is sure that the listener can take his intentions for granted has little incentive to elaborate his meanings and make them explicit and specific. Middle-class culture, in contrast, tends to place the "I" over the "we," and the resultant uncertainty that meanings will be intelligible to the listener forces the speaker to select among syntactic alternatives and to differentiate his vocabulary. The result is the

development of an 'elaborated code' oriented to the communication of highly individuated meanings.[26]

Because "one of the effects of the class system is to limit access to elaborated codes"[27] and because schools operate in accordance with the symbolic order of elaborated codes, working-class children are at a significant disadvantage. "Our schools are not made for these children; why should the children respond? To ask the child to switch to an elaborated code which presupposes different role relationships and systems of meaning . . . may create for the child a bewildering and potentially damaging experience."[28] By conceptualizing the social structure as a system of class inequality, tracing this structure's implications for language, and demonstrating the ways in which schools value the elaborated codes and other linguistic devices characteristic of the upper classes, Bernstein puts forth a theory that focuses on a powerful mechanism of social reproduction.

WILLIS: THE LADS AND THE EAR'OLES

Like Bernstein, Paul Willis, author of *Learning to Labor*, insists on the relative autonomy of the cultural sphere. In this impressive ethnographic study of a group of disaffected, white, working-class males in a British secondary school, Willis undertook extensive participant observation in order to grasp this "counter-school culture's" distinctive pattern of cultural practices. Willis found that the complex and contradictory nature of the "sources of meaning" on which these boys draw and the determinants of their behavior "warns against a too reductive or crude materialist notion of the cultural level."[29]

This is not to say, however, that Willis denies the importance of structural influence. On the contrary, writing in the Marxist tradition, Willis believes that these boys' class background, geographical location, local opportunity structure (job market), and educational attainment influence their job choice. But he reminds deterministic Marxists that these structural forces act through and are mediated by the cultural milieu. If we are to understand social reproduction, we must understand

> *how* and *why* young people take the restricted and often meaningless available jobs in ways which seem sensible to them in their familiar world as it is actually lived. For a proper treatment of these questions we must go to the cultural milieu . . . and accept a certain autonomy of the processes at this level which defeats any simple notion of mechanistic causation and gives the social agents involved some meaningful scope for viewing, inhabiting, and constructing their own world in a way which is recognizably human and not theoretically reductive.[30]

By viewing social reproduction as it actually is lived out, we can understand the mechanisms of the process.

In his study of a working-class school, Willis finds a major division between the students. The great bulk of the students are the "ear'oles" who conform to the roles defined for students, aspire to middle-class occupations, and comply with the rules and norms of the school. The counterschool culture of the "lads," in contrast, rejects the school's achievement ideology; these nonconformist boys subvert teacher and administrator authority, disrupt classes, mock the ear'oles (to whom they feel superior), and generally exploit any opportunity to "have a laff," usually at the expense of school officials. In short, the lads use whatever means possible to display their open opposition to the school.

Willis directs almost all his attention to understanding the lads. Their rejection of school, according to Willis, is partly the result of some profound insights, or "penetrations," into the economic condition of their social class under capitalism. The lads believe that their chances for significant upward mobility are so remote that sacrificing "a laff" for good behavior in school is pointless. The lads repudiate schooling because they realize that most available work is essentially meaningless and that although individuals are capable of "making it," conformism for their group or class promises no rewards.[31] As Michael Apple puts it, "Their rejection of so much of the content and form of day to day educational life bears on the almost unconscious realization that, as a class, schooling will not enable them to go much further than they already are."[32] According to Willis, this type of insight into the nature of capitalism has the potential to catalyze class solidarity and collective action.

The promise of these cultural penetrations, however, is dimmed by certain "limitations" in the lads' cultural outlook. The lads equate manual labor with masculinity, a trait highly valued by their working-class culture; mental labor is associated with the social inferiority of femininity.[33] This reversal of the usual valuation of mental versus manual labor prevents the lads from seeing their placement in dead-end, low-paying jobs as a form of class domination. Instead, they positively choose to join their brothers and fathers on the shop floor, a choice made happily and apparently free from coercion. Val Burris, in a review of *Learning to Labor*, brings this point into sharp focus.

What begins as a potential insight into the conditions of labor and the identity of the working class is transformed, under the influence of patriarchal ideology, into a surprising and uncritical affirmation of manual labor. It is this identification of manual labor with male privilege which, more than anything else, ensures the lads' acceptance of their subordinate economic fate and the successful reproduction of the class structure.[34]

The lads' nonconformist cultural innovations, which ultimately contribute to the reproduction of the class structure, are often complex and contradictory. To understand these mechanisms of social reproduction requires an ethnographic approach based on a theory that postulates the relative autonomy of the cultural sphere. Although a Marxist, Willis eschews theories based on economic determinism or a correspondence principle as explanations for the perpetuation of class inequality. Rather, he gives explanatory power to the cultural level and the social innovations of the individuals involved. In this way, we can see how structural forces are mediated by the cultural sphere through which they must pass.

Willis insists that the cultural attitudes and practices of working-class groups are not necessarily reflective of, or even traceable to, structural determinations or dominant ideologies. Although the mode of production wields a powerful influence on the attitudes and actions of individuals, people do not simply respond to the socioeconomic pressures bearing down on them with passivity and indifference. The cultural level is marked by contestation, resistance, and compromise. Culture itself implies "the active, collective use and explorations of received symbolic, ideological, and cultural resources to explain, make sense of and positively respond to 'inherited' structural and material conditions."[35] Subordinate groups can produce alternative cultural forms containing meanings endemic to the working class. Termed "cultural production" by Willis, this process is by nature active and transformative. Still, these behavioral and attitudinal innovations, as the lads illustrate, are often ultimately reproductive. As Liz Gordon remarks in her review of Willis's work, it may seem contradictory to refer to cultural production as both transformative and reproductive, but "Willis wishes to move away from an oversimplistic either/or model. He points out that there is no clear separation between agency and structure; these cannot be understood in isolation from one another."[36]

GIROUX'S THEORY OF RESISTANCE

Bridging the division between structure and agency maintained by theories of social reproduction has been one of the ongoing theoretical concerns of Henry A. Giroux, who contends that separation of human agency and structural analysis either suppresses the significance of individual autonomy or ignores the structural determinants that lie outside the immediate experience of human actors.[37] Giroux insists on the need to admit "wider structural and ideological determinations while recognizing that human beings never represent simply a reflex of such constraints."[38] Structuralist theories, which stress that history is made "behind the backs" of the members of society, overlook the significance and relative autonomy of the cultural level and the human experiences of domination and resistance. "In the structuralist perspective human agents are registered simply as the effects of structural determinants that appear to work with the certainty of biological processes. In this grimly mechanistic approach, human subjects simply act as role-bearers."[39] Culturalist theories, on the other hand, pay too little attention to how structurally embedded material and economic forces weigh down and shape human experience. "Culturalism begins at the right place but does not go far enough theoretically—it does not dig into subjectivity in order to find its objective elements."[40]

Giroux argues for a rigorous treatment of ideology, consciousness, and culture in order to move reproduction theory past the theoretical impasse imposed by the structure-agency dualism. He proposes a dialectical treatment of subjectivity and structure in which structure and human agency are seen to affect each other and thinks it crucial "to understand more thoroughly the complex ways in which people mediate and respond to the interface between their own lived experiences and structures of domination and constraint."[41]

In exploring these issues, Giroux develops a theory of resistance. He takes as his starting point the ethnographic studies of Willis, Hebdige, and Corrigan, which analyze how socioeconomic structures work through culture to shape the lives of students.[42] Giroux follows their lead in examining student nonconformity and opposition for their sociopolitical significance. Giroux considers resistance a response to the educational system, a response rooted in "moral and political indignation,"[43] not psychological dysfunction. Student countercultures and their attendant social attitudes and practices, according to Giroux, need to be analyzed carefully for "radical significance"; not all forms of oppositional behavior stem from a critique, implicit or explicit, of school-constructed ideologies and relations of domination. The violation of a school rule is not in itself an act of resistance unless committed by a youth who, for example, sees through the school's achievement ideology and is acting on that basis. The logic of resistance runs counter to the social relations of schooling and calls for struggle against, rather than submission to, domination.[44] By insisting that oppositional behavior be scrutinized and that resistance be mined for its broader significance, Giroux sets the program for future studies in social reproduction.

Student resistance represents a fertile area for academic study because it offers the possibility of transcending the structure-agency dualism. Resistance theory examines the ongoing, active experiences of individuals while simultaneously perceiving in oppositional attitudes and practices a response to structures of constraint and domination. Taking Willis's concept of cultural production seriously, Giroux suggests that working-class subordination is not a simple reaction to the logic of capitalist rationality. Rather, oppositional cultural patterns draw on elements of working-class culture in a creative and potentially transformative fashion. Thus, the mechanisms of class domination are neither static nor final.

As Giroux is well aware, a thorough understanding of student resistance is difficult to come by. Oppositional behavior is not self-explanatory. It must be linked with the subjects' own explanations of their behavior and contextualized within the nexus of peer, family, and work relations out of which resistance emerges.[45] Unfortunately, Giroux himself undertakes no such investigation, and most studies of social reproduction concentrate on the role of schooling in the perpetuation of class inequality, thus giving only token consideration to the other vehicles of socialization.

SOCIAL REPRODUCTION IN CLARENDON HEIGHTS

This book intends to delve beneath the surface of teenage behavior to recover the interests, concerns, and logic that render it comprehensible. In *Learning to Labor,* Willis gives us a complete and sophisticated analysis of how the lads experience the process of social reproduction. But what of the ear'oles? Both groups are working class. What causes the lads to respond to the school and to the occupational structure in a completely different way than do the ear'oles? Are the ear'oles, as Burris suggests, prepared for their economic fate by passive submission to structural and ideological forces? Or do the ear'oles actively respond to structural pressures bearing down on them and develop their own novel cultural practices and meanings? If economic determinants have the overriding importance that theorists such as Bowles and Gintis suggest, how can two groups from the same social location embody two distinctly different cultural orientations? Will the educational and occupational outcomes be much the same for the lads and ear'oles, or will they differ? In the process of social reproduction, what is the relationship between structural forces and cultural innovation? How much autonomy do individuals have at the cultural level?

Although the British and American contexts are obviously different, such questions are crucial to our understanding of how social inequality is reproduced in the United States. The chapters that follow examine in an intensive fashion two very different groups from the same social location and in the process illuminate some of the mechanisms, both structural and cultural, that contribute to social reproduction. In particular, occupational aspirations, as a mediating link between socioeconomic structures (what society offers) and individuals at the cultural level (what one wants), play a crucial role in the reproduction of class inequality. At the interface between structural determinants and human agency, aspirations offer the sociologist a conceptual bridge over the theoretical rift of the structure-agency dualism. Bourdieu and Willis both emphasize the importance of aspirations in their theoretical writings. For Bourdieu, the relationship between aspirations and opportunity is at the root of "the educational mortality of the working classes."[46] We have seen that a disparity in aspirations is the major difference between the lads and the ear'oles. Indeed, of all the factors contributing to social reproduction (e.g., tracking, social relations of schooling, class-based differences in linguistic codes), the regulation of aspirations is perhaps the most important.

Now that we have familiarized ourselves with some of the major aspects of social reproduction literature—Bourdieu's concepts of cultural capital and habitus, Willis's notion of cultural production, and Giroux's theory of resistance—we are in a position to examine in depth the male teenage world of Clarendon Heights. The experiences of the Brothers and the Hallway Hangers, if properly elucidated, bear on the issues of social reproduction more directly than any sociological theory ever could. Thus, it is to the boys of Clarendon Heights that we now turn.

NOTES

1. Karl Marx, *Capital* (Harmondsworth: Penguin, 1976), p. 724.
2. Samuel Bowles and Herbert Gintis, *Schooling in Capitalist America* (New York: Basic Books, 1976), p. 56.
3. Ibid., p. 12.
4. Ibid.
5. Ibid., p. 129.
6. Ibid., p. 132.
7. Ibid., pp. 132–133.
8. Jerome Karabel and A. H. Halsey, eds., *Power and Ideology in Education* (New York: Oxford University Press, 1977), p. 40n.
9. Henry A. Giroux, *Theory & Resistance in Education* (London: Heinemann Educational Books, 1983), p. 85.
10. Ibid., p. 88.
11. Pierre Bourdieu, "Cultural Reproduction and Social Reproduction," in Karabel and Halsey, *Power and Ideology*, p. 496.
12. Ibid., p. 507.
13. David Swartz, "Pierre Bourdieu: The Cultural Transmission of Social Inequality," *Harvard Educational Review* 47 (November 1977):548.
14. Ibid.
15. Ibid., p. 554.
16. Pierre Bourdieu, *Outline of a Theory of Practice* (Cambridge: Cambridge University Press, 1977), pp. 82–83.
17. Ibid., p. 86.
18. Pierre Bourdieu and Jean-Claude Passeron, *Reproduction in Education, Society and Culture* (London: Sage, 1977), p. 156.
19. Bourdieu, *Outline of a Theory of Practice*, p. 79.
20. Swartz, "Pierre Bourdieu," p. 548.
21. Bourdieu, *Outline of a Theory of Practice*, p. 164.
22. Giroux, *Theory & Resistance*, p. 87.
23. Swartz, "Pierre Bourdieu," p. 553.
24. Paul Atkinson, *Language, Structure and Reproduction* (London: Methuen, 1985), pp. 66, 68, 74.
25. Basil Bernstein, "Social Class, Language, and Socialization," in Karabel and Halsey, *Power and Ideology*, p. 477.
26. Ibid., p. 63.
27. Ibid., p. 478.

28. Ibid., p. 483.

29. Paul E. Willis, *Learning to Labor* (Aldershot: Gower, 1977), p. 171.

30. Ibid., p. 172.

31. Ibid., pp. 126–129.

32. Michael W. Apple, *Education and Power* (Boston: Routledge and Kegan Paul, 1982), p. 99.

33. Willis, *Learning to Labor*, p. 148.

34. Val Burris, rev. of *Learning to Labor*, by Paul Willis, *Harvard Educational Review* 50 (November 1980):525.

35. Paul Willis, "Cultural Production and Theories of Reproduction," in *Race, Class and Education*, ed. Len Barton and Stephen Walker (London: Croom Helm, 1983), p. 112.

36. Liz Gordon, "Paul Willis—Education, Cultural Production and Social Reproduction," *British Journal of Sociology of Education* 5 (1984):113.

37. Giroux, *Theory & Resistance*, p. 119.

38. Ibid., p. 38.

39. Ibid., p. 136.

40. Ibid., p. 135.

41. Ibid., p. 108.

42. Ibid., pp. 98–99.

43. Henry A. Giroux, "Theories of Reproduction and Resistance in the New Sociology of Education: A Critical Analysis," *Harvard Educational Review* 53 (August 1983):289.

44. Ibid., p. 290.

45. Ibid., p. 291.

46. Bourdieu and Passeron, *Reproduction in Education*, p. 156.

3

TEENAGERS IN CLARENDON HEIGHTS: THE HALLWAY HANGERS AND THE BROTHERS

On any given day, except during the coldest winter months, the evening hours in Clarendon Heights are filled with activity. At one end of the housing development, elderly women sit on wooden benches and chat. In the center of the project, children play street hockey, kickball, stickball, or football, depending on the season. At the other end, teenage boys congregate in the stairwell and on the landing of one of the entries—doorway #13.

THE HALLWAY HANGERS: "YOU GOTTA BE BAD"

This doorway and the area immediately outside it are the focus of activity for the Hallway Hangers, one of the two main peer groups of high-school-age boys living in Clarendon Heights (the other group is called the Brothers). Composed of a core of eight youths, but including up to ten additional people who are loosely attached to the group, the Hallway Hangers are tough, streetwise individuals who form a distinctive subculture. Except for Boo-Boo, who is black, and Chris, who is of mixed racial parentage, the Hallway Hangers are white boys of Italian or Irish descent. The eight members considered here range in age from sixteen to nineteen. Five have dropped out of school, two graduated last year,[1] and one continues to attend high school. They all smoke cigarettes, drink regularly, and use drugs. All but two have been arrested. Stereotyped as "hoodlums," "punks," or "burnouts" by outsiders, the

Hallway Hangers are actually a varied group, and much can be learned from considering each member.

Frankie, the acknowledged leader of the Hallway Hangers, is of only medium height and weight, but his fighting ability is unsurpassed among teenagers in Clarendon Heights. Missing two front teeth from one of his few unsuccessful encounters, Frankie maintains a cool, calculating demeanor that only occasionally gives way to his fiery temper. He commands the respect of the other boys because he is a natural leader and because he comes from a family that is held in high esteem by the city's underworld. His brothers have been involved in organized crime and have spent time in prison; four of them were incarcerated at the time I conducted my research. Although Frankie is the ringleader of the Hallway Hangers, he has never been arrested—no small feat considering the scope of the group's criminal activity.

Whereas Frankie combines physical toughness and mental acuity, Slick, although no weakling, clearly possesses an abundance of the latter attribute. Very articulate and perceptive, Slick scored high on standardized tests and fared well in school when he applied himself (he dropped out last year). Slick gets along well on the street, where his quick wit and sharp tongue are major assets. Although his status falls short of Frankie's, Slick is accorded much respect by the other boys of Clarendon Heights.

As Slick is known for the strength of his intellect, Shorty is known for his physical toughness. When a teacher at the local high school remarked, "What makes someone tough has nothing to do with size or even muscle—it's the fear factor. If someone's fearless, crazy, he'll do anything," he doubtless had Shorty in mind. As his nickname implies, Shorty is small, but well built. His temper is explosive, and under the influence of alcohol or drugs, he has been known to accost strangers, beat up friends, or pull a knife on anyone who challenges him. On one occasion, he repeatedly stabbed himself in the head in a fit of masochistic machismo. Although Frankie and Slick also consider themselves alcoholics, Shorty's drinking problem is more severe. The county court ordered him to a detoxification center—an arrangement Shorty has slyly managed to avoid.

Like the other three boys, Chris is a self-professed alcoholic who also admits to being dependent on marijuana. Chris's father (who does not live at home) is black, and his mother is white, which gives Chris an ethnic heritage that makes his acceptance by the rest of the Hallway Hangers difficult. A tall, very slender youth, Chris is loud and talkative but without the self-confidence and poise of Slick or Frankie. He is often the object of the other boys' abuse, both verbal and physical, but nevertheless has some stature in the group largely because of his loyalty and sense of humor.

Boo-Boo, the other black member of the Hallway Hangers, is a tall, quiet, dark-skinned youth. His serious nature makes him a less frequent target of abuse, which begins as playful racial barbs but often degenerates into downright racial animosity. Like Chris, Boo-Boo is a follower. A sincere and earnest boy, his general demeanor is at odds with the violence and bluster that characterize the group as a whole. Nevertheless, Boo-Boo has been known to fight—and quite effectively—when seriously antagonized and generally is held in moderate esteem by the rest of the boys.

Like Boo-Boo, Stoney is a bit of a loner. The only Hallway Hanger to hold stable employment, Stoney works full time in a pizza shop. His regular income, which he recently used to buy a car, earns him a measure of deference from the other boys, but Stoney lacks the cockiness and bravado necessary for high stature within the group. Skinny and averse to street fights, Stoney perpetually but ineffectively strives to rid himself of the label "pussy." Stoney does share with the other boys an enthusiasm for beer and drugs; he has been arrested for possession of mescaline and is psychologically dependent on marijuana. He has a steady girlfriend (another anomaly for the Hallway Hangers, who generally reject serious relationships in favor of more casual romantic encounters) with whom he spends much of his time, but Stoney still values the friendship of the Hallway Hangers and remains an integral member of the group.

Steve, Slick's younger brother, is the stereotypical project youth. Constantly on the lookout for a free ride, Steve is insolent and loud but lacks his brother's sophistication. He is courageous, full of energy, and fights well, but Steve is not particularly popular with the other boys, who tolerate him as Slick's brother and as a person who can be counted on for support and loyalty in the most trying situations. Steve is the only Hallway Hanger still in school; he expects to graduate in two years (1986).

In contrast to Steve, Jinks is a sensitive, shy boy who shares with Stoney and Chris a psychological dependence on marijuana. Although he is considered immature and is taunted as a "mama's boy" by some of the Hallway Hangers, Jinks seems to have inner reserves of confidence and self-esteem that protect his ego from such assaults. Lighthearted and understanding of others, Jinks is the only white member of the Hallway Hangers who is not overtly racist. Although he takes a good deal of abuse from the others, especially Frankie and Shorty, Jinks's acceptance as a bona fide member of the group is beyond question.

These boys come together in the late afternoon or early evening after dinner and "hang" in doorway #13 until late at night. They come to "see what's up," to "find out what's goin' down," to "shoot the shit," and, generally, to just pass the time. Smelling of urine, lined with graffiti, and littered with trash and broken glass, this hallway is the setting for much playful banter, some not so playful "capping" (exchange of insults), and an occasional fight. The odors of cigarette smoke, beer, and marijuana are nearly always present. During the weekend, there may be a case or two of beer, a nearly constant circulation of joints, and some cocaine, mescaline, or "angel dust" (PCP). Late at night, one occasionally stumbles upon a lone figure shooting up heroin.

In an inversion of the dominant culture's vocabulary and value scheme, the subculture of the Hallway Hangers is a world in which to be "bad" is literally to be good. A common characteristic of lower-class[2] teenage peer cultures, this emphasis on being bad is inextricably bound up with the premium put on masculinity, physical toughness, and street wisdom in lower-class culture. Slick, in articulating the prominence of this value for the Hallway Hangers, states in definite terms what being bad often involves.

(*in an individual talk*)

SLICK: You hafta make a name for yourself, to be bad, tough, whatever. You hafta be, y'know, be with the 'in' crowd. Know what I mean? You hafta—it's just all part of growing up around here—you hafta do certain things. Some of the things you hafta do is, y'know, once in awhile you hafta, if you haven't gotten into a fight, if you have a fight up the high school, you're considered bad. Y'know what I mean? If you beat someone up up there, especially if he's black, around this way . . . if you're to be bad, you hafta be arrested. You hafta at least know what bein' in a cell is like.

(*in a group discussion*)

JM: So how is it that to be what's good down here, to be respected . . .

SLICK: You gotta be bad.

FRANKIE: Yeah, if you're a straight A student, you get razzed.

SLICK: Then you're a fucking weirdo, and you shouldn't be living here in the first place.

SHORTY: No, you got people down here who don't drink and don't smoke.

SLICK: Who? Name one.

SHORTY: Stern. John Stern.

FRANKIE: Yeah, but like he's sayin', whadda we think of John Stern?

SHORTY: Fucking shithead (*all laugh*).

Thus, good grades in school can lead to ostracism, whereas time spent in prison earns respect. To be bad is the main criterion for status in this subculture; its primacy cannot be overemphasized, and its importance is implied continually by the boys.

Frankie carries the notion of being bad to the extreme, despite its offensiveness to conventional American values. In June 1983, John Grace, a bartender in a pub across the city, shot two police officers and was himself wounded in a gunfight in Clarendon Heights. All three survived, and at the time of this interview, Grace was awaiting trial in a county jail where two of Frankie's brothers were also serving time. "Fucking Grace, he's my man. He's taken care of. My brother says he'll have a fucking joint when he see him in his cell. He's in lock-up, but they take care of him. He's a big fucking dude. He's respected up there, man. He's the baddest. He shot a fucking cop. He's golden, he's there. That's the best you can fucking do."

Although such a drastic view is seldom voiced or acted upon by the Hallway Hangers, success for members of the peer group does involve physical and emotional toughness. In addition, a quick wit is essential, for much time is spent capping on one another.

(in the hallway late one afternoon)

SHORTY: *(drunk)* Hey Steve, what are you doing tonight?

STEVE: Nuttin'. Why?

SHORTY: You wanna suck my dick?

STEVE: You're the only gay motherfucker around here.

SHORTY: Yeah? Ask your girlfriend if I'm gay.

STEVE: Yeah, well, you ask your mother if I'm gay.

This type of sportive banter is common, a diversion to interrupt the boredom inherent in hanging in hallways for a good portion of the day.

JINKS: Everyone gets ragged on out there. It's just when you're high, y'know, you're drunk—you start ragging on people. Helps the time go by.

Sometimes, of course, real venom lies behind the words. In that case, size and strength are the crucial elements for success in an altercation. For behind all the posturing lies the reality of the pecking order, which is determined primarily by physical toughness. Fighting ability is the deciding factor for status demarcation within the group; those lacking in physical stature must compensate for it with aggressiveness and tenacity or learn to live with a lot of abuse, both verbal and physical.

For the Hallway Hangers, being bad entails the consumption of alcohol and the use of drugs on a regular basis. The boys are intoxicated for a good portion of almost every weekend and drink heavily during the week. During the summer, the level of drinking reaches staggering proportions, often involving the consumption of two or more "beer balls" (the equivalent of two and a half cases of beer pressurized into a plastic ball about two feet in diameter) a day for a group of eight or ten boys. Although none of the Hallway Hangers is drunk constantly, Frankie, Shorty, Slick, and Chris all consider themselves alcoholics.

FRANKIE: See, the way we are right now, technically we are alcoholics. Y'know, I can go days without drinking alcohol. It ain't like I need it, but right now I want it, y'know; it helps me get through. Y'know, get through problems, whatever; it helps me get through. Take away all the fucking problems down here, and there would be no problems with alcohol.

Shorty is honest about the debilitating effects of his dependence on alcohol.

(in a group discussion)

SHORTY: I think when you're an alcoholic like me, man, you ain't gonna be able to hold no fucking job. You say things you fucking forget.

FRANKIE: Yeah, yeah. I hear ya.

SHORTY: I mean, I don't remember trying to stab my own brother in the back; my other brother caught me. That's when I knew I was dead-up an alcoholic. Then I stabbed myself and three other people.

JM: How'd you get to be an alcoholic in the first place?

SHORTY: Being with these motherfuckers (all laugh). These got me going. Frankie always used to drink before me. I only used to drink about a beer a night, and I used to get buzzed every night. It's like this now: six pack—Monday through Friday. Friday, it's a case, and when summer comes, it's . . .

ALL: Beer balls!

Most of these boys began drinking beer regularly at the age of thirteen or fourteen; their preferences now include whiskey and Peppermint Schnapps.

The Hallway Hangers also began smoking marijuana when they were twelve or thirteen years old, a tendency that has led many to use an assortment of heavier drugs as well. Most of them describe stages in their adolescence during which they used PCP, mescaline, valium, or THC (the chief intoxicant in marijuana). Only Chris admits to having used heroin; Frankie's experience is more typical of these boys.

(in a group interview)

FRANKIE: My drug was, my freshman and sophomore year, I was into THC, right? And you get a tolerance and shit, and you start doing three and four hits.

SLICK: Frankie was a junkie.

FRANKIE: Well, yeah, I didn't boot it [shoot it up], but I was addicted to it, definitely.

Having moderated what they now see as their youthful enthusiasm for different drugs, the Hallway Hangers generally limit themselves to marijuana and cocaine. All the Hallway Hangers smoke a great deal of marijuana; Chris, Jinks, and Stoney acknowledge their dependence on the drug. Marijuana joints circulate in doorway #13 almost as often as cans of beer, and all admit they get high before and during school.

(in an individual interview, before he dropped out of school)

JM: Chris, you get high a lot in school?

CHRIS: Oh, yeah. I'm high every time I go to school. I gotta be. Sometimes I even drink before I go—I'll have a few beers. It's too much if you don't. I'm a fucking alcoholic. I do a lot of cocaine. I'll do up cocaine whenever I can get it. Fucking expensive though.

Despite their own widespread use of marijuana and occasional consumption of cocaine, the Hallway Hangers have no respect for junkies or "dustheads," those who are addicted to heroin or angel dust.

(in an interview with Shorty and Slick)

SHORTY: Little Tony and them, fuckin' ten, twelve years old, smoking pot, taking drugs. And that ain't good, at that age, cuz me and him don't do drugs, maybe coke, y'know? Coke and pot. But a lot of other dudes out here, they'll be taking; they'll be shooting up and everything. We don't even bother with them.

Obviously, underage drinking and drug use are illegal, and the Hallway Hangers have made their share of trips to the police station and the courthouse. Stoney has three convictions, twice for possession of narcotics and once for passing stolen property. Boo-Boo has been arrested for "hot boxes" (stolen cars). Chris has assault with a deadly weapon in addition to some less serious convictions on his record. Shorty has been to court for larceny, assault with a deadly weapon, and other less substantial crimes. One of the older teenagers on the fringes of the Hallway Hangers was convicted of rape and sentenced to eighteen months in the maximum security state prison after his sophomore year in high school.

These, of course, represent only the crimes at which the Hallway Hangers have been caught. Their criminal activity is actually much more widespread. Those trusted by the Hallway Hangers are occasionally approached with offers for good deals on bicycles, stereo equipment, or musical instruments, all of which have been stolen. Chris makes a lot of money dealing drugs; Shorty did. Many of the others make small amounts of cash selling drugs to friends and acquaintances.

JINKS: We all know how to make a fast buck on the street. Buy the pot, roll up joints, sell 'em for two bucks a joint. Pay thirty for a bag; get twenty-five bones out of a bag—there's fifty bucks for thirty bucks.

Jimmy Sullivan, an experienced and perceptive teacher of the adjustment class in which Frankie, Shorty, and Steve are, or were at one time, enrolled, gives a good description of the Hallway Hangers' criminal careers.

JS: One thing about these kids: Crime pays, and they know it. . . . It's so easy to go over to the hallowed halls across the street there [a large university] and pick up a bike. I know three or four stores in the city that will pay thirty to forty dollars for a good bike, no questions asked. They'll turn it over for 150 or 200 bucks. What do these kids need money for? What do they care about? Beer, sneakers, joints. They're not going to work when they can make easy money through virtually riskless criminal enterprises. Only suckers are gonna work for that. As long as their expectations stay low and they only need a hundred bucks a week—as Steve said, "All I want is my beer money"—they're all set. Up to when they're seventeen years old there's no risk. But when they turn about eighteen, the peer group doesn't accept that anymore. If they could go on stealing bikes for the rest of their lives, I think they would. But when you're seventeen or eighteen and someone says, "Hey man, where'd you get the cash?" it's unacceptable to say, "Oh, stealing bikes, man." You've got to be into cars, dealing drugs, or holding people up. That's when the risk and fear start coming into it. For many of them, the easiest route is to get a job. Of course, some of them don't, and they end up in jail.

Although this dynamic certainly plays a role in the Hallway Hangers' rationale, the legal system's distinction between a juvenile and an adult is more important in their determination of whether or not crime pays.

(in a group interview)

JM: Most of you are seventeen or over now?

SLICK: Only Chris is sixteen.

JM: Doesn't that make a big difference in terms of what you're doing to get money?

SHORTY: Hey, I'm doin' good. I don't deal no more, Jay. I got a good job coming at the weapons lab; most likely I'm gonna get my brother one there.

FRANKIE: Yeah, you slow down. Seventeen—you're an adult.

SLICK: Yeah, at seventeen you start slowing down.

SHORTY: You gotta start thinking.

(in a separate interview)

FRANKIE: Now that I think about it, I should've did more crime when I was a juvenile cuz when you're a juvenile you get arrested a good eight or nine times before they put you away. So I could've did a lot more crime, but I don't really mind. It was all right. But yeah, that's what most people do is once they go to seventeen, they smarten up and say that's big-time prison. And I've had many good examples of what not to do. I know jail ain't no place for nobody, even though some of my brothers make a living out of it.

Like many urban slums, the teenage underworld of Clarendon Heights is characterized by predatory theft, and some of the Hallway Hangers specialize in "cuffing" drugs, stolen merchandise, and money off those who themselves are involved in illegal activity. Shorty and Frankie have sold hundreds of fake joints, robbed other drug pushers, and forced younger or less tough boys to give them a share of their illegal income. The consensus among the Hallway Hangers is that this type of thievery is morally more defensible than conventional theft. More importantly, there is less risk of detection, for the authorities are unlikely to become involved.

(in a group discussion)

SLICK: You chump off thieves, and then you're like a hero. At least you got him back, y'know? You steal off a fucking thief who makes his life off stealing off other people, then its like you're fucking . . .

FRANKIE: You rip off illegal people, y'know? You rip off dealers.

SHORTY: That's why if you deal, you gotta be able to kill.

FRANKIE: Yeah, sometimes it could mean your life if you get caught. But you can't get put in jail.

For those raised with a strong sense of law and order, these attitudes are difficult to fathom. The Hallway Hangers, for their part, however, cannot understand the contempt and disdain the upper classes display for their lifestyle and launch a counterattack of their own.

(*in a group interview*)

SLICK: All right, you get people making fucking over fifty thousand dollars, and they fucking ask us why do we hang there? What the fuck, man?

CHRIS: What else are we gonna do?

JINKS: They can go fuck themselves.

CHRIS: They want us to deal the drugs so they can buy them.

SLICK: See, they don't know what the deal is. See, they're just doing what we're doing, except they're doing it in a more respectable way. They're ripping off each other up there. That's all they're doing. They're all ripping each other off up there. But they're doing it in a fucking legal way.

FRANKIE: Yeah, check this out.

SHORTY: We ain't doin' it behind anybody's back.

FRANKIE: All them fucking businessmen, man. All them stockbrokers and shit in New York. All them motherfuckers are out to rip people off. There's more fucking scamming going on up there. They're like legally ripping everyone off.

SLICK: We're just doing it illegally.

This is an insightful, if incomplete, critique of the social order, but not one about which the Hallway Hangers get particularly upset. Rather, they accept it as a simple fact of life with an acquiescent attitude that is typical of their outlook.

An important characteristic of the subculture of the Hallway Hangers is group solidarity. Membership in the Hallway Hangers involves a serious commitment to the group: a willingness to put out for others and to look out for the rest of the group's well-being as well as one's own. This loyalty is the glue that holds the group together, and honoring it is essential. The requirements and limits of this commitment to the group are seldom expressed, but are such that Slick would not leave Shorty "hanging with the cops," even though to stay with Shorty resulted in his own arrest.

SHORTY: See, that's how Slick was that day we were ripping off the sneakers [from a nearby factory]. He figured that if he left me that would be rude, y'know? If he just let me get busted by myself and he knew I had a lot of shit on my head, that's what I call a brother. He could've. I could've pushed him right through that fence, and he coulda been *gone*. But no, he waited for me, and we both got arrested. I was stuck. My belly couldn't get through the fucking hole in the fence.

This cohesion between members of the Hallway Hangers is a striking characteristic of their subculture and one to which they constantly draw attention. Not only are they proud of their adoption of communitarian values, but they also see their "brotherhood" as inconsistent with conventional middle- and upper-class attitudes.

(*in a group discussion*)

SLICK: What it is, it's a brotherhood down here. We're all fucking brothers. There's a lot of backstabbing going on down here, down in the streets. But we're always there for each other. No shit. There's not a guy in here that wouldn't put out for one of the rest of us. If he needs something and I got it, I'll give it to him. Period. That's the way it works. It's a brotherhood. We're not like them up there—the rich little boys from the suburbs or wherever. There's a line there. On this side of the line we don't fuck with each other; we're tight.

FRANKIE: We'd chump them off [rob] on the other side, though.

SLICK: Fucking right. If he's got four hundred bucks in his pocket, there's more where that came from. Fuck him. But they also chump each other off; only they do it legally. How do you think they got rich—by fucking people over. We don't do that to each other. We're too fucking tight. We're a group. We don't think like them; we think for all of us.

FRANKIE: That's the fucking truth. If you don't have your fucking buddies, where are you? You're fucking no one. Nuttin'.

SLICK: If I had the choice, and this isn't just me but probably everyone in here, if I had the choice between being a good person and making it, I'd be a good person. That's just the way I am. If I had my bar exam tomorrow and these guys needed me, I'd go with them. That's just the way it is down here.

SHORTY: Yeah, you wanna be here with your family, with your friends; they're good people. You're comfortable with them. You don't feel right with these other people. I dunno. . . . You wanna be like them, y'know? You see they're rich; you wanna be rich. You can't be the poor one out of the crowd. You got all the crowd, and places like that—the suburbs—they're all rich. Y'know, a lot of places, they say quiet places; around here, you'll just be able to hang together, and nobody has that much money.

SLICK: But I'll tell you right now, you cannot find better friends because everybody's in the same boat. You'll find a few assholes, rats, whatever, but mostly when you have all of us, we all know everybody's poor. You're not better than me; I'm not better than him, y'know? Like, say if I have a hundred dollars or he has a hundred dollars, y'know, it's not just his or mine—it's *our* money. It goes between us, y'know what I mean? Like up there, it's not as tight. People aren't tight up there. I just came back from Fort Lauderdale, and I seen it up there. Real rich people, it's not like this at all.

These comments bear ample testimony to the solidarity that characterizes the subculture of the Hallway Hangers. This solidarity is not an ideal to which they only pay lip service; shared money, shared drugs, and shared risks in criminal activity are all facts of life in doorway #13.

At the same time that these boys affirm the lifestyle and values of people in their neighborhood, they assert with peculiar constancy their deeply felt desire to move with their families out of Clarendon Heights. Many of them want to make enough money to get their families out of the projects forever.

(all in separate discussions, unsolicited by me)

SLICK: Most of the kids down here, most of 'em wanna make money so they can help their families and help themselves to get out of this place. . . . My main concern is to get my family out of the projects.

CHRIS: I just wanna get my mother out of the projects, that's all.

SHORTY: All's I'm doing, I'm gonna get enough money, save enough money to get my mother the fuck out of here.

These statements are evidence of the stigma the Hallway Hangers, as public housing tenants, feel as a matter of course. Their pride in their lifestyle is pierced by the dominant culture's negative judgments. One implication of the culture's achievement ideology is that those of low socioeconomic stature are personally deficient. This negative evaluation and the inability of the Hallway Hangers to shield themselves completely from it combine to produce the deep ambivalence the boys feel toward themselves and their community.

Daily life for the Hallway Hangers is marked by unrelieved boredom and monotony. The boys are generally out of work, out of school, and out of money. In search of employment or a "fast buck on the street," high or drunk a good deal of the time, many are preoccupied with staying out of prison—a struggle some already have lost—and with surviving from one day to the next.

(in a discussion with Shorty and Slick)

SLICK: All through the teenage years around here, you hafta learn to survive, before you learn to do anything else.

SHORTY: Nobody learns anything from school around here. All it is is how to survive and have money in your pocket.

SLICK: You hafta learn how to survive first.

SHORTY: This is the little ghetto.

SLICK: Y'know, you hafta learn how to survive; if you can't survive, especially around here, that's why you see so many people who are just down and out. It's tough. That's what it is. It's tough.

Growing up in Clarendon Heights is indeed tough, and the frustrations of project life find release through the racist attitudes held by the boys. Racism among members of the Hallway Hangers runs very deep. Frankie and Shorty are violent in their prejudice against black people, while Slick, Steve, and Stoney are racist in a less strident manner. Only Jinks has a measure of empathy and respect for blacks.

According to the Hallway Hangers, their antipathy toward blacks stems from an incident in the early 1970s. At that time, a full-scale riot erupted in Clarendon Heights between the project's mostly white residents and black youths from the predominantly black Emerson Towers housing project a half mile away. The conflict lasted several days and involved the National Guard and riot police. Frankie describes how this event crystallized his own racist attitudes.

JM: So why is it, why is there like this tension between the whites and the blacks?

FRANKIE: Well, when I grew up here, when I was fucking second, third grade, there was racial riots right in front of my window every night. My brothers, I have seven brothers, were all out there, y'know, stabbin' niggers, beating niggers up. I was brought up thinking fucking niggers suck. Went over to Hoover School, no fuckin' black people there at all. Y'know, third grade, we had one black kid. His name was Sonny. Y'know, everyone fucked him up. So it was this through the racial riots. I was brought up to hate niggers.

Although the riots contributed to the racism of the Hallway Hangers, surprisingly enough, they also account for the acceptance of Boo-Boo and Chris into the group.

(in an interview with Jinks and Chris)

JM: Now Chris, you're an interesting case cuz, except when Boo-Boo's around, you're the only black guy out there. How'd that come about?

CHRIS: It goes back to the days of the riots.

JINKS: Back in the days of the riots, when the whites used to fight the blacks at the Heights . . .

CHRIS: Nobody fucked with my family.

JINKS: Chris's family was always like neutral. They'd help out anybody. And besides, as he's grown older, I've related to him more because my brother married a black lady. And I got nieces and nephews that are like him: mulatto. I've just related to him more. I see things from his point of view more. Cuz I know how he feels when people start capping on him: "Hey Breed."

JM: So that's how it came about with you?

CHRIS: Yeah. When the riots were going on, right, they'd be out there: the niggers against the whites; I'd be sleeping over his house and shit, y'know? His brothers would be fucking hating niggers, man; like his brother John, they'd be killing them.

Boo-Boo also gives a similar reason for his membership in the Hallway Hangers.

JM: What happened with your family during the riots?

BOO-BOO: My father knew both. He used to have all the kids in the house and shit.

JM: What happened with Chris's family?

BOO-BOO: People they knew wouldn't do nothing. If someone was hurting real bad and needed a towel or something, they'd get it. They knew both. Y'know, Chris's mother is real nice—she'd help both the whites and blacks.

Other factors have contributed to Chris's and Boo-Boo's affiliation with the Hallway Hangers. Boo-Boo's family was one of the first black households to be moved by the city's Housing Authority into the Heights. When he was growing up, he naturally made friends with white youngsters. His younger brother Derek went to a private grammar school; most other black youths who now live in Clarendon Heights had yet to move in. Boo-Boo's expressed reason for being a Hallway Hanger is simple: "I grew up with them, since I was real small."

The situation was much the same for Chris; in addition, his acceptance into the Hallway Hangers has been facilitated because he is half white.

(in a group interview)

FRANKIE: It ain't like he's living with his black daddy; he's living with his white mommy.

SHORTY: His white brothers.

(in a separate discussion)

JINKS: My brothers alway liked his family though . . .

CHRIS: Cuz my brothers were white, y'know.

JINKS: His brothers were mulatto, but they looked like a white person. . . . It just looked like he had a nice tan all year round. And he was one of my brother's best friends. Y'know, it's just families hanging around.

Although both Chris and Boo-Boo are full members of the Hallway Hangers, their position often seems tenuous because of their race. Both take a lot of ribbing for their skin color. Chris routinely is referred to as nigs, nigger, breed, half-breed, or oreo; Boo-Boo gets less direct abuse but is the butt of racist jokes and occasional taunts. Both tend to deal with it in the same way: They "play it off," make a joke of it, or ignore it.

(in an individual discussion)

JM: So you naturally hung with Frankie and them. Are there any problems with you being black?

BOO-BOO: No. They say things but they're just fooling around. I take it as a joke. They're just fooling around. It doesn't bother me at all. If they hit me or something, that's a different story.

Chris occasionally will play along with the other Hallway Hangers by agreeing with their racist statements and denigrating other blacks.

One balmy night in late autumn, I walked into doorway #13 at about eleven o'clock to find Frankie, Chris, and two older guys on the fringes of the Hallway Hangers, Joe and Freddy, smoking a joint and drinking a beer. I struck up a conversation with Frankie, but I was interrupted by Joe, a twenty-three-year-old man whose six-foot frame boasts a lot more brawn than mine. "Hey Jay," he said in a mocking, belligerent tone, glancing sharply up at me from his two empty six packs of Miller, "You're a fucking nigger. You're a nigger. You play basketball with the niggers. You talk like a nigger. You're a fucking nigger." This reference to a basketball game a few days earlier in which I played with the Brothers demanded a response that would not provoke a fight but would allow me to maintain some poise and dignity in front of the others. (I had learned long since that to confront the Hallway Hangers' racism was a fruitless exercise and not particularly conducive to entry into the group.) In the end, although I escaped with my pride and body intact, Chris was not so lucky. The exchange that followed highlights his deep ambivalence toward his ethnic identity.

JOE: Did you hear me? I said you're a nigger, a motherfucking nigger.

JM: What, you'd rather play four on six? It's not my fault we won; maybe it's yours.

JOE: You're a nigger, a fucking nigger. You act like a nigger.

JM: You must be really rat-assed drunk or that must be really good herb, cuz it isn't that fucking dark in here. My skin looks white to me.

FRANKIE: (in an attempt to steer the conversation away from confrontation) No, really though Jay, you don't have to have black skin to be a nigger.

CHRIS: Yeah, look at me. My skin is black, right? But I ain't a nigger. I ain't. It's not cool. The Brothers, I don't like them. I ain't like them. I ain't a nigger.

FRANKIE: Chris, you're a fucking nigger.

CHRIS: No, I ain't, Frankie. You know that.

Chris will go so far as to shout racial epithets at fellow blacks and to show enthusiasm for fighting with the Hallway Hangers against other black youths.

Much of this attitude, however, is expedient posturing that enables Chris to maintain his sometimes tenuous status in the group. His real feelings are quite different.

CHRIS: I've lived here for fourteen years. I've always hung with these guys. I dunno, maybe it's cuz I never knew many black people back then. These guys are all right though. They fuck with me some, but not like with some kids. I mean, after fourteen fucking years you get used to them calling you nigger every ten minutes. It doesn't do no good to get upset. I just let it slide. Fuck it. I've gotten used to it. I'm glad you're not prejudiced though. The only time they get real bad is when they've been drinking; then I gotta watch myself. I know how these guys think. That's something, too—understanding how they think. I've been here fourteen fucking years, and I know how these motherfuckers think. Like, I can tell when they're gonna fuck with me. When they're trashed, they'll be looking at me a certain way and shit. Then another one will do it. I get the fuck out of there because I know they're gonna fuck with me. Yeah, when they're drunk, they'll get like that. Fucking assholes. But when they haven't been pounding the beers, they're the most dynamite people around. Really.

The rest of the Hallway Hangers are quick to deny any animosity toward Chris.

(*in a group interview*)

JM: Chris, it can't be easy coming from down here and being half black and half white.

SHORTY: The blacks bother him cuz he hangs with whites—us.

JM: Yeah, and you fuck with him cuz he's black.

FRANKIE: No, see, cuz we just razz him because he's black.

SHORTY: We done that all his life and he knows it.

CHRIS: It don't bother me.

Nevertheless, outright hostility toward Chris does come to the surface at times, especially when people are under the influence of alcohol or drugs. It seems that whenever Chris threatens the status of others in the group with his street hockey ability, his knack for making a fast buck selling drugs, or his success with girls, racial antagonism comes to the fore. One particular incident is illustrative of this dynamic. Frankie and I were talking in the doorway when we noticed two white girls giving Chris a few lines of cocaine on the landing above us. As they came down the stairs on their way out, Frankie demanded in a very abrasive tone, "What are you getting that fuckin' *nigger* high for? You don't fucking do that." As the door slammed behind them, Frankie muttered, "They want to suck his black cock, that's why. Fuckin' cunts."

Although the Hallway Hangers attribute their racist attitudes to the riots that occurred in Clarendon Heights during their childhoods, such an explanation cannot account for the racial antagonism that gave rise to the riots in the first place. Racism in Clarendon Heights is a complex phenomenon that does not lend itself to easy interpretation or explanation. Nevertheless, in the attitudes and comments of the Hallway Hangers, it is possible to discern evidence in support of the proposition that racism in lower-class communities stems from competition for scarce economic resources.[3] Shorty, for example, bitterly attributes his brother's unemployment to affirmative action policies: "He got laid off because they hired all Puerto Ricans, blacks, and Portegis (Portuguese). It's cuz of the fuckin' spics and niggers." In a separate discussion of the harshness of unemployment, Smitty, an older youth on the fringes of the Hallway Hangers, put forth a similar view.

SMITTY: All the fuckin' niggers are getting the jobs. Two of them motherfuckers got hired yesterday [at a construction site]; I didn't get shit. They probably don't even know how to hold a fuckin' shovel either.

FRANKIE: Fuckin' right. That's why we're hanging here now with empty pockets.

The perceived economic threat blacks pose to the Hallway Hangers contributes to their racism. The racial prejudice of the Hallway Hangers, a subject of academic interest in its own right, also has important ramifications for social reproduction. In Chapter 8 we see how it not only harms blacks but is ultimately self-destructive as well.

Although the Hallway Hangers can be hostile to Boo-Boo and Chris, their real racial venom is directed against the Brothers, the black peer group at Clarendon Heights. Interestingly, when considering each member of the Brothers individually, the Hallway Hangers admit respect and esteem for a number of them. Considered as a group, however, there is little feeling aside from bitter racial enmity. As with Chris, the enmity is at its sharpest when the Brothers are perceived as threatening in some way. The following interview segment, quoted at length, captures the essence of the Hallway Hangers' attitude toward the Brothers.

JM: What do you think of Super and the rest of them?

SLICK: Fuck 'em, they're niggers.

FRANKIE: Fuck 'em, they're niggers, that's right.

SHORTY: They're niggers, man.

FRANKIE: Pretty soon, pretty soon, we're gonna be beefing [fighting] them motherfuckers, and they're not gonna like it.

SLICK: Once they're ready to take a beating, that's when . . .

FRANKIE: No, no. I'll tell you. They're ready; they're ready. Summertime. Summertime, we'll be fighting.

SLICK: Yeah, this summer we'll be fighting them.

FRANKIE: Definitely, we'll be fighting them.

SHORTY: Even though we did before, and they were the same age as us, but if we beat them up bad, they'd fucking, y'know . . .

SLICK: They'd call the cops and shit.

SHORTY: (sarcastically) Or their big tough fathers would come out. You see what we'll do to their fathers. We'll fight their fathers worse than we'll fight them.

JM: (with my disgust undisguised) So why are you so into that?

SHORTY: No, we ain't into it. We don't like their attitude.

FRANKIE: They don't like us, man. What're you crazy? They're niggers.

SHORTY: They move in here. We don't bother them. Once they start with us . . .

FRANKIE: Hey, they're coming on our fucking land. Fuck them motherfuckers. They don't like us, man, and I sure as hell don't like them.

SHORTY: I've lived here all my fucking life, and no new nigger is gonna move in and fucking start [a fight] with me.

FRANKIE: And I'll tell ya, I'll stick any of them; I'll beat any of them. Fuck them fucking niggers.

SHORTY: Jay, listen to this. They move in here, right?

JM: But how do they move in here, huh?

SHORTY: They just move in here, y'know?

JM: But wait. Into the projects? It's not like you pick which one you wanna move into.

SHORTY: Bullshit!

JM: I think they said, "There's too many white people in here and people been complaining." So they started moving black people in here.

FRANKIE: (*still yelling*) Yeah, that's what happened last time. They moved too many fucking niggers in, and then in '71 and '72 we had the fucking riots.

SHORTY: The last time they did that was ten years ago. Watch!

JM: All's I'm sayin' is that it's not their fault that they moved in. It's the Housing Authority that sends 'em in.

SHORTY: Will you fucking listen, Jay?

JM: Yeah, but I mean, if you were black, would you wanna live here? I fucking wouldn't.

FRANKIE: (*very angrily*) They come in here with a fucking *attitude*, man. They ain't gettin' no [inaudible] attitude. Fucking niggers are getting *hurt* this summer. I'm telling you, man.

SHORTY: Jay, *listen*. When they first moved in here, they were really cool and everything. We didn't bother them. But once more and more black families moved in, they said, "Wow, we can overrun these people. We can overpower them." That's what their attitude was.

SLICK: Slowly but surely, man, they're trying to fucking fuck us over. It's gonna be '71 and '72 all over again.

SHORTY: They come in here walking with their buddies now with sticks and shit and look at us and laugh. Y'know what we could do to them so bad? It's just that a lot of us don't fucking wanna . . .

SLICK: No one can really afford to get arrested anymore, or we'll go away. No one wants to go away. No one wants to go to fucking jail.

FRANKIE: Yeah, but I'll tell you. Them niggers, man. It's just about time. This summer.

The resentment the Hallway Hangers feel toward blacks and the destructive consequences that flow from this hatred could not be more plainly exposed. By pointing to the economic and social factors that feed this racism, I do not mean to absolve the Hallway Hangers of responsibility for their racist attitudes and beliefs, much less for the violence to which these give rise. Racism is a sickness that rots American society, but those who see it simply as a matter of individual pathology overlook the social conditions that contribute to its outbreak and spread. We can blame the Hallway Hangers, but we also must blame the economic and social conditions of lower-class life under competitive capitalism.

THE BROTHERS:
CONSPICUOUS BY THEIR CONVENTIONALITY

In contrast to the Hallway Hangers, the Brothers accommodate themselves to accepted standards of behavior and strive to fulfill socially approved roles. It is the white peer group from Clarendon Heights that is at odds with mainstream American culture. Nonconformity fascinates the sociologist, and if in this book undue attention is given to the distinctive cultural novelty of the Hallway Hangers, it should be borne in mind that the Brothers also pose an interesting and in many ways exceptional case. However, because my primary interest is the role that aspirations play in social reproduction, and because the Hallway Hangers undergo the process of social reproduction in a unique fashion, my emphasis in both the presentation of ethnographic material and in its analysis inevitably falls on the Hallway Hangers.

The most obvious difference between the two peer groups is in racial composition: The Brothers have only one white member. When one considers that this peer group emerges from the same social setting as do the Hallway Hangers, other striking differences become apparent. Composed of a nucleus of seven teenagers and expanding to twelve at times, this peer group is not a distinctive subculture with its own set of values defined in opposition to the dominant culture. The Brothers attend high school on a regular basis. None of them smokes cigarettes, drinks regularly, or uses drugs. None has been arrested.

Craig is a quiet, tall, dark-skinned youth with a reserved manner and easy smile, except on the basketball court. A graceful athlete, he is on the varsity basketball team at the high school. He moved to the projects six years ago and was one of three black children to attend the neighborhood grammar school. His family is tightly knit; he lives with his parents, four brothers and sisters, and two stepsiblings. Self-assured and agreeable, Craig maintains a leadership role in the peer group, although such status demarcations are much less clearly defined among the Brothers than among the Hallway Hangers.

In contrast to Craig, Super is a fiery, loud, yet often introspective lad who, despite his medium size, never backs down from a fight. Hesitant in speech and uncomfortable with written material, Super struggles in the classroom. He is, however, a natural athlete. His speed, quickness, and agility lend themselves to football and basketball, but his carefree attitude toward sport and his flare for flashy moves do not sit well with high school coaches and have prevented success in these areas at the varsity level. Super's home life is turbulent; his temper, apparently, is matched by his father's, and the confrontations between father and son have prompted Super to leave home for safer environs for a week or two on at least three occasions.

Originally from the Dominican Republic, Juan is the only Brother to have finished school, but he currently is unemployed. He is slight of build, a sincere and sensitive youth. Juan speaks in somewhat broken English, was not particularly successful in school, and is not a good athlete. His loyalty, kind manner, and sense of fair play, however, are attributes that have earned him respect. Such remarks as these are typical of him: "Yup," he said, as he left one evening to meet his girlfriend, "there's the three things everyone needs—a job, a car, and a girl. And the girl's the most important. Because otherwise you'd be lonely. You need someone to talk to and somebody to love." In a neighborhood notorious for its toughness, such a comment is remarkable for its honesty and tenderness.

Mokey is a quick-tempered boy whose impatience with others often borders on insolence. Stocky and of medium height, Mokey commits himself with vigor and enthusiasm to whatever he is pursuing but has difficulty sustaining this drive for an extended period of time. One week he is enthused about his prospects on the school football team, but two weeks later he has quit the squad and exhibits a newfound zeal for track and field. Full of energy and constantly on the move, Mokey chafes against the tight rein his mother keeps on him but generally accedes to her wishes. When necessary, his father, who does not live with the family, is called in to straighten out any problems.

James, a junior at the high school, is very small for his age. He manages to compensate for his diminutive size, however, with a quick and caustic tongue. He is not as well integrated into the group as the other boys, perhaps because of a long, involved relationship with a girl that recently ended. A year ago, James was a fixture in one of the city's video arcades during school hours; now he attends school every day as well as on Thursday evenings to make up for failed subjects. This turnabout resulted from a serious talk with his father, whose presence in the household is sporadic. James's wit, sense of humor, and toughness have earned him the esteem of the Brothers.

Derek is Boo-Boo's half brother. The two boys have different friends, interests, and attitudes and are not particularly close, but they do maintain an amiable cordiality outside their home, which is a considerable achievement in view of the animosity between the Brothers and Hallway Hangers. (I take up the siblings' substantially divergent outlooks and membership in different peer groups in Chapter 8.) Their paths parted when, as a third grader, Derek's scholastic achievements enabled him to secure a government scholarship to a prestigious private school. Derek attended Barnes Academy through the eighth grade with great success; his grades were good, and he had many friends. Nevertheless, he decided to attend the city high school, where he has continued his academic achievement. Although lacking in athletic prowess, Derek is admired by the other boys for his scholastic success and personal motivation.

Mike is the sole white member of the Brothers. He lives with his mother and grandmother and rules the household. His large frame and strength have made him a valuable asset to the high school's football, wrestling, and track and field squads. His athletic ability and an aversion to drugs and alcohol inculcated by his mother as well as a strong and lasting friendship with Super all account for Mike's allegiance to the Brothers. He takes some abuse from his white peers on this account, but his self-confidence is not punctured by such ribbing.

The Brothers, in contrast to the Hallway Hangers, are not a distinctive subculture with its own set of shared values. The Brothers accept the dominant culture's definitions of success and judge themselves by these criteria. A night in the city jail would permanently tarnish a Brother's reputation rather than build it up. In the eyes of the Brothers, John Grace, the bartender who was involved in the shootout in Clarendon Heights, only would be worthy of disdain, and perhaps pity, rather than the respect Frankie accords him. While the Hallway Hangers have little concern for the judgments of the dominant culture, the Brothers become uncomfortable and embarrassed when recounting disciplinary problems they have had at home or in school. Such a "confession" for a member of the Hallway Hangers, on the other hand, might be accompanied by laughter and a sense of triumph.

Just as the Brothers accept the values of the dominant culture, their behavior generally conforms to societal expectations. Whereas the Hallway Hangers are conspicuous in their consumption of cigarettes and beer, the Brothers reject both. Although many of the Brothers drink beer in moderation every once in a while at a party or on a similar occasion, their consumption of alcohol is very limited. Likewise, although most of the Brothers have tried marijuana, they rarely smoke it, and they never use other drugs.

The Brothers are uncomfortable with simply "hanging"; they cannot tolerate such inactivity. They often can be found playing basketball in the park or the gym. If a pick-up game of basketball cannot be mustered in the immediate neighborhood, they often will walk a half mile to the Salvation Army gym or another housing project. Energetic and spirited, the Brothers dislike the idleness of the Hallway Hangers.

DEREK: I would never hang with them. I'm not interested in
  drinking, getting high, or making trouble. That's about all they do.
  . . . I don't like to just sit around.

Although the Brothers do not adopt those practices that symbolize rejection of authority or basic societal values, their peer group does have its own distinctive attributes. The Brothers carry themselves in ways familiar to most urban black Americans, although somewhat scaled down. Their style of dress, mode of speech, and form of greeting clearly set them apart from other residents of Clarendon Heights. However, the caps, neck chains, and open shirts so prevalent among teenagers in the predominantly black sections of the city are lacking among the Brothers, whose residency in a white neighborhood has important implications for much more than their dress.

Athletics is one activity into which the Brothers channel their energies. Many excel in organized youth, church, and school basketball leagues as well as in regular pick-up games. Mike, Super, and Mokey also play on the school football team. Only Juan and Derek are not good athletes, and even they maintain an interest in sports, often rounding out the teams for a pick-up game of basketball.

Girls also claim much of the Brothers' time. A frequent topic of conversation, their interest in girls seems much more widespread than is the case for the Hallway Hangers. While the Hangers tend to go out with girls on a casual basis (typically for a weekend), the Brothers often have steady girlfriends, with whom they are constantly speaking on the phone, to whose house they are forever headed, and about whom they always are boasting. Whereas the Hallway Hangers focus on their beer and drugs, the Brothers have their basketball and girlfriends.

Since Juan bought an old worn-out Vega for two hundred dollars and fixed it up complete with paint job and functioning engine, cruising the streets also has become a favorite pastime for the Brothers. It gives them access to the "Port" and the "Coast," the black sections of the city. Considering the tense racial atmosphere of the Clarendon Heights community, it is no wonder that the Brothers do not spend as much time in the vicinity of the Heights as the Hallway Hangers do and instead prefer the black neighborhoods.

In addition to being the objects of many of the Hallway Hangers' racist slurs and insults, the Brothers suffer from even more substantive racial abuse. Super tells how the windows in his family's car have been broken year after year and how one morning last spring he awoke to find "KKK" drawn in spray paint on the side of the car. Juan recounts with anger accompanied by matter-of-fact acceptance how his mother was taunted by some members of the Hallway Hangers, which led his father into a confrontation with them. His father was lucky to escape unharmed from the ensuing argument. Juan has a measure of understanding for the Hallway Hangers: "When they call me a nigger, I usually don't let it bother me none. They drunk or high, y'know. They don't know what they're doing." In his freshman year of high school, however, Juan was beaten up by Shorty for no apparent reason; he still bears the scar on his lip from the fight, and the memory of it burns in his mind, fueling the resentment he feels toward the Hallway Hangers.

Although the Brothers are not submissive in the face of racial animosity from the Hallway Hangers, they are outnumbered and outmatched, and they usually find it expedient to walk away before a confrontation explodes into a street fight. They are accustomed to the violent racial prejudice of the Hallway Hangers. In fact, Craig, instead of being upset that a simple basketball game threatened to erupt into a racial brawl, merely commented, "That was good of Shorty to come over and tell us we better leave before his friends start all sorts of trouble." Although the Brothers are hesitant to answer openly the insults of the Hallway Hangers, they do vent their contempt for the Hallway Hangers in private discussions.

(all in separate interviews)

JUAN: I don't like their attitude, their gig, what they do. . . . They'll be there, hanging in front of the Heights, fighting and arguing and stuff like that. . . . It wasn't until I moved here that I heard the word "nigger." I had heard about people in the projects; I knew they'd be a pain in the ass sometimes. . . . I swear, if I ever see one of them touching my mother or doing something to my car, I don't care, I'll kill them. Cuz I don't like none of them. I'm afraid I'm gonna hurt one of them real bad. Every time I hear them call me nigger, I just don't say anything, but I can't take the pressure of people getting on my case every time, y'know?

CRAIG: I don't know why they just hang out there being crazy and getting drunk and bothering people. Maybe cuz they need attention or something. They got nuttin' better to do so they might as well cause trouble so people will think they're bad and stuff. They're just lazy. They wanna take the easy way out—that is, hang around outside all day.

JAMES: They're not gonna get anywhere except for standing at that same corner going (*imitating someone who is very benumbed*), "Hey man, got some pot, man? Hey Frank, let's get high."

DEREK: We just have different attitudes. We like to stay away from the projects as much as possible, or they'll give us trouble. That's about all they do: make trouble.

SUPER: They smoke reefer; they drink. They ain't friendly like people, y'know what I'm sayin'? They go around the street laughing at people, ragging them out, y'know what I mean? They just disrespect people.

MIKE: They're just a bunch of fuck-ups.

Such perceptions are often voiced by the Brothers. The situation between the two peer groups, however, is not one of constant strife. Rather, there is a constant underlying tension that surfaces occasionally—often during basketball games or when the Hallway Hangers have been drinking excessively—but that threatens to erupt into considerable violence.

Aside from racial factors, the character of the two peer groups differs markedly in other ways. The Brothers have no pecking order based on fighting ability. Although Craig is generally respected most, there is no hierarchy in the group, hidden or otherwise; the Brothers do not playfully abuse each other, physically or verbally. Loose and shifting cliques develop among the members and sometimes encompass outsiders. Friendships wax and wane according to the season and the extracurricular activities and responsibilities of the boys. During the winter, for example, Craig is so tied up with the basketball team that he effectively drops out of the group, and his best friend, Super, becomes closer to Derek and Mokey. During the school day, the Brothers often see little of each other and, once out, invariably break up into smaller friendship groups, coming all together only once in awhile. In short, the Brothers are no more than a peer group, whereas the Hallway Hangers are a much more cohesive unit with its own subculture.

The Hallway Hangers, who reject the values of the dominant culture and subscribe to their own distinctive cultural norms, have a sense of solidarity that is noticeably absent from the Brothers' peer group. Internal cohesion and the adoption of communitarian values, in which the Hallway Hangers take pride, are missing among the Brothers. Although all the Brothers would support each other in a fight, the ties that bind them are not as strong and are not as strongly affirmed as those that bind the Hallway Hangers.

The Brothers do not compare themselves to members of the upper classes, nor do they feel as keenly the stigma or shame associated with life in public housing. (An explanation of these differences is undertaken in Chapter 7.)

Daily life for the Brothers is far less circumscribed than it is for the Hallway Hangers. Active, enthusiastic, and still in school, the Brothers are not preoccupied with mere survival on the street. Their world extends into the classroom and onto the basketball court, and it extends into the home a great deal more than does the world of the Hallway Hangers, as we shall see in the next chapter.

NOTES

1. All temporal citations have as their reference point March 1984, when the first draft of the book was written. Thus, "presently" and "currently" refer to late winter 1984 and "graduated last year" means June 1983. The present tense is used throughout the book, and no developments after February 1984 are included as part of the research.

2. *Lower class*, as the term applies to public housing residents, is not used in this book as an analytical construct but as a descriptive term that captures their position at the lower end of the socioeconomic spectrum. Similarly, the term *upper classes* is used to refer to all those whose position is higher on the socioeconomic scale; *middle class* refers more specifically to white-collar workers, including professional and managerial personnel.

3. See, especially, David T. Wellman, *Portraits of White Racism* (Cambridge: Cambridge University Press, 1977); and Donald Neal, "A Theory of the Origin of Ethnic Stratification," *Social Problems* 16 (Fall 1968):157–172.

$$4$$

THE INFLUENCE
OF THE FAMILY

As the focal socializing agency, especially in the early years of a child's life, the family plays a crucial role in the process of social reproduction. In this chapter, we consider the particular circumstances of each boy's family and how the family influences his expectations for the future. In describing the families of these boys, we must be attentive to a number of factors, such as the presence of a father in the household,[1] the occupational histories of parents and older siblings, and the length of the family's tenancy in public housing.

All families living in Clarendon Heights are lower class. For a family of four to qualify for federal housing projects, its annual income must not exceed $14,000; for state housing developments the limit is approximately $1,500 lower. These are, of course, the upper boundaries; the annual income of most families living in Clarendon Heights is well below the limit.

THE HALLWAY HANGERS' HOUSEHOLDS

Chris lives with his white mother and two younger sisters. Their father, who is black, moved out of the house a few years ago. "I kicked my father out," boasts Chris in a group interview. Chris also has two half brothers and one half sister who live on their own. His brothers work in unskilled, manual labor jobs; his sister is a part-time secretary. Chris seems to have free run of the household. His mother, a kind, friendly woman who has never married, has been pleading with Chris for two years to attend school regularly, but to no avail. Although she does not work regularly, for much of the year she babysits in her home for one and sometimes two young children from working-class families. In exchange for her labors (nine hours per day), she receives a small wage.

Chris's family has lived in Clarendon Heights for sixteen years, prior to which his mother lived with her other children in private housing.

Boo-Boo also has lived in Clarendon Heights for his entire life. He and his older brother have a different father than his younger brother Derek (a member of the Brothers) and his younger sister. Derek's father is dead; Boo-Boo's father has lived out of state for the past five years. Their mother, a high school dropout, nevertheless has stable employment assembling computer and electronic parts in a nearby suburb. Boo-Boo's father, who graduated from high school, has been in the merchant marine "for a long, long time." Boo-Boo's older brother has a drug dependency problem. He dropped out of high school a few years ago, recently has joined the army reserves and is struggling to acquire a General Equivalency Diploma (G.E.D.) so that he can join the army.

Stoney's mother's occupational history is a modest success story. She attended St. Mary's Catholic High School in the city but had to drop out during her freshman year to find work after her mother died. She subsequently earned a G.E.D. as well as a secretarial degree and has worked her way up to a supervisory position as head secretary of a department in a state welfare office. Stoney's father's experience has been altogether different. Confined to the county house of correction a year and a half ago for passing a bad check, he broke out with only a month remaining on his sentence. With no place to go and unable to see his family, however, he subsequently turned himself in. After serving the remainder of his sentence plus some additional months for the escape, he has now found short-term work cleaning carpets. But like so many others from Clarendon Heights with a criminal record, Stoney's father probably will have a difficult time securing stable employment and is likely to end up back behind bars. Stoney's family moved to the Clarendon Heights neighborhood only three years ago; before that time they lived in Emerson Towers housing project, where Stoney's mother grew up. In contrast to the rest of the Hallway Hangers, Stoney's mother has a strong influence on him. A strict disciplinarian, she sets a nightly curfew for him, which he respects with diligence.

Frankie's family lived in the Heights for thirty years, and although his mother recently moved to another project in the city, Frankie spends nearly all of his time in the Clarendon Heights community. His mother and father both grew up in separate working-class neighborhoods in the city. Frankie's father attended City Tech for a few years before quitting school. He died when Frankie was seven years old. Frankie is the only Hallway Hanger whose mother graduated from high school; she currently works full-time at a camera factory. His sister also graduated from high school, but none of his seven brothers has earned a diploma. As mentioned earlier, all of Frankie's brothers have served time in prison; four of them presently are scattered around the state in various institutions. When out of prison, they find work in construction, landscaping, or painting. One of his brothers tends bar at the local pub, where recently he was shot trying to break up a fight. Most of Frankie's brothers work irregularly; at any given time, one or two may be unemployed.

Slick and Steve are the only members of the Hallway Hangers whose family has moved recently to public housing. Although their mother grew up only a few blocks from the Heights, the family lived in a neighboring city until they moved to Clarendon Heights about six years ago. Their father has never lived with the family, his background is hazy, and Steve's feelings about him are ambivalent. "I haven't seen that bastard for a long time. . . . I think he got put away when he was a kid." Neither parent graduated from high school. "My mom quit in the ninth or tenth grade. She quit cuz she had to put money in the house. And, y'know, she was on her own by the time she was eighteen," declares Slick. Currently out of work due to ill health, their mother, an aggressive and strong-willed woman, usually is employed as a nurse's aide. Slick and Steve have a brother and sister, both younger.

Jinks, like Frankie, is part of a large family that has lived in Clarendon Heights for close to thirty years. Both of his parents grew up in the city and are currently employed full-time. His father has worked for the city maintenance department for nearly thirty years, while his mother has been employed at a hotel as a chambermaid for six or seven years. Neither parent graduated from high school, nor did five of his six older siblings, including his only sister. The one high school graduate is in the navy; of the other three brothers, one paints houses, one works in a factory assembling clothes racks, and one is unemployed, having himself completed a stint in the navy. Jinks's fifth brother died of natural causes at the age of sixteen. His sister recently obtained her own apartment in Clarendon Heights; she has a small daughter to look after and consequently does not work. Given that the largest apartment in Clarendon Heights contains only three bedrooms, Jinks's family must have been very cramped before his sister and her daughter moved out. Even now, six people live in the unit.

Shorty's family is even larger. He has ten older brothers and sisters, three of whom have graduated from high school.

SHORTY: I got seven brothers. We lived here for thirteen years. . . . I mean, we been through the riots and everything. My brother Joe had to quit school when he was sixteen years old, just because my father was an alcoholic. He had to go out and get a job. My [other] brother, he was a bikey; he had to sell pot. But Joe was out gettin' a job at sixteen to support all the kids. . . . He [went back to school and was subsequently employed as] a cop for two months; he got laid off. He was working at the weapons lab as a security guard. You ask him. He's our father. That's what he really is—he's our father. My father got put away for nine months. He didn't live with us for six years. Every fucking penny that my brother got he threw right into the family, right into the house. Cuz my mother can't work. She almost died three times; she has a brain tumor.

Aside from this account, information on Shorty's family is very sketchy, as he will very seldom speak about his home life. In a separate interview, however, Shorty did mention that with the exception of Joe, all the boys in his family have at one time or another been in the military service, as was his father.

Despite the difficulty inherent in generalizing about such diverse family histories, it is clear that the Hallway Hangers share certain family characteristics that may affect their aspirations. Foremost among these are the duration of these families' tenancy in public housing. With the exception of Slick and Steve, all the Hallway Hangers and their families have lived in the projects for many years: Shorty for thirteen years, Chris for sixteen, Boo-Boo's family for at least eighteen, Jinks's family for twenty-seven years, and Frankie's and Stoney's families for thirty years. Like most of the project residents, the educational attainment of these boys' parents and older brothers and sisters is very low; of their parents, only Boo-Boo's father and Frankie's mother graduated from high school. The sporadic employment record of family members is another common characteristic. For those who are able to find employment at all, it is typically menial, low paying, and unstable. Other less widespread commonalities between the families of these boys include the fathers' absence from the household, the large size of the families, and the numerous encounters of family members with the law.

THE BROTHERS' FAMILIES

Super's family has lived in public housing for eighteen years. The family moved to Clarendon Heights only five years ago but prior to that lived in a large housing project in a nearby city. Super's mother and father came to the north from South Carolina and Tennessee respectively in the early 1960s. Neither graduated from high school. Super's mother does not work; his father is a general laborer in construction but currently is unemployed, a typical predicament for low-level employees in the seasonal construction business. Super has two younger sisters and an older sister who attends a Catholic high school. Super has left home repeatedly, citing his parents' strict and inflexible disciplinary code as the reason. Although many parents in Clarendon Heights use physical intimidation when disciplining their children, Super is the only boy discussed in this book who admits he is abused physically by his parents.

Details about Mokey's home life are scarce. Mokey is not sure whether or not his parents graduated from high school. Apparently a heavy drinker, Mokey's father is a custodian in an office building in the commercial and financial district of the city. Although his father moved out of the house at least four years ago, Mokey frequently meets him at work to help with the evening cleanup, especially during the summer. His mother works part-time at a nearby day care center. He has a brother who is two years younger than he is and a five-year-old sister who has just entered kindergarten. His family lived in a very small public housing development before moving into Clarendon Heights.

James has lived in the Clarendon Heights community for his entire life. His mother, who is originally from Georgia, quit school when she was in the eighth grade. She is unemployed temporarily because she injured her shoulder about six months ago, but she usually works as a nurse's aide for the elderly. James's father graduated from high school and currently works in a factory that manufactures zippers and buttons. When asked if his father lives in the household, James shakes his head no, but adds, "He didn't really move out. He comes and he goes." James is the oldest child; his two younger sisters are excellent students, but his thirteen-year-old brother has a much more lackadaisical attitude toward his education. As noted previously, James's approach to school recently has undergone a dramatic change from ambivalence to commitment.

Craig's family came to this country from Haiti about eleven years ago and has lived in the Clarendon Heights neighborhood for six years. Although the educational system is somewhat different in Haiti, both his parents attained the equivalent of a high school diploma. His mother works part-time as a "homemaker"; she prepares meals, cleans, and performs other domestic chores for an elderly couple. Craig's father works as a janitor for an engineering company. Craig took pains to explain to me that his father has worked his way up to a supervisory role in the maintenance department.

CRAIG: I think he's a supervisor.

JM: So what exactly does he do?

CRAIG: Before he used to do it himself—cleaning—but now he makes sure others do it.

Craig lives with his parents and six brothers and sisters. "Actually, I got four brothers and sisters, right? But since my father was messin' around, I got six brothers and sisters." The half siblings as well as his four full brothers and sisters all live in the household. His two older sisters have been very successful academically; there seems to be a supportive atmosphere for academic achievement in his home. His brother is in his second year at a technical college. One of the older sisters, who was a straight-A student in high school, is studying medicine at a local college.

Juan's family is also from the West Indies, in this case the Dominican Republic. His mother and father were divorced there, at which time Juan's mother came to the United States. Juan and his younger sister came to join her ten years ago; their three brothers preferred to remain in their home country. At some point, his mother remarried, and the family of four moved into Clarendon Heights in 1978. Juan's stepfather is presently unemployed.

JUAN: He can't find a job.

JM: What's his trade?

JUAN: He used to work in a hotel, like in management—a boss. He decided to quit, and then he went to another hotel. Then the same thing happened: He decided to quit. Don't know why.

Juan's mother does not work either. Both his stepfather and mother graduated from high school in the Dominican Republic. He sorely misses his older brothers and hopes to return to his homeland in the near future.

Mike lives with his unmarried mother and grandmother. His father, an Italian immigrant, was a very successful professional wrestler, but Mike knows of him only from television. Mike has lived in public housing since he was two years old, first in Emerson Towers and, since 1977, in Clarendon Heights. His grandmother retired from her work in a local factory a few years ago. His mother, a high school dropout, has held a series of jobs. Most recently, she worked at Woolworth's and subsequently on the night shift at a large hotel. She found that job physically draining and currently is employed as a homemaker who takes care of elderly people. Neither woman has much success disciplining Mike; periodically, however, his uncle is brought in to help with the task, which Mike loathes. A navy veteran, Mike's uncle is the stereotypical tough, no-nonsense, blue-collar worker. His uncle recounts stories of painful encounters with his own father when his self-discipline slipped perceptibly and threatens Mike with the same type of punishment.

UNCLE: When my father said something, he meant it. When he said to be in at eleven o'clock, he meant eleven o'clock. I can remember being out with the boys one night and running all the way home—got in at 11:05. My old man was sitting there waiting for me. He looked at me, looked at the clock, and that was it. He knocked the shit out of me.

MIKE: (grimacing) That's crazy. Jay, tell him that's crazy.

UNCLE: It worked. And it'll work on you too. Damn right it will.

Indeed, the approach does have the desired effect, for now his mother exercises more control of Mike by intimidating him with the threat of summoning his uncle.

In general terms, the Brothers' families are typical of lower-class households and are much like the families of the Hallway Hangers.

Family structure is not of the conventional nuclear type; most are "broken homes." Educational achievement is low, and employment, for those who have a job, is typically in nondescript, uninteresting, unskilled work. There are, however, some differences between the families of the Brothers and of the Hallway Hangers in these areas. Whereas among the Hallway Hangers only Jinks's father lives regularly in the household, three of the Brothers have a male authority figure living with them. Nearly half the parents of the Brothers have graduated from high school; of the Hallway Hangers, only Boo-Boo and Frankie have a parent who has obtained a high school diploma. With the exception of Derek, all the Brothers are either the oldest male sibling or have older brothers and sisters whose educational achievement is significant; for the Hallway Hangers, on the other hand, it is more typical to find that an older sibling has been sent away to prison. In addition, all the Brothers' fathers work except Juan's, whereas among the Hallway Hangers, only Jinks's father works regularly. Moreover, the Hallway Hangers' families have lived in public housing for at least twenty years, and some are second-generation tenants (Stoney's, Jinks's, and Frankie's). The Brothers' families have lived in public housing for five to thirteen years (the exceptions are James, whose family has been in public housing for sixteen years, and Derek, who is Boo-Boo's brother). An even more pointed contrast arises when we consider how long the families of each peer group have lived in the Clarendon Heights neighborhood. Of the Hallway Hangers, only Steve's and Slick's family has moved to the area within the last twelve years. The opposite is true of the Brothers. Only James's family (and, of course, Derek's) has lived in Clarendon Heights for more than six years. In analyzing the feelings of hopelessness, immobility, and stagnation that plague the Hallway Hangers, this contrast will prove important.

The subjective side of these structural elements also shapes the boys' aspirations. Although rejection of parental authority is a common attribute of adolescent subcultures, the Hallway Hangers seem to respect the views of their parents, even though their parents do not play a large role in their lives. What we see in most cases is an unspoken but mutually accepted limitation of the parental role. At sixteen, seventeen, and eighteen years of age, these boys have gained a maturity from years of hard living on the street that is incommensurate with their chronological age. It appears that both they and their parents respect the notion that parental authority is incompatible with this maturity.

The boys' comments point to the limited role their parents play in their lives. In describing his mother's influence, Frankie says, "She wants me to do what I want to do." But, although she has little direct control of her son and does not exercise much authority, Frankie respects her wishes. He knew, for example, how badly she wanted one of her sons to graduate from high school. For reasons that will become clear in the next two chapters, Frankie wanted to leave school. "The only reason I got my diploma wasn't for me; it was for my mother. My mother wanted a diploma." The limited influence Slick's mother had concerning the same issue is apparent from the following exchange.

(in a discussion with Slick and Shorty)

JM: So did she [his mother] pressure you at all to stay in school when you decided to quit?

SLICK: No. She wanted me to stay in high school, but at the time, things were tough, y'know?

SHORTY: She knows his attitude is all right.

SLICK: She knows what I want, and she's not gonna stop me from getting it my way.

This type of interaction is typical of the relationship between parent and son among the Hallway Hangers.

The respect these parents have for the autonomy of their sons extends to the way in which they influence their sons' occupational aspirations. When asked about the effect their parents have on their ambitions, the Hallway Hangers are unanimous in their declaration that such a determination is left up to them alone. Indeed, even Stoney's mother, the most authoritarian of the parents, does not feel it is her place to sway Stoney's aspirations. She thinks it inappropriate to foster high aspirations in her children, fearing that unrealistically high goals only will result in disappointment, frustration, and feelings of failure and inadequacy. "It's not like he's growing up in the suburbs somewhere. Sure, he could probably make it if everything went right for him, but lemme tell you, the chances aren't great. He's got his goals, and they're probably good, realistic ones. I personally think he should've stayed in school. I think he fucked up by dropping out. But he didn't think it was worth it, and what the hell, maybe it isn't."

Other parents also are hesitant to encourage hefty ambitions in their children; as the Hallway Hangers tell it, there is little stimulus from home to raise their aspirations.

JM: What kind of work does your mother [do your parents] want you to do for a living?

(all in separate interviews)

BOO-BOO: Anything. She doesn't really care, as long as I'm working.

FRANKIE: She don't fucking care. I mean, I'm sure she cares, but she don't push nothing on me.

SLICK: She wants me to make a buck so I can move for myself.

STEVE: Anything, man. Somethin'. I dunno. Just a fuckin' job.

JINKS: They don't talk about it. They hardly ever talk about it. Just as long as I'm not out of work. My mother hates when I'm unemployed.

If such an attitude is widespread among parents in Clarendon Heights, then the conventional sociological wisdom requires revision. The premise that lower-class parents project their frustrated ambitions onto their children in an attempt to reach their goals vicariously is a widely accepted notion among social psychologists and one to which Robert Merton alludes in his essay "Social Structure and Anomie." Citing work he and some colleagues undertook on the social organization of public housing developments, Merton reports that a substantial portion of both black and white parents on lower occupational levels want their children to have professional careers.[2] Before we challenge the sociological perspective on intergenerational mobility, however, we should consider the attitude of the Brothers' parents toward this issue.

In contrast to the Hallway Hangers, the Brothers' parents exercise a good deal of authority over them. All the Brothers have a relatively early curfew, which they conscientiously obey. They are expected to perform up to a certain standard at school, both in terms of academic achievement and discipline. Furthermore, they are expected to respect prohibitions against smoking cigarettes, drinking alcohol, and using drugs. Failure to meet expected standards of behavior invariably results in punishment. In these instances, the youth is confined to his family's apartment for specified times during the day. Sometimes one of the Brothers will be restricted to his room after school, occasionally for periods as lengthy as one month. By their obedience and consent to these restrictions the Brothers acknowledge the control their parents exercise. Comparable manifestations of parental authority are altogether absent among the Hallway Hangers. In fact, Craig explicitly made this point in comparing the differences in attitude and behavior between the Brothers and the Hallway Hangers. "I guess our parents are a lot tighter than their parents. Y'know, at least they tell us what to do and stuff. From the very beginning, ever since we were born, y'know, they'd always be telling us, 'Do this; do that.' Always disciplining us. As far as their parents go, I can't really say their parents are bad, but their parents aren't helping any."

Parental influence on the Brothers' aspirations accords with Merton's findings. James, for instance, feels that his parents project their own frustrated educational and occupational ambitions onto him.

JAMES: My father had to quit school when he had to go to work. But he went back to school. He was one of the top people in his class; he could've went to college. But he didn't have the money to go to college. He had to go to work. So now he wants us all to go to college.

(*later in the same interview*)

JM: What do your mother and father want you to do for a living?

JAMES: They wanted me to be a lawyer when I was a little kid. They wanted me to grow up and be a lawyer.

James also attributes his dramatic turnaround in school performance to his father's influence.

JM: So how'd you get back on track then? Why've you started working hard now? This year.

JAMES: I decided I need to have good marks, so . . .

JM: Did anyone help you decide that or just . . .

JAMES: *Yeah*. My father.

JM: Yeah?

JAMES: He didn't hit me or anything; he just talked to me. Told me I wouldn't be able to go and do what I want to when school's over. Wouldn't be able to get no good job.

Other members of the Brothers indicate that similar processes are at work in their families.

SUPER: One thing I know they want me to do, they're always sayin' is finish school. They want me to go to college.

JM: They want you to finish high school and college?

SUPER: Uh-huh. . . . They want me to get a good job; I know that. And not no job with hard labor, y'know, standin' on my foot; they want me sittin' down, y'know, a good job, in an office.

Derek, Juan, and Craig also mention that their parents have high hopes for them. Craig's parents were the key figures in his decision to try becoming an architect. Juan's father wants him to get a job where "you can keep yourself clean." Derek's family nurtured hopes their son would enter a professional career. "They wanted me to be a lawyer. Ever since I went to Barnes Academy."

In addition to the Brothers' accounts, we have further evidence from the parents themselves. Mokey's mother, for instance, feels that her expectations heavily influence Mokey and undoubtedly will play a large part in whatever he decides to do. She insists that he pursue a career "which gives a successful future," such as management or ownership of a small business. She also believes that Mokey should "plan to be a success and reach the highest goal possible. The sky's the limit. That's what my mother told me, and that's what I tell my children. The sky is the limit."

Thus, the Brothers present a significant contrast to the Hallway Hangers with respect to their parents' influence in their lives. The Brothers' parents wield a substantial degree of authority, both in the present and in shaping their children's educational and occupational aspirations. These parents may be projecting their own unfulfilled occupational ambitions onto their children by nurturing in them high hopes for the future.

Some of the Brothers also have older siblings who serve as role models. Craig, Super, and James all have older brothers and sisters who have achieved at least moderate success in school. These three boys see that the path to academic achievement can be followed. Juan, Mokey, and Mike have no older siblings; they see a path that is as yet untried. In contrast, the Hallway Hangers, with the exception of Stoney and Slick, have older siblings who have failed in school; thus, the Hallway Hangers see a tortuous path that is difficult to negotiate. The Brothers all may not have older brothers and sisters who are high academic achievers, but, with the exception of Derek, at least they are not confronted exclusively with examples of academic failure, as most of the Hallway Hangers are. This difference between the two peer groups also has a significant impact on the boys' hopes for the future, which are the subject of the next chapter.

NOTES

1. The sociological literature on delinquency and deviance cites the absence of a male authority figure as an important factor in the socialization of teenage boys. That the absence of a father figure affects boys' (and girls') upbringing and development is beyond doubt, but the tendency to view single-parent families as pathological must be resisted. Familial structures are culturally and historically specific. Lower-class and black family structures are often not conventional, but, as Errol Lawrence argues in the Centre for Contemporary Cultural Studies' *The Empire Strikes Back* (London: Hutchinson, 1982), the conventional nuclear family is not the natural or universally applicable form of household organization. Rather, the nuclear family is the specific achievement of the white bourgeoisie (p. 120). To maintain that households headed by single women are inherently weak or unstable is to assume that women are incapable of raising children on their own, a view I do not share.

2. Robert K. Merton, *Social Theory and Social Structure* (New York: Free Press, 1968), p. 213.

5

THE WORLD OF WORK: ASPIRATIONS OF THE HANGERS AND BROTHERS

Given that work determines one's social class, the perpetuation of class inequality requires that boys like the Hallway Hangers and the Brothers go on to jobs that are comparable in status to the occupations of their parents. Thus, the attitudes of these boys toward the world of work are critical to our understanding of social reproduction. In this chapter, their previous employment records, their general impressions of work, their aspirations and expectations, and their perceptions of the job opportunity structure are considered.

Before describing the boys' orientation toward work, I would like to make an analytical distinction between aspirations and expectations. Both involve assessments of one's desires, abilities, and the character of the opportunity structure. In articulating one's aspirations, an individual weighs his or her preferences more heavily; expectations are tempered by perceived capabilities and available opportunities. Aspirations are one's preferences relatively unsullied by anticipated constraints; expectations take these constraints squarely into account.[1]

THE HALLWAY HANGERS: KEEPING A LID ON HOPE

Conventional, middle-class orientations toward employment are inadequate to describe the Hallway Hangers' approach to work. The notion of a career, a set of jobs that are connected to one another in a logical progression, has little relevance to these boys. They are hesitant when asked about their aspirations and expectations. This hesitancy is not the result of indecision; rather it stems from the fact that these boys see little choice involved in getting a job. No matter how hard I pressed him, for instance, Jinks refused to articulate his aspirations: "I think you're kiddin' yourself to have any. We're just gonna take whatever we can get." Jinks is a perceptive boy, and his answer seems to be an accurate depiction of the situation. Beggars cannot be choosers, and these boys have nothing other than unskilled labor to offer on a credential-based job market.

It is difficult to gauge the aspirations of most of the Hallway Hangers. Perhaps at a younger age they had dreams for their futures. At ages sixteen, seventeen, and eighteen, however, their own job experiences as well as those of family members have contributed to a deeply entrenched cynicism about their futures. What is perceived as the cold, hard reality of the job market weighs very heavily on the Hallway Hangers; they believe their preferences will have almost no bearing on the work they actually will do. Their expectations are not merely tempered by perceptions of the opportunity structure; even their aspirations are crushed by their estimation of the job market. These generalizations may seem bold and rather extreme, but they do not lack ethnographic support.

The pessimism and uncertainty with which the Hallway Hangers view their futures emerge clearly when the boys are asked to speculate on what their lives will be like in twenty years.

(*all in separate interviews*)

STONEY: Hard to say. I could be dead tomorrow. Around here, you gotta take life day by day.

BOO-BOO: I dunno. I don't want to think about it. I'll think about it when it comes.

FRANKIE: I don't fucking know. Twenty years. I may be fucking dead. I live a day at a time. I'll probably be in the fucking pen.

SHORTY: Twenty years? I'm gonna be in jail.

These responses are striking not only for the insecurity and despondency they reveal, but also because they do not include any mention of work. It is not that work is unimportant—for people as strapped for money as the Hallway Hangers are, work is crucial. Rather, these boys are indifferent to the issue of future employment. Work is a given; they all hope to hold jobs of one kind or another in order to support themselves and their families. But the Hallway Hangers, like the lads in Willis's study, believe the character of work, at least all work in which they are likely to be involved, is essentially the same: boring, undifferentiated, and unrewarding. Thinking about their future jobs is a useless activity for the Hallway Hangers. What is there to think about?

For Steve and Jinks, although they do see themselves employed in twenty years, work is still of tangential importance.

JM: If you had to guess, what do you think you'll be doing twenty years from now?

(*in separate interviews*)

STEVE: I don't fucking know. Working probably. Have my own pad, my own house. Bitches, kids. Fucking fridge full of brewskies. Fine wife, likes to get laid.

JINKS: Twenty years from now? Probably kicked back in my own apartment doing the same shit I'm doing now—getting high. I'll have a job, if I'm not in the service, if war don't break out, if I'm not dead. I just take one day at a time.

Although the Hallway Hangers expect to spend a good portion of their waking hours on the job, work is important to them not as an end in itself, but solely as a means to an end—money.

In probing the occupational aspirations and expectations of the Hallway Hangers, I finally was able to elicit from them some specific hopes. Although Shorty never mentions his expectations, the rest of the Hallway Hangers have responded to my prodding with some definite answers. The range of answers as well as how they change over time are as significant as the particular hopes each boy expresses.

Boo-Boo's orientation toward work is typical of the Hallway Hangers. He has held a number of jobs in the past, most of them in the summer. During his freshman year in high school Boo-Boo worked as a security guard at school for $2.50 an hour in order to make restitution for a stolen car he damaged. Boo-Boo also has worked on small-scale construction projects through a summer youth employment program called Just-A-Start, at a pipe manufacturing site, and as a clerk in a gift shop. Boo-Boo wants to be an automobile mechanic. Upon graduating from high school, he studied auto mechanics at a technical school on a scholarship. The only black student in his class, Boo-Boo was expelled early in his first term after racial antagonism erupted into a fight. Boo-Boo was not altogether disappointed, for he already was unhappy with what he considered the program's overly theoretical orientation. (Howard London found this kind of impatience typical of working-class students in the community college he studied.[2]) Boo-Boo wanted hands-on training, but "all's they were doing was telling me about how it's made, stuff like that." Boo-Boo currently is unemployed, but he recently had a chance for a job as a cook's helper. Although he was not hired, the event is significant nevertheless because prior to the job interview, Boo-Boo claimed that his ambition now was to work in a restaurant. Here we have an example of the primacy of the opportunity structure in determining the aspirations of the Hallway Hangers. One job opening in another field was so significant that the opening prompted Boo-Boo to redefine totally his aspirations.

In contrast to the rest of the Hallway Hangers who are already on the job market, Steve wants to stay in school for the two years required to get his diploma. Yet he has a similar attitude toward his future work as do the other youths. He quit his summer job with the Just-A-Start program and has no concrete occupational aspirations. As for expectations, he believes he might enlist in the air force after graduation but adds, "I dunno. I might just go up and see my uncle, do some fuckin' construction or something."

Many of these boys expect to enter military service. Jinks and Frankie mention it as an option; Stoney has tried to enlist, but without success. Although Jinks refuses to think in terms of aspirations, he will say what he expects to do after he finishes school.

JM: What are you gonna do when you get out?

JINKS: Go into the service, like everybody else. The navy.

JM: What about after that?

JINKS: After that, just get a job, live around here.

JM: Do you have any idea what job you wanna get?

JINKS: No. No particular job. Whatever I can get.

Jinks subsequently quit school. He had been working twenty hours a week making clothesracks in a factory with his brother. He left school with the understanding that he would be employed full-time, and he was mildly content with his situation: "I got a job. It ain't a good job, but other things will come along." Two weeks later, he was laid off. For the past three months he has been unemployed, hanging full-time in doorway #13.

Shorty has worked construction in the past and has held odd jobs such as shoveling snow. Shorty, an alcoholic, has trouble holding down a steady job, as he freely admits. He was enrolled in school until recently. Ordered by the court to a detoxification center, Shorty apparently managed to convince the judge that he had attended enough Alcoholics Anonymous meetings in the meantime to satisfy the court. He has not returned to school since, nor has he landed a job. Given that Shorty is often on the run from the police, he is too preoccupied with pressing everyday problems to give serious thought to his long-term future. It is not surprising that my ill-timed query about his occupational aspirations met with only an impatient glare.

Stoney is one of the few Hallway Hangers with a definite ambition. In fact, he aspires to a middle-class occupation—to own his own pizza shop. Although Stoney's goal is exceptionally high for a Hallway Hanger, ownership of one's own business, according to Ely Chinoy, is a common ambition for at least part of the blue-collar workforce.[3] Still, Stoney himself considers his aspiration unusually ambitious and is automatically defensive about his chances for success.

JM: What's your ambition?

STONEY: To *own* a store. One of these days I will. Watch. People might laugh at me now, but one of these days I will. It might be in fifty or sixty years. No, after a few years—if I'm about thirty years old, I can get a loan to get a store easy. Really. Get me some financial credit, buy me a little shop, work my way up.

Averse to both heavy manual work and "sitting behind a desk—I'd hate that," Stoney went straight to a local pizza establishment when he was put on a special work-study arrangement at school. He worked twenty-five hours per week, attending school in a special class from three to six in the afternoon. Stoney finally "got real sick and tired of school" and started working full-time, only to be fired soon thereafter. "I was working part-time anyway and I could work more if I wanted, so I told him [the boss] to put it up to thirty [hours per week] and I cut down my school more. Then I went up to forty. That's when I quit school. Then I got fired (*laughs*)."

Stoney can afford to laugh. In contrast to Jinks, he has a marketable skill—making pizza—and immediately found another job in a small pizza shop in a different part of town. He soon left that "gig," returning to his original job. Shortly thereafter, he was fired once again for "being mouthy." The very next day, he was hired by a third pizza shop. Stoney has worked there for the past seven months, earning $5.00 per hour under the table. He likes his boss, the small size of the operation, and the good wage.

A year ago, however, when Stoney was employed by the larger establishment, was working for a boss he did not like, and was making only slightly more than minimum wage, he tried to join the navy. "I wanted to get into the navy and travel for awhile. For two years, see the world, travel. I just found out real quick that they weren't gonna take me cuz of my drug record." Stoney was arrested last year for possession of mescaline. Although he could still have joined the army, he was not interested: "I don't want no bullshit army." According to Stoney, it is just as well that he was not accepted into the navy. "I like what I'm doing now, so I'll probably be here for awhile."

Like most of the Hallway Hangers, Slick already has held quite a few jobs. Between the ages of nine and thirteen Slick worked under the table in a supermarket that his uncle managed. He also has worked construction and as a clerk in a shoe store as well as odd jobs such as snow shoveling and minor landscaping. Slick quit school his junior year and began bagging groceries in another supermarket. "I just decided I had to put any kind of money away; whatever was available I would do, right? When I went down there (*pointing to doorway #13*), a lot of people would say, 'Well, fuck it; it's just bagging,' y'know? But you ain't gonna get no $20,000 a year job right off the streets anyway. You have to start somewhere, doin' somethin'."

Just the same, Slick could not take bagging groceries for long. He quit that job last June and enlisted in the army the next day. Slick really wanted to join the marines, but without a high school diploma, one must score exceptionally high on the standardized tests the marines administer to potential recruits. Slick missed by one point.

Once he was reconciled to entering the army, Slick was disappointed to find that without a high school diploma, he did not qualify for many of the benefits. Not one to accept a setback so easily, Slick did something about it. "I started talkin' about the bonuses and shit [with the recruiter], cuz I seen them on the paper up there, and I asked him. He said 'Well, you have to have your high school diploma.' So right across the street was the Somerville Adult Education Center." He enrolled in some classes at considerable cost but managed to have a bona fide diploma by midwinter. Although originally scheduled to report for service in October, Slick postponed his entry until late December when he expected to have his diploma.

By December, however, Slick had what he considered a better job lined up as a security guard at a local defense contracting firm the Hallway Hangers call "the weapons lab." Although he would not be able to start that job until mid-January, Slick somehow managed to cancel his enlistment. Shortly thereafter, however, his contact at the weapons lab was fired, and with him went Slick's prospective job. He currently is unemployed and, like Jinks, spends much of his time hanging at the Heights.

Despite these setbacks, Slick dreams of becoming a lawyer. Apparently, I was the first person to whom he voiced this hope. In a subsequent group interview in which five of the Hallway Hangers were discussing their plans for the future, an embarrassed Slick mentioned his aspiration in front of the group. The manner of this disclosure, which amounted to a confession, and the response of the group are instructive.

SLICK: (*sheepishly*) I'm gonna be a lawyer.

(*This response elicits surprise and whistles from the group.*)

CHRIS: My boy ain't talkin' no petty cash.

SHORTY: My boy wants to be a lawyer. He ain't even graduated from high school. Got himself a shit-ass diploma. Signed up for the army.

FRANKIE: I know. My boy bought his diploma and shit.

Slick himself is the first person to admit that he is not likely to achieve this goal, although his pride prevents him from expressing his reservations to the group. Slick, like Jinks and the rest of the Hallway Hangers, realizes that there is usually little room for choice in occupational decisions. "Well, *if I had the choice*, if I couldn't be a lawyer, I'd like to either do landscaping or construction (*my emphasis*)." Although his expectations are far different from his aspirations, Slick is the only Hallway Hanger who aspires to a professional career.

Like so many of the Hallway Hangers, Frankie's aspirations and expectations are in a constant state of flux. What follows are Frankie's comments on his occupational expectations on four separate occasions spanning a one-year period.

(2/22/83)

FRANKIE: I'm getting out [of school] this spring.

JM: What are you gonna do then? I mean for work.

FRANKIE: I don't fucking know. Probably work construction. That'll be good. I'll make like seventy-five bucks a day. Under the table. Sixty or seventy-five bucks a day. I could do that for the rest of my life. I get paid cash, every day. My brother sets it up for me.

(4/15/83)

JM: Have any idea what you'll be doing for work when you graduate, Frankie?

FRANKIE: I don't fucking know. If I can't get anything else, I'll just join the fucking service.

On May 13, 1983, the day he graduated, Frankie was feeling very strongly the sense of uncertainty surrounding his prospects for future employment.

FRANKIE: (*unsolicited*) I gotta get a job, any fucking job.

JM: What about the construction?

FRANKIE: Yeah, I can work with my brother, but that's under the table. Besides, he's in Bradford [state prison] now.

During the summer, when he was unemployed, Frankie was on the verge of joining the army. Finally, he landed a temporary job as a garbage collector for the city. He was laid off in November and since that time has been out of work.

In an in-depth interview in December, Frankie articulated a new occupational aspiration, which he presently nurtures. "My kind of job is like, y'know, I did a lot of construction. That's the kind of job like I want. What I want to do is save up some money and go to tractor trailer school and take heavy equipment. I don't wanna drive no eighteen wheeler, but I want to do heavy equipment like payloading. Hopefully, some day I can do it. I got to get up the cash first."

An aspiration to blue-collar work, such as this, is not easy to achieve. Coming up with the cash, Frankie realizes, is no easy task. In addition, even if he were able to get his heavy equipment license, there would be no guarantee that he will land the job he envisions. Frankie is aware of the problems; the scenario he foresees contains many "ifs." "If I do get my license, and say if I get a job with a construction company, I'll tell 'em I got my license, but I'm starting off as a laborer anyway. Gettin' in fuckin' holes, y'know. Then if higher jobs come up in it, I'd have a better chance than anyone, instead of them sending someone to school. Y'know, 'This kid already got his license, give him a couple of days to get back in the swing of things.'" Considering these contingencies, it is no wonder Frankie has yet to act on these hopes.

Whereas Frankie is lucid about his aspiration and how to achieve it, Chris is in doubt about his future. He never has held a steady job for any significant period of time and presently makes his money dealing drugs (mostly marijuana and cocaine) in the Clarendon Heights neighborhood. He works quite hard, actively seeking out customers and making himself available through the afternoon and evening hours. Because he is currently the sole major outlet of drugs for the teenagers of Clarendon Heights, Chris makes a good deal of money (about $150 per week). Although dealing pays well, the risks are high. He admits that the police seem to be watching him closely, and if he is convicted of another offense, he may well be sent away. The threat of violence from other kids trying to make a fast buck is an additional and sometimes greater risk, one brought home to Chris when he mentioned his occupational aspirations in a group interview.

CHRIS: I wanna sell cocaine, no lie. I wanna deal cocaine, be rich.

SLICK: (*somewhat dubiously*) That's what he wants to do.

CHRIS: I'm just tellin' you the truth, man. That's what I'm s'posed to do, right man?

SLICK: He's gonna get fuckin' blown away (*laughter*).

FRANKIE: I'll cuff off him a thousand dollars.

Like Frankie, who also used to make his money illegally (and still does to a lesser degree), Chris may weigh the risks and alter his aspirations, or he may take his chances and try to make a future out of selling drugs.

One cannot help but be struck by the modesty of the Hallway Hangers' hopes for the future. Only Slick aspires to a professional career; Stoney is the only other individual who aspires to a middle-class job. Refusing the risk of hope, the remainder adjust their occupational goals to the only jobs that they perceive to be available—unskilled manual work.

Many expect to enter military service, not because they find it particularly appealing but because of the paucity of other opportunities. The concept of an aspiration is essentially alien to the Hallway Hangers. Most simply expect to take whatever they can get.

The Hallway Hangers are quite honest about their occupational expectations and aspirations, but it is not comforting to look closely at one's future when bleakness is its main characteristic. When free of the psychological complications inherent in considering one's own future, the Hallway Hangers predict even more inauspicious outcomes for the peer group in general.

JM: What sorts of jobs do you think the rest of the guys will have?

(*all in separate interviews*)

STONEY: Shitty jobs. Picking up trash, cleaning the streets. They won't get no good jobs.

SLICK: Most of the kids around here, they're not gonna be more than janitors or, y'know, goin' by every day tryin' to get a buck. That's it. . . . I'd say the success rate of this place is, of these people . . . about twenty percent, maybe fifteen.

STEVE: I dunno. Probably hanging around here. I dunno. Shit jobs.

JINKS: I think most of them, when and if a war comes, they're all gone. In the service. Everyone's going. But for jobs—odds and ends jobs. Here and there. No good high-class jobs. I think they'll all end up working for the city, roofers, shit like that.

In Frankie's answer to the same question, we get a real feel for the deep sense of pessimism that dominates the Hallway Hangers' outlook on their future. Listening to him talk, one can detect a poignant fear for his own destiny.

FRANKIE: Well, some of them are gonna do okay, but, I dunno, some of them are just gonna fuck up. They'll just be doing odd jobs for the rest of their lives, y'know. Still be drinking, y'know; they'll drink themselves to death, what's some of 'em'll do. That's what I hope I don't do. Yeah, some of them are gonna drink themselves to death, but some of them, y'know, they're gonna smarten up. Get married, have some kids, have a decent job. Enough to live off anyways, to support a wife and kids. But some of them, they're gonna fuck up; they'll be just a junkie, a tramp. They'll be sitting out on the lawn for the rest of their life with their fucking bottle. Going to work every morning, getting laid off. Fucking, y'know, they're just gonna fuck up. That's what I hope I don't do. I'm trying not to anyways.

The definitions of aspirations and expectations given at the beginning of this chapter suggest that an assessment of the opportunity structure and of one's capabilities impinge on one's preferences for the future. However, the portrait of the Hallway Hangers painted in these pages makes clear that "impinge" is not a strong enough word. But are the leveled aspirations and pessimistic expectations of the Hallway Hangers a result of strong negative assessments of their capabilities or of the opportunity structure?

This is not an easy question to answer. Doubtless, both factors come into play, but in the case of the Hallway Hangers, evaluation of the opportunity structure has the dominant role. Although in a discussion of why they do not succeed in school, the Hallway Hangers point to personal inadequacy ("We're all just fucking burnouts"; "We never did good anyways"), they look to outside forces as well. In general, they are confident of their own abilities.

(in a group interview)

JM: If you've got five kids up the high school with all A's, now are you gonna be able to say that any of them are smarter than any of you?

SLICK: *(immediately)* No.

JM: So how'd that happen?

SLICK: Because they're smarter in some areas just like we're smarter in some areas. You put them out here, right? And you put us up where they're living—they won't be able to survive out here.

SHORTY: But we'd be able to survive up there.

FRANKIE: See, what it is—they're smarter more academically because they're taught by teachers that teach academics.

JM: Not even streetwise, just academically, do you think you could be up where they are?

FRANKIE: Yeah.

CHRIS: Yeah.

SHORTY: Yeah.

JM: When it comes down to it, you're just as smart?

FRANKIE: Yeah.

SLICK: *(matter-of-factly)* We could be smarter.

FRANKIE: Definitely.

CHRIS: On the street, like.

FRANKIE: We're smart, we're smart, but we're just smart [inaudible]. It's fucking, y'know, we're just out to make money, man. I know if I ever went to fucking high school and college in a business course . . .

SLICK: And concentrated on studying . . .

FRANKIE: I know I could make it. I am a businessman.

JM: So all of you are sure that if you put out in school . . .

FRANKIE: Yeah! If I went into business, I would, yeah. If I had the fucking money to start out with like some of these fucking rich kids, I'd be a millionaire. Fucking right I would be.

Although these comments were influenced by the dynamics of the group interview, they jibe with the general sense of self-confidence the Hallway Hangers radiate and indicate that they do not have low perceptions of their own abilities.

If their assessments of their own abilities do not account for the low aspirations of the Hallway Hangers, we are left, by way of explanation, with their perceptions of the job opportunity structure. The dominant view in the United States is that American society is an open one that values and differentially rewards individuals on the basis of their merits. The Hallway Hangers question this view, for it runs against the grain of their neighbors' experiences, their families' experiences, and their own encounters with the labor market.

The Clarendon Heights community, as a public housing development, is by definition made up of individuals who do not hold even modestly remunerative jobs. A large majority are on additional forms of public assistance; many are unemployed. Like most old housing projects, Clarendon Heights tends to be a cloistered, insular neighborhood, isolated from the surrounding community. Although younger residents certainly have external points of reference, their horizons are nevertheless very narrow. Their immediate world is composed almost entirely of people who have not "made it." To look around at a great variety of people— some lazy, some alcoholics, some energetic, some dedicated, some clever, some resourceful—and to realize all of them have been unsuccessful on the job market is powerful testimony against what is billed as an open society.

The second and much more intimate contact these boys have with the job market is through their families, whose occupational histories only can be viewed as sad and disillusioning by the Hallway Hangers. These are not people who are slothful or slow-witted; rather, they are generally industrious, intelligent, and very willing to work. With members of their families holding low-paying, unstable jobs or unable to find work at all, the Hallway Hangers are unlikely to view the job opportunity structure as an open one.

The third level of experience on which the Hallway Hangers draw is their own. These boys are not newcomers to the job market. As we have seen, all have held a variety of jobs. All except Steve are now on the job market year round, but only Stoney has a steady job. With the exceptions of Chris, who presently is satisfied with his success peddling drugs, and Steve, who is still in school, the Hallway Hangers are actively in search of decent work. Although they always seem to be following up on some promising lead, they are all unemployed. Furthermore, some who were counting on prospective employment have had their hopes dashed when it fell through. The work they have been able to secure typically has been in menial, dead-end jobs paying minimum wage.

Thus, their personal experience on the job market and the experiences of their family members and their neighbors have taught the Hallway Hangers that the job market does not necessarily reward talent or effort. Neither they nor their parents, older siblings, and friends have shared in the "spoils" of economic success. In short, the Hallway Hangers are under no illusions about the openness of the job opportunity structure. They are conscious, albeit vaguely, of a number of class-based obstacles to economic and social advancement. Slick, the most perceptive and articulate of the Hallway Hangers, points out particular barriers they must face.

SLICK: Out here, there's not the opportunity to make money. That's how you get into stealin' and all that shit.

(*in a separate interview*)

SLICK: That's why I went into the army—cuz there's no jobs out here right now for people that, y'know, live out here. You have to know somebody, right?

In discussing the problems of getting a job, both Slick and Shorty are vocal.

SLICK: All right, to get a job, first of all, this is a handicap, out here. If you say you're from the projects or anywhere in this area, that can hurt you. Right off the bat: reputation.

SHORTY: Is this dude gonna rip me off, is he . . .

SLICK: Is he gonna stab me?

SHORTY: Will he rip me off? Is he gonna set up the place to do a score or somethin'? I tried to get a couple of my buddies jobs at a place where I was working construction, but the guy says, "I don't want 'em if they're from there. I know you; you ain't a thief or nothing."

Frankie also points out the reservations prospective employers have about hiring people who live in Clarendon Heights. "A rich kid would have a better chance of getting a job than me, yeah. Me, from where I live, y'know, a high crime area, I was prob'ly crime-breaking myself, which they think your nice honest rich kid from a very respected family would never do."

Frankie also feels that he is discriminated against because of the reputation that attaches to him because of his brothers' illegal exploits. "Especially me, like I've had a few opportunities for a job, y'know. I didn't get it cuz of my name, because of my brothers, y'know. So I was deprived right there, bang. Y'know they said, 'No, no, no, we ain't havin' no Dougherty work for us.'" In a separate discussion, Frankie again makes this point. Arguing that he would have almost no chance to be hired as a fireman, despite ostensibly meritocratic hiring procedures, even if he scored very highly on the test, Frankie concludes, "Just cuz fuckin' where I'm from and what my name is."

The Hallway Hangers' belief that the opportunity structure is not open also emerges when we consider their responses to the question of whether they have the same chance as a middle- or upper-class boy to get a good job. The Hallway Hangers generally respond in the negative. When pushed to explain why, Jinks and Steve made these responses, which are typical.

(*in separate interviews*)

JINKS: Their parents got pull and shit.

STEVE: Their fucking parents know people.

Considering the boys' employment experiences and those of their families, it is not surprising that the Hallway Hangers' view of the job market does not conform to the dominant belief in the openness of the opportunity structure. They see a job market where rewards are based not on meritocratic criteria, but on "who you know." If "connections" are the keys to success, the Hallway Hangers know that they are in trouble.

Aside from their assessment of the job opportunity structure, the Hallway Hangers are aware of other forces weighing on their futures. A general feeling of despondency pervades the group. As Slick puts it, "The younger kids have nothing to hope for." The Hallway Hangers often draw attention to specific incidents that support their general and vague feelings of hopelessness and of the futility of nurturing aspirations or high expectations. Tales of police brutality, of uncaring probation officers and callous judges, and of the "pull and hook-ups of the rich kids" all have a common theme, which Chris summarizes, "We don't get a fair shake and shit." Although they sometimes internalize the blame for their plight (Boo-Boo: "I just screwed up"; Chris: "I guess I just don't have what it takes"; Frankie: "We've just fucked up"), the

Hallway Hangers also see, albeit in a vague and imprecise manner, a number of hurdles in their path to success with which others from higher social strata do not have to contend.

Insofar as contemporary conditions under capitalism can be conceptualized as a race by the many for relatively few positions of wealth and prestige, the low aspirations of the Hallway Hangers, more than anything else, seem to be a decision, conscious or unconscious, to withdraw from the running. The competition, they reason, is not a fair one when some people have an unobstructed lane. As Frankie maintains, the Hallway Hangers face numerous barriers: "It's a steeplechase, man. It's a motherfucking steeplechase." The Hallway Hangers respond in a way that suggests only a "sucker" would compete seriously under such conditions.

Chris's perspective seems a poignant, accurate description of the situation in which the Hallway Hangers find themselves.

CHRIS: I gotta get a job, any fucking job. Just a job. Make some decent money. If I could make a hundred bucks a week, I'd work. I just wanna get my mother out of the projects, that's all. But I'm fucking up in school. It ain't easy, Jay. I hang out there [in doorway #13] 'til about one o'clock every night. I never want to go to school. I'd much rather hang out and get high again. It's not that I'm dumb. You gimme thirty bucks today, and I'll give you one hundred tomorrow. I dunno. It's like I'm in a hole I can't get out of. I guess I could get out, but it's hard as hell. It's fucked up.

THE BROTHERS: READY AT THE STARTING LINE

Just as the pessimism and uncertainty with which the Hallway Hangers view their futures emerges when we consider what they perceive their lives will be like in twenty years, so do the Brothers' long-term visions serve as a valuable backdrop to our discussion of their aspirations. The ethos of the Brothers' peer group is a positive one; they are not resigned to a bleak future but are hoping for a bright one. Nowhere does this optimism surface more clearly than in the Brothers' responses to the question of what they will be doing in twenty years. Note the centrality of work in their views of the future.

(all in separate interviews)

SUPER: I'll have a house, a nice car, no one bothering me. Won't have to take no hard time from no one. Yeah, I'll have a good job, too.

JUAN: I'll have a regular house, y'know, with a yard and everything. I'll have a steady job, a good job. I'll be living the good life, the easy life.

MIKE: I might have a wife, some kids. I might be holding down a regular business job like an old guy. I hope I'll be able to do a lot of skiing and stuff like that when I'm old.

CRAIG: I'll probably be having a good job on my hands, I think. Working in an office as an architect, y'know, with my own drawing board, doing my own stuff, or at least close to there.

James takes a comic look into his future without being prompted to do so. "The ones who work hard in school, eventually it's gonna pay off for them and everything, and they're gonna have a good job and a family and all that. Not me though! I'm gonna have *myself*. I'm gonna have some money. And a different girl every day. And a different car. And be like this (*poses with one arm around an imaginary girl and the other on a steering wheel*)."

The Brothers do not hesitate to name their occupational goals. Although some of the Brothers are unsure of their occupational aspirations, none seems to feel that nurturing an aspiration is a futile exercise. The Brothers have not resigned themselves to taking whatever they can get. Rather, they articulate specific occupational aspirations (although these often are subject to change and revision).

Like all the Brothers, Super has not had extensive experience on the job market; he only has worked at summer jobs. For the past three summers, he has worked for the city doing maintenance work in parks and school buildings through a CETA-sponsored summer youth employment program. During the last year, Super's occupational aspirations have fluctuated widely. His initial desire to become a doctor was met with laughter from his friends. Deterred by their mocking and by a realization of the schooling required to be a doctor, Super immediately decided that he would rather go into business: "Maybe I can own my own shop and shit." This aspiration, however, also was ridiculed. "Yeah, right," commented Mokey, "Super'll be pimping the girls, that kinda business." In private, however, Super still clings to the hope of becoming a doctor, although he cites work in the computer field as a more realistic hope. "Really, I don't know what I should do now. I'm kinda confused. First I said I wanna go into computers, right? Take up that or a doctor." The vagueness of Super's aspirations is important; once again, we get a glimpse of how little is known about the world of middle-class work, even for somebody who clearly aspires to it. Of one thing Super is certain: "I just know I wanna get a good job."

Although Super does not distinguish between what constitutes a good job and what does not, he does allude to criteria by which the quality of a job can be judged. First, a good job must not demand that one "work on your feet," a distinction, apparently, between white and blue-collar work. Second, a good job implies at least some authority in one's workplace, a point Super makes clearly, if in a disjointed manner. "Bosses—if you don't come on time, they yell at you and stuff like that.

They want you to do work and not sit down and relax and stuff like that, y'know. I want to try and be a boss, y'know, tell people what to do. See, I don't always want people telling me what to do, y'know—the low rank. I wanna try to be with people in the high rank." Although Super does not know what occupation he would like to enter, he is certain that he wants a job that is relatively high up in a vaguely defined occupational hierarchy.

Mokey has not given as much thought to his occupational aspirations as have most of the Brothers. His contact with the job market has been minimal. His only job has been part-time janitorial work with his father. Mokey plans to attend college and does not envision working full-time until after graduation, several years from now.

JM: So what do you think you wanna do when you get out of school?

MOKEY: I have no idea really.

JM: Don't think about it that much?

MOKEY: Not really. Before, I wanted to be a motorcyclist, like motocross. That was it.

JM: Didn't you tell me mechanic?

MOKEY: And mechanic. That was when I wanted to be a motor mechanic. For motorcycles. I wanted to be a motocross, that's what I wanted to be.

JM: How'd you decide on that?

MOKEY: I seen a motorcycle race before and I've ridden a couple of minibikes before, and I just decided.

Usually, the aspirations of the Brothers reflect more thought than those Mokey articulates. Although his mother reports that he is interested in "general management, of his own or someone else's business," Mokey's aspirations are sketchy and contradictory.

In contrast to Mokey, James's aspirations are defined clearly. Since his eighth grade class visited the high school and James viewed the computer terminals, he has aspired to design video games. This is a goal to which James is strongly committed. His plans are well developed; he has even considered his prospective employers: Atari, Intelevision, or Colecovision. His enthusiasm for his foreseen occupation is unmatched by the other boys. "I like jobs that are fun and make money too. Like making computer games; it would be fun. . . . I want computers. I love computers. I fell in love with computers, so I know I want to do computers."

James is confident that he will achieve his occupational goal, despite the difficulty he has had finding any kind of summer employment. Last summer, after a two-month job search, James did maintenance work for the city recreation department. Paid and hired through the CETA job program, he spent the summer clearing parks and buildings.

The only boy whose plans are more definitively developed is Derek. Derek has never worked in his life; his summers have been spent traveling with a wealthy friend from Barnes Academy. Since he was a young boy, however, Derek has dreamed of joining the military. He wants to learn electronics and become a helicopter pilot, an aspiration Derek took a big step toward fulfilling by enlisting in the navy this past summer. He is on delayed entry until he receives his diploma this June; then he will report to basic training in July and will serve for six years.

Considering that the decision to enter the service is usually a last resort for most Heights teenagers, it is noteworthy that Derek aspires to a career in the navy, particularly given his success in high school and at Barnes Academy. Of all the Brothers and Hallway Hangers, he seems to have the best educational credentials and the best chance to move on to high-status employment. But Derek does explain his choice.

DEREK: At first, they [his parents] wanted me to be a lawyer. Ever since I went to Barnes. But there's no way I could do that. I need a job that has action. I need to be active. I couldn't sit behind a desk all week to make a living; that wouldn't be right.

JM: What do you mean, it wouldn't be right?

DEREK: I just couldn't do it. I like all the activities the navy has. And, y'know, sometimes I like to take orders. Carry them out. I don't want to just sit around.

This devaluation of white-collar work as inactive and boring, according to Paul Willis, is the main cultural innovation of the nonconformist lads that deters them from entering, or even trying to enter, white-collar work. This distaste for office work, which is bound up inextricably with the working-class culture's ideal of masculinity, serves to level the aspirations of the lads, thereby spurring them to work on the shop floor. A close examination of the Hallway Hangers and Brothers, however, reveals no such definitive cultural process at work, although we can detect traces of such an attitude among the Hallway Hangers (and with Derek). However, Super and his parents denigrate work that would require that he stand on his feet, a view shared by Juan.

Juan, whose previous employment record consists of a number of summertime jobs, aspires to be a cook. Like Super, he hopes to avoid manual work (a hope his father shares). "I like clean job, y'know, where you can keep yourself clean. That's what my father said. 'You should get a job where you can keep yourself clean.' I found out that the one that was better off for me was cooking. I like mechanic, but, no man, too rough for me."

Despite this aversion to auto mechanics, which Juan expressed last summer, he currently is seeking employment in precisely that area. The only Brother to have graduated from high school and thus currently on the job market, Juan has been unable to find work in food preparation. Although he retains his aspiration to be a cook because "it's fun; I like it," the unpleasant experience of unemployment for eight months has forced Juan to lower his expectations.

Craig, who like most of the Brothers has "never held a real job, just, y'know, summer jobs," hopes to be an architect. Craig has been a good artist since his earliest years and his father suggested that he consider architecture as a career. Craig has nurtured this aspiration since sixth grade and sees himself working for an architecture firm in the future. He adds, however, that if he is frustrated in his attempt to find employment in this field, he would like to be a computer operator or programmer.

This tendency to express contingency plans in case of failure is articulated fully by Mike. During the course of a year, Mike has revealed a hierarchy of aspirations and expectations. Mike's dream is to be a professional athlete: a wrestler, like his father, or a football player. He realizes this would come about only "if I get a big break." The occupational aspiration about which he talks the most is in the computer field, apparently a common aspiration for these boys because of the emphasis put upon the subject in high school. One step below that on his hierarchy of occupational preferences is more traditional blue-collar work, particularly as an electrician. Finally, he says, "If I don't make it in like, anything, if I flunk out or something, I'll probably join the service or something."

Like most of the Brothers, Mike is very concerned about the quality of his future employment. "Mostly," he comments, "I just wanna get ahead in life, get a good job." Specifically, he wants to avoid the dull, monotonous type of work he experienced last summer as a stock boy in a large hardware warehouse. "It's for fucking morons," he exclaims. Mike also has held a summer job in which he learned some carpentry skills doing weatherization work for the City Action to Save Heat project, another CETA program. He hated taking orders from a strict supervisor who, Mike recalls, "just sat on his fat ass all day anyway. Then again," he added upon reflection, "I wouldn't mind doing that."

Despite the Brothers' absorption with athletics and the status of professional sports in American culture, the Brothers have few illusions about the extent to which sports are a ticket to success. While their younger siblings speak incessantly about "making it in the pros," the Brothers no longer aspire seriously to a career in professional athletics. Only Mike and Craig see sports as a means to get a college education.

Although not all the Brothers aspire to professional or managerial work, all do have hopes for the future. The notion of a career makes sense when applied to their visions of future employment. They are committed to acting on their hopes, and although they realize that there is no guarantee that their dreams will come to fruition, they are not resigned to failure. In short, the Brothers are optimistic about their future employment, while the Hallway Hangers are deeply pessimistic about their prospective occupational roles.

In contrasting the Brothers and the Hallway Hangers, however, we must resist the temptation to define the two groups only in relation to one another. Certainly in comparison to the Hallway Hangers, the Brothers have high aspirations. To assert that the Brothers aspire to middle-class jobs while the Hallway Hangers do not, however, would be overly simplistic. In a society in which the achievement of a prestigious occupation is considered a valid goal for everyone, it is significant that a few of the Brothers have only modest goals.

The Brothers display none of the cockiness about their own capabilities that the Hallway Hangers exhibit. Instead, they attribute lack of success on the job market exclusively to personal inadequacy. This is particularly true when the Brothers speculate about the future jobs the Hallway Hangers and their own friends will have. According to the Brothers, the Hallway Hangers (in Super's words) "ain't gonna get nowhere," not because of the harshness of the job market but because they are personally lacking. The rest of the Brothers share this view.

JM: Some of those guys who hang with Frankie, they're actually pretty smart. They just don't channel that intelligence into school, it seems to me.

CRAIG: I call that stupid, man. That's what they are.

JM: I dunno.

CRAIG: Lazy.

(in a separate interview)

SUPER: They think they're so tough they don't have to do work. That don't make sense, really. You ain't gonna get nowhere; all's you gonna do is be back in the projects like your mother. Depend on your mother to give you money every week. You ain't gonna get a good job. As you get older, you'll think about that, y'know. It'll come to your mind. "Wow, I can't believe, I should've just went to school and got my education."

(in a separate interview)

MOKEY: They all got attitude problems. They just don't got their shit together. Like Steve. They have to improve themselves.

In the eyes of the Brothers, the Hallway Hangers have attitude problems, are incapable of considering their long-term future, and are lazy or stupid.

Because this evidence is tainted (no love is lost between the two peer groups), it is significant that the Brothers apply the same criteria in judging each other's chances to gain meaningful employment. James thinks Mokey is headed for a dead-end job because he is immature and undisciplined. He also blames Juan for currently being out of work. "Juan's outa school, and Juan does *not* have a job (*said with contempt*). Now that's some kind of a senior. When I'm a senior, I'm gonna have a job already. I can see if you're gonna go to college right when you get out of school, but Juan's not doin' nothin'. He's just stayin' home." Juan, in turn, thinks that Mokey and Super will have difficulty finding valuable work because of their attitudes. He predicts that Derek and Craig will be successful for the same reason.

These viewpoints are consistent with the dominant ideology in America; barriers to success are seen as personal rather than social. By attributing failure to personal inadequacy, the Brothers exonerate the opportunity structure. Indeed, it is amazing how often they affirm the openness of American society.

(all in separate interviews)

DEREK: If you put your mind to it, if you want to make a future for yourself, there's no reason why you can't. It's a question of attitude.

SUPER: It's easy to do anything, as long as you set your mind to it, if you wanna do it. If you really want to do it, if you really want to be something. If you don't want to do it . . . you ain't gonna make it. I gotta get that through my mind: I wanna do it. I wanna be somethin'. I don't wanna be livin' in the projects the rest of my life.

MOKEY: It's not like if they're rich they get picked [for a job]; it's just mattered by the knowledge of their mind.

CRAIG: If you work hard, it'll pay off in the end.

MIKE: If you work hard, really put your mind to it, you can do it. You can make it.

This view of the opportunity structure as an essentially open one that rewards intelligence, effort, and ingenuity is shared by all the Brothers. Asked whether their chances of securing a remunerative job are as good as those of an upper-class boy from a wealthy district of the city, they all responded affirmatively. Not a single member of the Hallway Hangers, in contrast, affirms the openness of American society.

This affirmation of equality of opportunity is all the more astounding coming from a group of black, lower-class teenagers. Only Juan mentioned racial prejudice as a barrier to success, and this was a result of personal experience. Juan's mother was forced out of her job as a clerk in a neighborhood grocery store when some of the customers complained about the color of her skin. "Most of the time it depends on the boss, whether or not he has something against black. If they judge by the attitude, by the way they act, then that's it; there'll be an equal chance, but it's not usually that way."

Whereas the Hallway Hangers conclude that the opportunity structure is not open, the Brothers reach an entirely different, and contradictory, conclusion. Considering that both groups share neighbors and that the families of the boys have similar occupational histories, this discrepancy is all the more problematic. Indeed, we have uncovered quite a paradox. The peer group whose members must overcome racial as well as class barriers to success views the occupational opportunity structure as essentially open, whereas the white peer group views it as much more closed. The Brothers, whose objective life chances are probably lower than those of the Hallway Hangers, nevertheless hold positive attitudes toward the future, while the Hallway Hangers harbor feelings of hopelessness. To unravel this paradox is a challenge, one that we shall face in Chapter 7.

If the Hallway Hangers view their predicament as a race in which they, as members of the lower class, must jump a number of hurdles, while the rest of the pack can simply sprint, the Brothers see it as an even dash. The Hallway Hangers believe a strong finish, given their handicap, is out of the question and drop out of the race before it begins. They cannot understand why the Brothers compete seriously. Apparently, explains Slick, the Brothers do not see the hurdles. "It's a question of you wanna see it, and you don't wanna see it. They might not wanna see all the obstacles. In the long run, it'll hurt them. You hafta hear what's going on, or it's gonna hurt you later on."

The Brothers, for their part, are lined up at the start, unsure of their ability, but ready to run what they see as a fair race. They do not understand why the Hallway Hangers fail to take the competition seriously. It is, after all, the only game in town.

DEREK: I don't know. I really don't. I guess they just don't realize what they have to do. It just doesn't get through to them. I dunno. I don't think anyone has really told them straight out what it takes to make it, to be a winner.

Before we analyze how the same race can be viewed in two fundamentally different ways, we must investigate how the two peer groups prepare themselves for the competition. School is the training ground, the place where this preparation takes place. As we might expect, the boys who plan to run the race competitively approach their training in a fundamentally different way than do those who already have conceded defeat.

NOTES

1. Kenneth I. Spenner and David L. Featherman, "Achievement Ambitions," *Annual Review of Sociology* 4 (1978):376–378.

2. Howard B. London, *The Culture of a Community College* (New York: Praeger, 1978).

3. Ely Chinoy, *Automobile Workers and the American Dream* (Boston: Beacon Press, 1955).

6

SCHOOL: PREPARING
FOR THE COMPETITION

School is an institution in which the Hallway Hangers and the Brothers are forced into daily contact. Many of the attitudes we already have uncovered are played out in school, and made manifest in the boys' conduct. Before we can consider this intriguing cultural and institutional mix, however, we must familiarize ourselves with the school itself.

Almost all the teenagers from Clarendon Heights who attend school go to Lincoln High School (LHS). LHS, a comprehensive school of more than 2,800 students and 300 faculty, is organized into four regular academic houses (A,B,C,D), four alternative programs (Enterprise Co-op, Pilot School, Achievement School, Fundamental School), and a separate Occupational Education Program that offers both academic and vocational courses. Two additional programs—the Building Trades and Services Program (BTS) and the Adjustment Class—also come under our purview.

Lincoln High School students from all four grades in the main academic program are sorted randomly into the four main houses of the school, as are staff members from all the academic areas. These 400–500 students and approximately 50 teachers are each assigned to one area of the building—their house. Freshmen and sophomores take most of their subjects within their house, while juniors and seniors often cross over to other houses as their elective program expands. The house system is designed to create a smaller setting that promotes better communication and accountability; it also is intended to build strong relationships between students' families and the administrators and counselors who work with the students all four years. In House D, in addition to the more than 300 students in the conventional curriculum, the Bilingual Program teaches the standard course work to about 200 students in their native languages: Portuguese, French-Haitian, Spanish, and Chinese.

According to the course catalogue, the Occupational Education Program provides new options to secondary school students: a high school diploma as well as marketable skills in an occupation of one's choice. Karen Wallace, a career counselor at the school, describes the Oc. Ed. Program as "a spinoff from the old technical school. It's for kids who like to work with their hands." Students enrolled in Oc. Ed. carry an academic program that meets LHS graduation requirements, but they also carry a full vocational program that according to the course catalogue "insures access to a career at a skilled level."

As freshmen, students in Occupational Education spend two periods each day in the exploratory program, in which they sample each of the twelve shops: auto body, auto mechanics, carpentry, computers, culinary arts, drafting, electrical, electronics, machine, metals, printing, and welding. According to Bruce Davis, guidance counselor for the Occupational Education Program, at the end of the year each freshman lists three shops in which he or she prefers to major. In consultation with the shop teachers, the guidance counselors decide, on the basis of the interest, aptitude, and behavior each student has demonstrated, each student's shop major. Most of the students, claims Davis, end up with their first choice. During their sophomore year, students spend three periods per day in their shop. "During the third and fourth years," explains Davis, "they spend three periods in shop plus three periods per week in what we call a theory class where they learn about the occupation itself." The Occupational Education Program enrolls approximately 300 students.

Enterprise Co-op is an alternative, career-oriented program that includes student-run businesses for dropouts and potential dropouts. The curricula of the standard English, math, and social studies courses also include academic work relating directly to the students' experiences in the businesses. A wood shop and extensive food services are operated in an atmosphere that simulates the real business world. Students receive shares in the co-op based on their productivity, and their dividend checks reflect the increase or decrease in profits for a particular pay period. "It is anticipated that, after one year of participation in Enterprise Co-op," states the course catalogue, "a student will be prepared either to re-enter the mainstream high school program, or to secure entry-level employment in a career of his/her choosing."

The Pilot School, founded in 1969, is an alternative high school program that accommodates approximately 200 students. According to Wallace, the Pilot School came into being when a group of parents decided that the curriculum and atmosphere of the high school were too regimented. "The teachers act as counselors to the students; there are weekend trips and lots of outdoor activities. You have a much closer teacher/pupil relationship. The onus of responsibility is on the student to take charge for his work." Candidates for admission are selected at random after steps have been taken to ensure that the student body approaches a representative cross-section of the school population with respect to geographical area, race and/or ethnic background, sex, academic interest, and parental occupation. The course catalogue bills the Pilot School as an attempt to create a community of students, parents, and educators accountable to each other for the goals of the program and the successful operation of the school.

The Fundamental School, which originated when a group of parents decided that the high school was not regimented enough, employs an educational philosophy at the other end of the spectrum. The school (with 400–500 students) "emphasizes basic academic requirements with few frills." The catalogue describes this alternative program as one that "stresses academic excellence and student accountability and enlists parental involvement and support in reinforcing the discipline code." For Stephen, a ninth grader who at his parents' insistence has chosen to go into the Fundamental School as did his brother Mokey, the Fundamental School is simply a lot stricter than the regular program: "I mean, you can't cut class in Fundamentals. If you do, bang, you'll get caught."

"The Achievement School," according to Wallace, "is for kids who haven't quite made it out of elementary school, but who are old enough to be in high school." With a maximum student population of forty, the Achievement School is designed to provide intensive compensatory education in the basic academic subjects for students with special needs (e.g., underachievers, perceptually handicapped). Wallace explains that kids "do cross over and are mainstreamed, but they have their own graduation."

Like Enterprise Co-op, the Building Trades and Services Program enrolls "high risk" students: dropouts and potential dropouts with truancy and disciplinary problems. Students from grades nine through twelve attend classes in math, science, English, history, and social studies in a small, self-contained environment from 8:00 until 11:30 A.M. A lunch break follows; then from 12:00 until 2:30 P.M. the students learn carpentry skills and occasionally travel to work at small-scale construction sites around the city. Teachers seldom mention the program, and when they do, it is typically in a negative vein: "There's Building Trades with very easy academics. I don't know what the hell you learn to do there, be a janitor or something."

Like all public high schools in the state, LHS has provisions for those students who are considered emotionally disturbed. These students are required to meet regularly with an adjustment counselor. Depending on a psychiatrist's perception of the severity of the problem, a student meets with his or her adjustment counselor weekly, daily, or for two periods each day. Adjustment counselors have more flexibility than do guidance counselors, which enables them to spend a lot more time and energy on each of their assigned students. According to Wallace, "He'll (the adjustment counselor) go to court with them, make sure they see their probation officer, and that type of thing. The student is required to spend a block of time with his adjustment counselor each week."

Those with severe problems are enrolled full-time in the Adjustment Class, the last step before residential schooling or institutionalization.

Whereas secondary school adjustment programs, according to state statutes, serve emotionally disturbed students, the teachers describe the youngsters assigned to the programs in a different manner. Wallace portrays them simply as "kids whose academics are very poor or who are in trouble" and "who are really into drugs, have bad home lives, or things like that." The students in the Adjustment Class realize they are classified as emotionally disturbed, but if the seriousness with which they take their mandatory appointments with the school psychiatrist is any indication, they are none too concerned about the designation.

FRANKIE: I would toy with him more than he'd try to fuck with me. Y'know, like once I caught him with a tape recorder in his drawer. It would've been cool if he told me it was on. But he didn't tell me, and like I knew it was on, so I waited five minutes. He was asking me "What bothers you?" I said, "You wanna know what bothers me? I'm pretty pissed that you fuckin' put that tape recorder on." I slammed open his drawer and shut the fucker off. I said, "That's what's pissing me off and I don't feel pissed off no more," and I sat back down. And like one time, y'know, I seen *Caine Mutiny*, and I went and I got some marbles. Y'know, Humphrey Bogart, he was a paranoiac, and he went in there always playing with marbles. So I went in there and played with marbles. The guy asked me why I was doing it. I says, "Cuz I know you're getting paid eighty-five bucks for this one hour, and I'm gonna make you work for it for once."

Jimmy Sullivan, the teacher of the adjustment class for fourteen years, describes his students variously as those "who've been in fights and are general pains in the ass," as "kids who have had emotional problems in the past and have shown an inability to be mainstreamed," as "those who couldn't hack the other programs," and "kids who are tough, from very, very rough backgrounds." Sometimes, he simply refers to those in his class as "crazy."

That the adjustment class is unique is beyond doubt. Walking into the room after school, one beholds a large, sand-filled punching bag suspended from the ceiling, weights and barbells sprinkled on the floor, magazines such as *High Times, Sports Illustrated,* and *Soldier of Fortune* left on the easy chairs and couches that line the room and a small punching bag in one corner. Both Jimmy and his assistant have black belts in karate; the twelve kids in the class are encouraged to work out with the weights and to learn martial arts. Posters of Bruce Lee adorn the walls to provide further inspiration.

The program is very flexible. Students must arrive at school by 9:30 in the morning and leave by 12:30. Upon arrival, the boys (there are no girls in the class) pick up their folders, which contain their daily assignments in math, reading, vocabulary, history, and a lesson from a job opportunities book. Most of the reading is on a fifth grade level; the daily math assignment includes basic addition, subtraction, multiplication, and division as well as work in decimals and fractions. In an interview, Jimmy expressed his teaching philosophy and gave an indication of the atmosphere that predominates in the class.

JS: The kids are judged on their ability to get the work done. They've got the folder; that's it. It doesn't matter if they have this problem or that problem; everybody's got a fucking problem. Regardless of the problems, you've got to get your work done. I'd say the work can usually be done in two hours. Y'know, they come in here, some take a nap on the couch, some get a cup of coffee over at the store. There's a lot of freedom, but they have to get the work done. If you come in three days but only did the work two days, that's a forty percent. . . . They'll get twenty-five credits each semester for being in here; you need 180 to graduate. They can get ten extra credits for my version of work-study. I didn't give any work-study credits this year. I mean, you have to hold a job for more than a fucking week.

With its unique approach, the Adjustment Class deserves a separate in-depth study of its own. Although we shall temporarily reserve judgment on the effectiveness of the class, considering the positive attitudes of the enrolled students toward the class and the respect they accord Jimmy, the class is, by the school's standards, unusually successful. In contrast to the other programs, the boys attend regularly and control themselves while in class.

LHS formally practices tracking (as do 80 percent of the country's public high schools); classes in almost all programs are organized so students of similar learning achievement or capability are put together. According to their performance in each subject area in grammar school, pupils are placed into tracks, which also are called ability groupings and streams. Almost all the subject areas are divided into general, intermediate, and advanced level courses. Of the basic academic subjects, only the Social Studies Department, reflecting a commitment to heterogeneous classroom populations, offers a significant number of non-leveled courses. Even outside the core academic areas, most courses in business education, home economics, art, photography, dramatic arts, music, and physical education are leveled according to ability or achievement. Classes in the Fundamental School as well as academic classes in the Occupational Education Program also are leveled. Only classes within the Pilot School are all heterogeneous and untracked. But at Lincoln High School there are actually two levels of tracking—among programs (with Oc. Ed., Enterprise Co-op, BTS, and the Adjustment

Class at the bottom) and within them. The practice of tracking on both levels has widespread implications for students' academic achievement, self-esteem, and postsecondary school educational and occupational plans, implications that are considered later in this chapter.

Although racial tension at LHS never has been as severe as at schools in a city such as Boston, Massachusetts, an incident in 1980 nevertheless focused attention on the severity of the problem at Lincoln. In a fight between black and white students on school grounds, a white boy was stabbed fatally. The ensuing review of the school's policies revealed a significant shortage of black teachers. When the school system moved to rectify the problem by bringing in more black staff, a backlash from a number of white students accompanied the changes. Wallace, who is black, reports that white students, especially those from the Clarendon Heights neighborhood, "resented the fact that the black students now had somewhere to go, someone to relate to. And they did come—in droves. The white kids thought they were getting special attention." Indeed, the Hallway Hangers continue to believe that black students are favored at the high school, which is evidence that racial tension still exists.

THE BROTHERS: CONFORMITY AND COMPLIANCE

Super, like all other pupils, had to decide in the middle of eighth grade what high school program he wanted to enroll in. As part of this process, the high school sends a guidance counselor down to each eighth grade grammar school class to explain the various programs and curricula at the high school. Booklets detailing the programs and their constituent courses are distributed to students; tours of the high school by all eighth grade classes are arranged; and parents are invited to the high school for an information night, during which high school counselors present each program and answer questions. Finally, a high school guidance counselor meets individually with every eighth grader to discuss what the LHS course catalogue calls his or her "high school choice, occupation or career plans, sports, interests and hobbies, and personal concerns." Considering the importance of the student's program choice and the implications it may have for his or her future, the provisions the high school makes to ensure an informed, carefully weighed decision are understandable. For thirteen and fourteen year olds, however, the choice of programs is not always based exclusively on logic or long-term considerations. Super's expressed rationale for entering the Occupational Education Program is typical: "Really, I picked Oc. Ed. because my friends picked it. That's why, y'know."

In contrast to the rest of the Brothers, Super changed his program after he entered LHS. Super was involved in several fights stemming from racial tension in the predominantly white Occupational Educational Program and was suspended from school (another anomaly among the

Brothers) three months into his first term. Subsequently, he enrolled in House C, part of the regular academic program.

Super is now well integrated into the school. He respects his teachers and truly wishes to be successful academically. Super accepts the disciplinary code of the school. He occasionally cuts classes but openly chastises himself for this weakness in self-resolve. Similarly, although he later expresses regret, Super often ignores his homework for the pursuit of more pleasurable activities—playing basketball and flirting with girls. Super's scholastic performance is mediocre; his grade average (on the standard scale whereby sixty is the lowest passing mark) during the one-and-a-half year period he has been enrolled in the high school hovers just below a seventy.

A natural athlete, Super has been involved in sports at LHS, which is further evidence of his successful integration into the school. This past fall he played on the junior varsity football team; last year he made the freshman basketball team but quit when he found the daily practices too time consuming. Super's earnest involvement in both academic and athletic pursuits, with only fair success in each, typifies the Brothers' approach to school.

Mokey undergoes the rigors of schooling in a similar way. Enrolled in the Fundamental School at his mother's insistence, he is generally obedient and hard working. Despite his positive attitude, Mokey's grades have not been good. He failed a course last year, thereby prompting him, again at his mother's urging, to apply to the Upward Bound Program, into which he was accepted. Upward Bound, a year-round, federally sponsored program for underachieving high school students, stresses development of academic skills and motivation for students who traditionally are not considered college bound. Mokey attended an overnight summer school at a nearby college campus and presently spends three hours every Thursday afternoon in the program. Although he now names four colleges he would like to attend, Mokey actually has fared less well in school since his participation in the program, having failed two classes in the fall semester of his junior year. Despite his unsatisfactory performance, Mokey's attitude toward school is positive. His conduct and effort seem to be at a high level, and, like Super, he enjoys playing on the junior varsity football team.

James's attitude toward school has fluctuated dramatically during the past three years. After a dismal sophomore year, during which he cut nearly all his academic classes and only attended his computer shop for three periods daily, James has made a real turnaround. He now attends every class assiduously and is making up last year's failed classes after school on Thursdays. Whereas last year James spent school hours playing video games in a local sub shop, this year he recently was elected president of the science club despite having failed his science course in the fall semester.

Of all the boys from Clarendon Heights, Derek's educational history is the most unusual. After finishing third grade at the neighborhood grammar school, Derek was selected to attend Barnes Academy, a prestigious prep school located on the outskirts of the city. At Barnes, Derek enjoyed great success. He earned A's and B's and immediately gained the respect of students and staff. Nevertheless, instead of attending grades nine through twelve at Barnes, Derek chose to attend Lincoln High School. Tired of the heavy workload, sick of the pressure to achieve in order to requalify for his scholarships, and bored with his subjects, he transferred to House D in Lincoln.

DEREK: I like to work, but not too much. That's why I quit Barnes after eighth grade. I just lost interest. It got to be too much—all the bills and everything.

JM: You were on a scholarship though. Didn't it pay for everything?

DEREK: Yeah, as long as I kept my grades up, then the government would pay for it.

Derek's scholastic achievement at the high school has been quite high; he has been on the honor roll several times and maintains a strong B average.

Although his grades are not as high as Derek's, Craig works very hard in school. Self-disciplined and conscientious, Craig spends a good deal of time each evening on his homework, often passing up pick-up basketball games in favor of studying. Presently a senior, Craig picked the Fundamental School in eighth grade in part because it was at the time housed in a separate building located in the northern reaches of the city. By entering the Fundamental School, Craig hoped to avoid the racial tension in the main high school, a hope that went unrealized when the Fundamental School was moved into the Lincoln building just prior to his freshman year.

JM: You're in the Fundamental School, right?

CRAIG: Fundamental, yeah.

JM: Now, why'd you choose that one, way back in eighth grade?

CRAIG: Cuz I heard their reputation was something.

JM: What's their reputation?

CRAIG: Their reputation was that they have very good teachers and stuff. My sister and her friends said it was a very good school.

JM: Do they have technical drawing in Oc. Ed.?

CRAIG: In Oc. Ed.—oh, they have a lot of that stuff.

JM: How come you didn't decide to go into there?

CRAIG: I didn't know Oc. Ed. was like that. . . . I didn't want to go into it cuz I thought, I thought, really, I thought most of the kids in there are stupid.

JM: Do you think that now?

CRAIG: No, they're smarter than I am.

JM: In technical drawing?

CRAIG: Yeah, they went through a better program. See, if I was in Oc. Ed. I'd have like three periods each day.

JM: All this wasn't clear to you back in the eighth grade?

CRAIG: Well, to be truthful, the main reason I picked Fundamental was cuz the main high school was real tense. Y'know, there was fights up there—a white kid got stabbed to death, and when I was in the eighth grade it was still pretty bad. See, the Fundamental School used to be way up by, uh . . .

JM: Columbia Street?

CRAIG: Yeah, I thought by going up there I'd miss all the hassles. But then they moved the year I was graduating [from eighth grade]. They just moved into Lincoln.

Craig, during the course of his three and a half years at the school, has maintained a seventy-five average.

Juan, a 1983 graduate of the high school, studied culinary arts in the Occupational Education Program. Describing his performance in school as "pretty good," Juan never failed a subject and once received a ninety-four in a class for his efforts. In his honest, sincere, and straightforward manner, Juan describes his behavior in school. "I wasn't any angel in the class; most of the time I was okay. I was in between, because sometimes I came in a bad mood in some classes. But usually I wouldn't bother nobody, because I wasn't ready to go through no hassle. . . . Most teachers knew me as a nice kid. I don't know if I was a nice kid (smiles widely), but they know me as a nice kid." Although many of his black friends, like Super, eventually dropped out of the Occupational Education Program, Juan stuck with it.

Mike is generally obedient and disciplined, although he periodically cuts classes and occasionally sneaks down into the school basement with his girlfriend. Nevertheless, he respects the rules of the school; like many of the Brothers, he becomes embarrassed and almost apologetic when recounting episodes of misbehavior. Mike's academic performance is mediocre. Last year he failed English, which prompted his enrollment in a six-week summer school course. His grades have not improved much this year; his first semester's marks were a B, two C's, and two D's. While his performance in the classroom has been poor, Mike has excelled on the athletic fields. As a sophomore, he has made the varsity football, wrestling, and track teams.

In general, the Brothers are integrated fully into the school. Although many of them turn in only fair academic performances, they honor and respect the standards, conventions, and judgments of the school. They show no evidence of disrespect for teachers or other school officials, and their disciplinary records are for the most part clean. Their course of study is stable; once they choose a particular program, most of them stay with it until graduation. Their participation in extracurricular activities, especially athletics, gives them a chance to excel in an activity that is sometimes prized as highly as academics. In short, the Brothers are typical high school students.

THE HALLWAY HANGERS: TEACHER'S NIGHTMARE

For the most part, Frankie exemplifies the Hallway Hangers' attitudes toward school; he is unusual only in that he graduated. Placed in a special program limited to fifty students his freshman year (which has since been discontinued), Frankie was expelled from the high school for repeated fights, especially with black students, and for striking a teacher in the face. He was prevented from gaining entry into any alternative program and thus was barred from the school altogether. He then attended the King School, a certified, tuition-free, private, alternative high school for low-income youths that employs a politically radical educational philosophy and curriculum. Dissatisfied with the teachers, whom Frankie variously terms "fuckin' liberals," "flakes," and "burnouts from the sixties," he left the King School after one year. When Frankie threatened to take Lincoln High School to court for refusing to readmit him, he gained entry into the Enterprise Co-op Program. Although he did well at first, he was struggling to stay in the program after the first month because of a drug problem that severely impaired his performance. Frankie was ingesting three and four "hits" of THC each day and was "gettin' real fuckin' high, veggin' out, not doin' my work." After a month, he was kicked out of Enterprise Co-op.

At that point, there was only one program in which Frankie could be enrolled—the Adjustment Class. A sympathetic guidance counselor who had gained Frankie's trust arranged for his admittance into Jimmy Sullivan's class. For the first time in his life, Frankie really admired and respected his teacher; he stayed in Jimmy's class for three years, graduating in 1983. The respect Jimmy elicits from his students is based on his toughness, his streetwise reputation, and the perception that his financial success (he has significant real estate holdings) is independent of his position as a teacher. In an interview before he graduated, Frankie comments on Jimmy's Adjustment Class.

FRANKIE: I didn't give a shit at the school. I used to tell teachers to their face to fuck themselves. That's why I like this class I'm in. Jimmy, he'll say, "You wanna fuck with me, then fight me." He's a fucking black belt in karate. . . . Jimmy makes more fucking money than anyone else in that school. He's a real estate broker.

(*in a separate interview*)

FRANKIE: I went there, y'know. It was cool, cuz like you went in there, fuckin' you talk to Jimmy, and you know Jimmy's real cool. I never had a teacher that says, "Fuck this and fuck that" and "I'll kick your ass if you fuck up." The teachers in the King School, they were flakes; they swore and shit, but you just told them to shut the fuck up, and they shut up. They were scared. Jimmy, he ain't scared of no one.

Faced with the simple choice of doing his daily two hours of academic work and getting credit or of not doing it and failing, he attended school conscientiously.

FRANKIE: Jimmy, he says to me, "Look, come in and do your work if you want to; if you don't, screw! Get the fuck out of here." . . . I listened to him, y'know, sat there until was fuckin' got through my head. I fuckin' realized, hey man, I gotta get my diploma, keep my moms happy. I started doing my work and, y'know, you fuck around and shit but Jimmy was cool. He let you fuck around—if you do your work you can do whatever you want to. I used to work out, used to do a lot of boxing and shit. . . . I was there for awhile, three years. It was pretty cool.

Frankie was the first Hallway Hanger to enter Jimmy's class. In fact, when Frankie was first accepted into the class, he was the only student not to have been sent there by the court system. Most of the students had come directly from prison; some were shuttled daily from the county jail where they were incarcerated. Now, however, the average age of the students has fallen from nineteen to seventeen, and most are referred to the class after having problems in other high school programs.

Steve, for example, made a similar trek through the different programs, finally landing in the Adjustment Class. He picked Occupational Education in the eighth grade "cuz all my friends were there and I thought it'd be all right." Steve lasted only a month in that program before he was switched to regular academics, House C, because of discipline problems and excessive truancy. He lasted only two weeks in House C before he was assigned to Enterprise Co-op. "I didn't go. And I told them to go to hell, and I left. I didn't show up for school for a *long* time. Then they transferred me over to Co-op. And then so I went there. It was all right, but I really didn't like it either. Then I just said the hell with

that and missed the whole rest of the year. Didn't get no credits either."
When he returned to school the next year, Steve kicked in a window
in a hallway, exclaiming that he wanted to be put in Jimmy's class.
The Hallway Hangers acknowledge that Steve's antic amounted to a
deliberate attempt to get into the Adjustment Class, and Steve himself
admits, "Yeah, I wanted to cuz they had me on the list and shit, so I
said fuck it, I'm in."

The effort paid off; Steve was admitted to Jimmy's class almost
immediately, has attended for one year, and plans to stay in it until he
graduates in two years. Like Frankie, he respects Jimmy and finds the
class superior to the other programs.

STEVE: Jimmy's class has been real good for me, man.

JM: Yeah? What's it like in there?

STEVE: Oh, it's bad. It's way better than the other school. Come in
at 9:30, get out at 11:30. The guy is just like us; he swears and
shit, tells all the other teachers to go fuck themselves; he don't
care. Got weights, punching bag; we get out early.

Aside from the streetwise teacher and the unique atmosphere of the
classroom, students in the Adjustment Class like the light academic
workload. As Jimmy himself admits, "This is the easiest way to graduate."
Whatever the reason, it is because of Jimmy's class that Frankie managed
to graduate and Steve has stayed in school.

For Shorty, however, Jimmy's class was not enough. Shorty was
admitted to the Adjustment Class because he was a chronic truant and
had a habit of threatening teachers. Shorty accounts for his downward
spiral into Jimmy's class this way.

SHORTY: You start school as a freshman and you start cutting one
class, right, and when that teacher starts giving you a hard time—
this is how it started with me: I wasn't good in history and
spelling and shit—and he wouldn't ever have got me a tutor or
nothing. So then I said, "Fuck it." He wasn't passing me so then I
stopped going to his class. Then he would spread the word
around to the other teachers, and they would give me a hard
time, and I'd stop going to their classes. Finally, I ended up in
Jimmy's class.

Although he successfully completed one year of the Adjustment Class,
Shorty, hearing that there was a warrant out for his arrest, became
convinced that he would be sent to a detoxification center or prison
and dropped out of school altogether this past November (1983). Although
he managed to avoid incarceration, Shorty never went back to school,
figuring he could not bring up his average enough to get credit for the
fall semester.

Slick has a somewhat different educational history. He lived in a neighboring city until sixth grade and scored well enough on a test to gain admission to Latin Academy, a public school for gifted students. He attended Latin Academy for one year, enjoyed the challenging academic work, and was disappointed with the local grammar school when his family subsequently moved to Clarendon Heights.

SLICK: When I was at Latin, it was fucking real hard, right? Then I moved here cuz my grandfather died and my mother wanted to be closer to my grandmother so we could help her out. So we moved over here, and it would've cost three thousand dollars for me to go there (*at Latin Academy, where nonresidents of the city in which it is located pay tuition*), and we ain't got that kinda money, so I couldn't go. I went here [the local grammar school] during my seventh and eighth grade and then up the high school. It was a big letdown from Latin. It was much slower, and I knew everything they were teaching me. So I just didn't go to the school.

Given the apparently high level of his academic training at Latin Academy, it is curious that Slick chose to enter the Occupational Education Program upon entering the high school. In answer to my query, he revealed his logic. "Because I was already working with my brain. I wanted to try to learn something with my hands, know what I mean? If I just kept on doing fucking academics, it wasn't gonna fucking help me anyways. It was stuff I already knew." In a separate interview, Slick intimated that he thought at the time that he needed to learn a trade to maximize his chances of getting a job.

Once at the high school, however, Slick was dissatisfied with Oc. Ed. and switched to regular academics before his sophomore year. During his second year, bored with his classes, he started to cut more frequently. Like many of his friends, Slick voices dissatisfaction with what he perceives as favoritism toward black students at the high school. Indeed, this is the expressed reason that Slick quit school in the middle of his junior year.

SLICK: The regular academics I didn't like because there was certain favoritism. By my junior year, I quit school. Went to work.

JM: What do you mean? What was the favoritism?

SLICK: You see, because of what happened a few years ago, they have to lean towards the minorities more. Because of, you know what happened, some kid got stabbed up there. So if there's like a fight between a white kid and a black kid, the white kid's always wrong. So I didn't like that; so I just quit school.

Jinks also began in the Occupational Education Program "because I wanted to learn a career for when I got out of school." As a field of specialization, he chose computers but left the program in favor of regular academics because he "couldn't deal with sitting at a desk all day typing. It was too fucking boring." Previously a strong B student (according to the other boys), Jinks started cutting most of his classes and spending his time at Pop's, a store about five blocks from the school. The Hallway Hangers and a number of other students frequent the back room of Pop's during school hours, playing cards, smoking marijuana, and drinking beer. This past fall, at the beginning of his senior year, Jinks dropped out of school. He already was working twenty hours per week and expected to be hired full-time. "I like working better than I like going to school. I just prefer working. Going to work, getting paid. I need the money. The holidays are coming; gotta buy them gifts. I got a part-time job now. When I quit school, it'll be a full-time job, my boss said." Shortly after Jinks quit school, he was laid off.

Aside from Frankie, Boo-Boo is the only other Hallway Hanger who has graduated from high school. He entered the Oc. Ed. Program "cuz everybody else was" and attended school diligently for two months before starting to cut most of his classes in favor of "smoking a few bones" at Pop's. Eventually, Boo-Boo stopped going to school at all for four months and did not receive so much as a phone call from the school authorities. Then Boo-Boo was arrested for auto theft in the middle of his freshman year (he was fifteen). After he was placed on probation as a result of his conviction in juvenile court, Boo-Boo's school performance was monitored by his probation officer. He was switched into the Building Trades and Services Program and began to attend school regularly. "I was only fifteen, and when you're on probation, you have to go to school. They kept giving me a hard time, and I didn't want to hear it, so I kept going." Boo-Boo stayed in BTS for four years and graduated in 1983.

Like many of the Hallway Hangers, Chris enrolled in Oc. Ed. his freshman year because he believed that knowing a trade would make it easier to get a job. During his freshman year, Chris was switched into BTS because "I was fucking up in Oc. Ed. I threw a chair at a teacher. I couldn't take the shit they were dishing out." Claiming that the academic work in BTS is far too simple ("We were just doing multiplication tables and shit—what a fucking joke"), Chris skipped all but his first two classes, hanging at Pop's the rest of the day. Unfamiliar even with the names of his afternoon teachers, Chris acknowledges that when he did attend school, he was impaired by drugs or alcohol. "Oh yeah, I'm high every time I go to school. I gotta be. Sometimes I even drink before I go; I'll have a few beers. It's too much if you don't." This past fall, Chris quit school altogether. Although he still frequents Pops to sell drugs and occasionally ventures onto school grounds for the same purpose, Chris is no longer subject to the school's authority, an arrangement he prefers.

Stoney chose to enter the regular academic program in the high school but attended classes for only two weeks before he started cutting regularly. "I never went. I'd go to a couple classes, and then I'd cut a class here, cut a class there, cut another class—before you know it, you got fifty cuts, detentions, and then I stopped going to school." According to Stoney, he was suspended a couple of times, and school administrators wanted to expel him, but because he was too young, they put him in a special after-school program. Working part-time and attending school from three to six in the afternoon, Stoney was satisfied with the situation until the middle of his junior year. Given the opportunity to work more hours and tired of the school routine from which he felt he was learning little ("We rarely did work in there. They thought I was stupid or something; they had us do stupid stuff"), he quit school completely and started working full-time.

As a group, the Hallway Hangers experience school in a way much different than the Brothers do. Whereas the Brothers are fully integrated into the school, the Hallway Hangers' attitudes toward the educational system can be summed up by Stoney's words: "Fuck school. I hate fucking school." Most of the Hallway Hangers have dropped out. While officially enrolled, most spent little time in school anyway, preferring the fun, companionship, and drugs at Pop's. When in class, they generally were disruptive and undisciplined. None of the Hallway Hangers participated in any extracurricular activities. By their own accounts, they were high or drunk much of the time they spent in school. No one picked a school program and stayed in it; they all switched or were switched into different classes, some spiraling down through the array of alternative programs at amazing speed, landing in the last stop on the line. Some stayed there; most have dropped out altogether.

What factors explain the wide discrepancy between the educational pattern of the Brothers and the Hallway Hangers? The school cites the personal problems with which the Hallway Hangers are burdened. They are slow, unmotivated, undisciplined, or emotionally disturbed. More sympathetic teachers, like Jimmy Sullivan, attribute this type of fundamental difference between students to the ability of some to "talk about themselves in the long range, to project themselves into the future." However, a deeper level of analysis is necessary to explain the Hallway Hangers' and the Brothers' different experiences in school.

THE UNDERLYING LOGIC OF STUDENT BEHAVIOR

As with many urban high schools, the Lincoln School is preoccupied with maintaining discipline. The team of security guards policing the hallways is ample evidence of this fact. Aside from specific sanctions (suspensions, detentions, parent notifications), teachers attempt to secure discipline by reinforcing the achievement ideology: "Behave yourself, work hard, earn good grades, get a good job, and make a lot of money." This line of reasoning rests on two assumptions: what I shall term the efficacy of schooling—the notion that academic performance is the crucial link to economic success—and the existence of equality of opportunity. Although used primarily to ensure proper behavior by highlighting its eventual rewards, the ideology has more than a disciplinary function.

Before we move on to consider the implications of this line of reasoning, we must address the question of how commonly it is used in the school. This task is not difficult, for both students and teachers draw attention to its prominence in securing discipline. Karen Wallace, the career counselor, in an unsolicited remark, mentioned that this argument is constantly reinforced by teachers: "We tell them that if they try hard enough, work hard enough, and get good grades, then anything is possible." On another occasion, Mike, excited about the prospects of securing a lucrative computer job, recounted the computer teacher's remark about a friend who makes two thousand dollars a week working with computers. The teacher assured his students that comparable jobs are available in the computer industry "for those who don't fool around and really learn the trade." In another unsolicited remark, Chris drew attention to this tendency of teachers to forge a secure link between success in school and success on the job market: "They tell you they'll get you a job when you're done. They say that to you right at the beginning. They say it to you all the time." The difference between Mike and Chris, and more generally, as we shall see, between the Brothers and the Hallway Hangers, is that Mike believes this line of reasoning, whereas Chris reacts to it with: "That's *bullshit*. They don't fucking give you shit."

Swallowing the Achievement Ideology

In the previous chapter, I noted the Brothers' widespread belief in the reality of equality of opportunity. Like most Americans, they view this society as an open one. Crucial to this widely held notion is a belief in the efficacy of schooling. As the achievement ideology propagated in school implies, education is viewed as the remedy for the problem of social inequality; schooling makes the race for prestigious jobs and wealth an even one. The Brothers have a good deal of faith in the worth of schooling.

The Brothers' belief in the equality of opportunity and the efficacy of schooling emerges very strongly from their responses to particular interview questions. When asked whether they feel they have an equal chance to do as well in school as would a wealthy boy from an affluent part of the city, the nearly unanimous response is "yes," as it is when they are asked if they have an equal chance to get as good a job as the same hypothetical wealthy boy would. With respect to their views on the efficacy of schooling, the Brothers' responses to the question of why they work hard in school are illustrative.

(*all in separate interviews*)

DEREK: I know I want a good job when I get out. I know that I have to work hard in school. I mean, I want a good future. I don't wanna be doing nothing for the rest of my life.

CRAIG: Because I know by working hard it'll all pay off in the end. I'll be getting a good job.

MIKE: Get ahead in life; get a good job.

When asked whether their academic achievement will influence the type of job they will be able to secure, the Brothers all agree that it will.

This viewpoint explains the Brothers' commitment to their school work and the relatively high level of effort that characterizes their academic participation. But whereas their acceptance of the achievement ideology accounts for the ease with which the Brothers are integrated into the school, their mediocre academic performance requires further explanation.

One cannot attribute the Brothers' lack of scholastic success to lack of effort; as we have seen, they try hard in school. Moreover, the Brothers generally are intelligent and able. Although their scores on I.Q. tests, which purport to measure intelligence, are not available, three years of acquaintance with the boys leaves me assured that, on average, they are not substantially less "gifted" or "clever" than my university classmates. What, then, accounts for the academic mediocrity of the Brothers?

In attempting to answer this question, we find ourselves in the company of many eminent sociologists who have tackled the problem of the "educability" of the lower classes. The consistent tendency of working-class children to perform less well in school than their middle-class counterparts is demonstrated by a wealth of empirical evidence,[1] but the actual processes and mechanisms by which this comes about remain almost completely obscured.

Many conventional sociologists look to the working-class family to explain differential academic performance by social class, an approach that has yielded little in the way of concrete results. As Olive Banks admits in *The Sociology of Education*:

> The consistent tendency of working-class or manual workers'
> children to perform less well in school, and to leave school sooner
> than the children of non-manual workers, calls for explanation, and it
> has seemed reasonable to look for that explanation in the working-
> class family.

It would, however, be far from the truth to conclude that the attention paid by sociologists in recent years to this problem has taken us very far towards a solution. We have many studies into the relationship between social-class background and educational achievement, and many different aspects of that background have been suggested as causal factors in the link between home and school, but up to now we have very little knowledge of the precise way in which these different factors interelate to depress intellectual performance.[2]

In addition to the inability of this approach to account for the problem of differential academic achievement, this emphasis on the family, in its extreme form, has produced some very dubious conclusions and destructive results. Propagated in the United States since the 1960s in an attempt to explain the low educational attainment of black and lower-class white children, the concept of cultural deprivation attributes their problems solely to the cultural deficiencies of their families. The view that the problem resides almost exclusively with the children and their families, and that some sort of cultural injection is needed to compensate for what they are missing, is not only intellectually bankrupt but also has contributed to the widespread popular notion that the plight of poor whites and minorities is entirely their own fault.

To understand the problems lower-class children face in the American educational system demands that attention be paid not just to their families but also to the school. Theories that give primacy to the family inhibit critical scrutiny of the nation's schools. The problem is not that lower-class children are inferior in some way; the problem is that *by the definitions and standards of the school*, they consistently are evaluated as deficient. The assumption of some mainstream sociologists that the problem must lie with the contestants, rather than with the judge, is simply unfounded.

Conventional sociologists as well as Marxist theorists have been singularly unable to put forth a convincing explanation of lower-class "educability." As Karabel and Halsey point out, the only explanation Bowles can muster is the vague assertion that the "rules of the game" favor the upper classes. Although this sentiment undoubtedly is true, he offers us no explanation of how the rules are biased and reproduced. Clearly, what is needed is a comprehensive analysis of how the educational system's curricula, pedagogy, and evaluative criteria[3] favor the interests of the upper classes.

Although such a formidable task has yet to be undertaken, the guiding theoretical concept for the endeavor has been provided by Bourdieu—the notion of cultural capital. To recapitulate: Bourdieu's theory maintains that the cultural capital of the lower classes—their manners, norms, dress, style of interaction, and linguistic facility—is devalued by the school, while the cultural capital of the upper classes is rewarded. As Halsey, Heath, and Ridge put it, "The ones who can receive what the school has to give are the ones who are already endowed with the requisite cultural attributes—with the appropriate cultural capital."[4] Although Bourdieu is primarily a theorist, Paul Dimaggio has substantiated Bourdieu's concept by analyzing data sets with measures for cultural attitudes, information, and activities for more than 2,900 eleventh grade boys and girls. He found that the impact of cultural capital on high school grades is "very significant," which confirms "rather dramatically the utility of the perspective advanced here [by Bourdieu]."[5]

Although neither Bernstein nor Nell Keddie self-consciously situates his or her empirical work within Bourdieu's theoretical framework, both provide analyses of actual classroom processes that enforce class-linked differences in educational achievement. These analyses fit nicely into Bourdieu's theoretical perspective. As we saw in Chapter 2, Bernstein actually demonstrates how class-based differences in speech patterns affect academic achievement and place working-class students like Frankie and Craig at a disadvantage with respect to their middle-class counterparts. Keddie's study also demonstrates how observed classroom phenomena—the different expectations teachers hold for students of different social origins, the determination of what counts as knowledge, teacher-student interaction, the tracking of courses—serve to handicap the performance of the lower classes.[6] As Karabel and Halsey remind us, because dominant social groups determine what is valued in the educational system, it should not surprise us that subordinate social groups are judged deficient by the criteria set by the powerful.[7]

These complex mechanisms of social reproduction are embedded deeply in the American educational system; they are well hidden, and thus the Brothers are unaware of the processes that work to hinder their performance. The Brothers believe in equality of opportunity and reject the idea that they have less of a chance to succeed in school than do middle- or upper-class students. Instead, the Brothers attribute their mediocre academic performance to personal inadequacy—laziness, stupidity, or lack of self-discipline.

(all in separate interviews)

SUPER: I would try—if I had more study skills, I bet you I'd be trying my hardest. I bet I'd be getting good grades. . . . I dunno; I just can't seem to do it.

MOKEY: I try my best to do as good as anyone else. But there's some real smart people up there, plus I can't seem to get myself to work, especially during football. It's hard.

MIKE: I did horrible [my freshman year in high school]. I used to do good. I got all A's in grammar school. Now I'm doing shitty. I guess I started out smart and got stupider.

If one accepts the equality of opportunity line of reasoning, those who are not "making it" have only themselves to blame.

Clearly, the self-esteem of the Brothers suffers as a result of their inferior academic performance. A careful review of the literature on the effects of academic achievement and particularly track placement on students' sense of self, undertaken by Maureen Scully in a 1982 unpublished essay, reveals that although we can expect academic self-esteem to vary according to scholastic performance, students' general self-esteem is often more resilient. Because some high school students do not value academic achievement very highly and instead emphasize nonacademic activities and values, their general sense of self-esteem is sheltered from the negative onslaughts of academic failure.[8] The Brothers, however, care a great deal about their academic performance, and thus their general self-esteem is sensitive to academic failure.

In summary, the Brothers believe that American society is an open one; equality of opportunity is perceived as a reality. Moreover, schooling is regarded by the Brothers as the means to economic success; consequently, they care about school, accept its norms and standards, and conform to its rules. As lower-class students, however, the Brothers are lacking in the cultural capital rewarded by the school system—hence their poor academic achievement and placement into low tracks. The Brothers blame themselves for the mediocrity of their scholastic performance. The implications of this dynamic are important to an understanding of the overall process of social reproduction (which will be taken up in the next chapter).

Spurning the Achievement Ideology

The school experiences of the Hallway Hangers suggest that they are a group of disaffected, rebellious, undisciplined boys who have been labeled "emotionally disturbed," "learning impaired," and "slow." Beneath their uncooperative conduct and resistance, however, lies a logic that makes sense to these boys and informs their attitudes toward school.

The Hallway Hangers do not "buy" the achievement ideology because they foresee substantial barriers to their economic success, barriers this ideology fails to mention. It is important to note that the Hallway Hangers could reject the notion that equality of opportunity exists but accept the reasoning that school can still help them. Just because one does not have the same chance to succeed in school or on the job market as a middle- or upper-class student does not mean necessarily that achievement in school will be of no use in securing a job. Indeed, the connection between schooling and occupational achievement is so deeply ingrained in the minds of most Americans that it is difficult to imagine people completely rejecting it.

The Hallway Hangers, however, challenge the conventional wisdom that educational achievement translates into economic success. In their view of the opportunity structure, educational attainment is of little importance. Convinced that they are headed into jobs for which they do not need an education, the Hallway Hangers see little value in schooling. Jinks perfectly summarizes this view: "Even if you get a high school diploma, that don't mean shit. A lot of people say, 'Oh, you need it for that job.' You get a high school diploma, and they're still gonna give you a shitty job. So it's just a waste of time to get it."

Because this point of view runs counter to a deeply rooted, collective belief, it offends our sensibilities. In fact, however, it is a rational outlook based on experience. Jinks looks at his four older brothers, one of whom graduated from high school, and observes that the one with the diploma is no better off than the rest of them. The brother who struggled through the four years of high school is in the navy, as was another who did not graduate.

Stoney feels the same way. He insists that school performance has no effect on what kind of job one will get. He argues instead that "fucking experience, man, it comes in handy," particularly in the case of his current job in a pizza shop.

STONEY: So the very next day, I went looking for another job. Went into this place, told him my experience, made a few pies. That was it; he hired me on the spot. No application or nothing.

JM: No high school diploma.

STONEY: That's right. He didn't want one.

JM: For your goals, how would it help you to have a diploma?

STONEY: (*immediately*) It won't, cuz I don't need no diploma to open a store. Like I said, if you know how to do something, you do it. If you don't, you don't.

JM: Do you think it would help you at all if you got fired tomorrow, and you went up to another pizza shop somewhere? Do you think it would help you if you could show them a diploma?

STONEY: No, it wouldn't help me. They wanna see what you got, what you can do. If you can do the job. I used to always get hired on the spot. They'd look at me and be real surprised a young kid can make pizza this good.

Relevant job experience is much more important than educational attainment for landing a job in food preparation, at least in Stoney's experience. The same logic holds true for a prospective construction worker or auto mechanic.

Shorty draws on the experiences of his brothers, much like Jinks, to reach a similar conclusion regarding the efficacy of schooling. Two of Shorty's brothers have graduated from high school; one of these apparently graduated from college as well. Nevertheless, neither has been able to secure desired employment. The college graduate is working security at a local research firm. Despite relatively high educational achievement, "they don't seem to be getting anywhere," comments Shorty.

Frankie need only look at his own experience to assert that schooling is generally incapable of doing much for the Hallway Hangers. In interviews, he constantly reiterates this theme.

JM: Okay, so why is it that some kids, even coming from down here, will go to school, and they'll work real hard, go to all their classes, and do all the work? Why do some kids take that route?

FRANKIE: Well none of my friends take that route. But I dunno. I never took that route. But I guess, I dunno, they're dopes. I dunno, I guess, y'know, they fuckin' think if they go through high school and go through college, they think they're gonna get a job that's gonna pay fifty grand a year. Y'know, a white-collar job. I don't think that's true.

JM: Do you think how you do in school is gonna affect what kinda job you get?

FRANKIE: I got my diploma, and you don't even need that. Y'know, my diploma ain't doing me no good. It's sitting in my bottom drawer. Y'know, it ain't gonna help me. I got my diploma, and you don't even need that. . . . All those Portegi [Portuguese] kids, they never went the fuck to school. Now they fuckin' got good jobs, cars—y'know, they fucking made it. They went out and fuckin' worked machinery and mechanics. So a high school diploma really isn't fucking shit.

(in a separate interview)

FRANKIE: They dropped out of school, and they got better fucking jobs than we do. I got my fuckin' diploma, and I ain't got jack shit. So it wasn't worth it for me to get my high school diploma. If I dropped out when I was sixteen—that was two years ago—I prob'ly would've already been through a job training program, and I'd already have a fucking job, saving me fucking money.

(following an assertion by me that schooling is of some use on the labor market)

FRANKIE: (angrily) But, but (stuttering because he is upset), still, I did, I did, I did the fucking, I did my school program, I went to school, I fuckin', I got my diploma, I went what you're s'posed to do. 'Cept you're s'posed to further your education—college and many more thousands of fucking dollars. Look how many fucking college graduates ain't got jobs. You know how fucking hard it is.

They got educations. What the fuck they doin' with it? They ain't doin' shit. So fucking school ain't paying off for no one.

This last assertion—that school does not pay off for anybody—is rather extreme and not one to which all the Hallway Hangers would give their support. Even Frankie, in a less tense moment, would agree that some kids do "make it" and that success in school is a crucial ingredient for economic and social advancement. Nevertheless, although exaggerated in this case, Frankie's comment is indicative of the general attitude of the Hallway Hangers.

The Hallway Hangers do not maintain that schooling is incapable of doing anything for anyone because they all know Billy. Billy used to hang with the Hallway Hangers, getting high every day before, during, and after school, drinking excessively, and stealing cars. During his freshman year and the early part of his sophomore year, however, Billy underwent a number of personal crises out of which he emerged a much different person. Part of a large family, Billy had a father who was an alcoholic and has a mother who is mentally ill. In the span of a year and a half, Billy's mother was deemed unfit by the Department of Social Services to have custody of her children, so Billy moved in with his father, who died shortly thereafter. At about the same time, Billy's best friend was murdered brutally in an abandoned building a few blocks from Clarendon Heights. Billy, who currently lives in a three bedroom apartment in Clarendon Heights with his aunt and uncle, three cousins, and a baby nephew, is a senior at Lincoln High School. Goalie of the varsity hockey team and recipient of a special college scholarship for "individuals of extraordinary ability and need," Billy has switched from Oc. Ed. to the Fundamental School in preparation for college.

The view among the Hallway Hangers is that Billy is "making it." He is living testimony to the fact that schooling can work, that it can pay off. So the Hallway Hangers are not of the view that success in school is irrelevant but rather that the odds of "making it" are simply too slim to bet on. In what can be likened to a cost-benefit analysis, the Hallway Hangers, much like Willis's lads, conclude that the possibility of upward social mobility is not worth the price of obedience, conformity, and investment of substantial amounts of time, energy, and work in school.

For the Hallway Hangers, perhaps the biggest cost of going to school every day is the deferred income from full-time work. As Giroux reminds us, the economic issue often plays the crucial role in a working-class student's decision whether to attend school full-time, part-time, or not at all.[9] The issue of potential work earnings entered into all the boys' decisions to drop out of school. Chris and Jinks comment on the tension between school and employment directly.

(in a joint interview)

CHRIS: Jay, lemme tell you how I feel about school. I wanna go to school; I'd like to go 'til like 11:30 and then at about twelve o'clock work until about five. Y'know, so I could go to school plus make some money.

JINKS: You won't like that brother, cuz that's what I do. That's what I do. He'll start going to work, getting a little money in his pocket, and he'll always want more.

(later in the same interview)

CHRIS: So Jay, people should fucking give us a break, y'know? *(laughing)* Pay us to go to school, y'know?

JM: How would that work?

CHRIS: Give us forty bucks a week to go to school 'til twelve o'clock. At twelve we go to work and make about fifty bucks.

JM: What would be in it for them?

JINKS: They'd get a lot of people to go *(laughing)*. They'd get a helluva lot more than they got now, I'm tellin' ya.

CHRIS: On Friday, I'd say, "Oh *yeah!* Got my job."

JINKS: Got my ounce all paid for.

This last comment is revealing. The world that the Hallway Hangers inhabit, with its preponderance of drugs and alcohol, demands financial resources. The pressure to come up with money is keenly felt by all these boys, a pressure to which Slick alludes often.

SLICK: *(motioning to doorway #13)* Hey, everyone out there has a goal. Their goal is one thing and that's money. You hafta have money, to make it. . . . That's what depresses them. That's what puts them into the pressure situation. They hafta make money; they know they hafta do it. The name of the game is money. You hafta get it. If you don't get it, there's no way you're gonna be able to do anything. You hafta make it.

Locked into the present by the pressing need for money, the Hallway Hangers, in contrast to middle-class teenagers, do not have the resources to bide their time while long-range educational or occupational plans come to fruition. Moreover, believing they have missed out on the indulgences of American consumerism, they are starved for immediate financial success.

(in a group interview)

SLICK: Y'know what it is, Jay? All of us down here, we just don't wanna make a buck; we wanna make a fast buck. We want it *now*. Right fucking now. And you know why? Not cuz we're stupid and can't wait for anything, but because we've never had it.

SHORTY: Fuckin' right. We're all poor as shit.

SLICK: No one in this room has thirty bucks in his pocket. Fuckin' right we want it. We've never had it.

The desire of these boys to go for the fast buck, to focus only on the present, becomes understandable in light of the uncertainty of the future and their bona fide belief that they may be in prison or dead.

In considering the experiences of the Brothers in school, we have seen that the effects of schooling on their self-esteem are significant. The Hallway Hangers also feel a measure of personal inadequacy with respect to their dismal educational attainment, but for them schooling is merely tangential to the overall experience of being a lower-class teenager in an urban setting. Hence, little of their self-esteem is tied up in school; academic performance has less effect on their sense of self. It is possible, however, that this apparent indifference toward school is itself in part a defense mechanism that protects the boys from assaults on their self-respect. Evidence for this type of failure-avoidance strategy has been documented in a number of quantitative studies of students' self-esteem.[10] For the Hallway Hangers, the prospects of failure in school and the accompanying feelings of inadequacy are further reasons not to invest themselves in education; the potential threat to self-esteem is another item on the cost side of the equation.

The cost of deferred work earnings, the price of obedience and conformity to rules and authority that run counter to the peer group's ethos, the risk of failure, and the investment of time and energy all make up the costs of school involvement for the Hallway Hangers. On the benefit side are improved prospects for social mobility resulting from educational achievement. For the Hallway Hangers, who see through the achievement ideology and have little faith in the efficacy of schooling, the improved prospects for social mobility are not worth the price that schooling exacts. Although their approach to school assuredly is not based on a rational cost-benefit analysis, these considerations do underlie their orientation toward education.

This logic dictates that the Hallway Hangers drop out of school or at least minimize their involvement with it. That most of the Hallway Hangers pursue this latter course is evident from their paths into the less demanding programs at Lincoln High School, such as BTS, the Adjustment Class, Enterprise Co-op, and the after-school program. With teachers for whom they have more respect, fewer rules, and lighter academic workloads, entry into these alternative programs sometimes minimizes the costs to the point where schooling becomes worthwhile.

Both high school graduates (Boo-Boo and Frankie) and the one boy currently enrolled in school (Steve) are or were in such alternative programs. Even for the boys in these programs, however, schooling often is not worth the price that must be paid, and thus most have dropped out. For Frankie to stay in school, for instance, the added benefit of "keeping my moms happy" was necessary to swing the balance in favor of schooling.

Whereas at first glance the rebellious behavior, low academic achievement, and high dropout rate of the Hallway Hangers seem to stem from lack of self-discipline, dullness of wit, laziness, or an inability to project themselves into the future, the actual causes of their rejection of school are quite different. Their unwillingness to partake of the educational system stems from an assessment of the costs and benefits of playing the game. Their view is not that schooling is incapable of propeling them up the ladder of social mobility, but that the chances are too slim to warrant the attempt. The Hallway Hangers' alienation from school rests not so much on a perceived lack of the means to succeed in school as of the means to convert that success into success on the labor market. Convinced that they are headed into dead-end jobs regardless of their educational attainment, the Hallway Hangers dismiss school as irrelevant.

Given this logic, the oppositional behavior of the Hallway Hangers is a form of resistance to an institution that cannot deliver on its promise of upward social mobility for all students. Furthermore, Lincoln High School, like almost all American schools, is essentially a middle-class institution. Its curriculum, grading system, and disciplinary code all reward middle-class traits, values, and skills. In coping with the difficulties of growing up poor in America, the Hallway Hangers have developed a set of survival skills of which they are very proud. These skills, however, are accorded little or no recognition in the school setting; instead, students must relinquish their street identities and move beyond their neighborhood ties. The Hallway Hangers resent the fact that the school, because of its middle-class orientation, ignores the skills they have picked up on the street. Thus, they do anything they can to express themselves in an institution that denies and violates their cultural identities.

The maturity and independence the boys have gained from years of hard living in Clarendon Heights clash with the authoritarian structure of the school. Teachers, as the agents of repression, are especially difficult for the Hallway Hangers to tolerate.

(all in separate interviews)

CHRIS: I hate the fucking teachers. I don't like someone always telling me what the fuck to do. Especially the way they do it. They make you feel like shit. I couldn't take their shit.

SLICK: It's with the maturity here—you wanna do what you want to do, and you don't want anyone to tell you what to do.

JINKS: You gotta get high to go to class. You gotta, to listen to the teaches talk their shit. Tell you, "Do this, do that, and do that" and a lot of people just say, "Fuck you. You do it yourself. I ain't doing shit for you."

Although teacher condescension and the institution's demand for unquestioning obedience to authority are sore points, the Hallway Hangers' resentment is not focused on teachers as a generic category as much as it is directed at middle-class teachers in particular. The Hallway Hangers constantly refer to the perceived social class disjuncture between themselves and the school's teaching staff. Jimmy Sullivan, who comes from the same class as these students and still displays many characteristics of that class culture, is respected because "he doesn't take no shit from anybody," including students. The middle-class teachers at the King School, in contrast, are held in contempt by Frankie because "they swore and shit, but you just told them to shut the fuck up and they shut up." The Hallway Hangers are willing to accept the authority of Sullivan and Harry Jones, a former resident of public housing. The same authority in the hands of other teachers, however, draws nothing but scorn from the boys.

(in a group interview)

JM: What about the teachers? You all seem to like Sullivan and Jones. What's the difference between them and the rest of 'em?

CHRIS: The other ones are all pussies.

SHORTY: Cuz they don't know how to deal with us kids.

FRANKIE: And the reason Harry Jones is cool is cuz Harry was brought up in the city his whole life; he used to live in Emerson Towers and his brothers and shit—they ain't all fucking angels, y'know. That's why he's cool. . . . And, y'know, there's a couple of other teachers that are fuckin' from around here and know what the fuck is happening. Y'know, but other teachers, they live in the suburbs and shit. They're coming into a city to work. They don't know what the fuck city kids are.

(in a discussion with Shorty and Slick)

SLICK: Certain teachers you can talk to up there. But most of the teachers that are up there, a lot of them are too rich, y'know what I mean? They have money, and they don't give a fuck about nobody. They don't know how it's like to hafta come to school late. "Why'd you come to school late?" "I had to make sure my brother was in school. I had to make sure certain things—I had to make sure that there was breakfast."

SHORTY: Responsibilities. See, that's what I mean. Now, the teachers will not understand. He ain't got no father, right? The father ain't living there, just like me. He's the oldest kid now. And he has big responsibilities at home because his brothers are growing up and his sister—he's got to keep an eye on 'em. Now you gotta do all that, and you got teachers giving you a hard fucking time?

SLICK: It's tough.

SHORTY: You got teachers like Harry Jones. They know; they understand where you come from, that you're trying to support your family.

SLICK: Like Harry Jones, when I got into his class, he talked to me, y'know? He'd understand what I'm doing.

SHORTY: He grew up around here all his life.

(*in a group interview*)

FRANKIE: Y'know, I'll admit I fucked up, y'know? Hey man, I got fucking problems, y'know? And the teacher just don't want to deal with it. Well, fuck them.

(*in a discussion with Jinks and Chris*)

JM: Do any of the teachers know the people?

JINKS: A few. Like Harry Jones, Jimmy Sullivan. All the rest are all bitchy. They don't understand us; they don't try to understand us.

Similar effects of social class differences between teachers and students have been found in other studies. In his analysis of the culture of a community college, Howard London found that subtle class antagonism between students and teachers was at the root of problems in conduct, absenteeism, and negative attitudes on the part of both toward the school.[11] The expressed antipathy of the Hallway Hangers toward middle-class teachers should not surprise us, for they are the most obvious symbols of the middle-class orientation of the school.

The school demands respect for its staff. But for the Hallway Hangers to show respect or even deference for individuals who by their standards do not deserve it is a real struggle. Thus, in trying to understand the approach the Hallway Hangers take toward school, we also must be cognizant of the costs involved in meeting the school's requirement of respect for teachers (loss of self-respect, condemnation from peers, forfeiture of feelings of ascendancy over other students).

The Brothers do not have problems with respecting teachers, for in many ways the teachers symbolize what the boys hope to become. Many of the Brothers aspire to middle-class jobs and, in any case, harbor no ill will toward middle-class values and norms. Indeed, the Brothers, consciously or unconsciously, emulate the middle-class traits of the teachers and endeavor to embody middle-class values. This phenomenon, termed "anticipatory socialization" by Robert Merton,[12] is an important source of dissimilarity between the Brothers and the Hallway Hangers.

In marked contrast to the Hallway Hangers, the Brothers feel that they are headed up the ladder of social mobility and believe that schooling is going to get them there. That two peer groups of the same social class, indeed from the very same neighborhood, hold such radically different attitudes toward school presents a challenging puzzle to the sociologist. In the next chapter, I attempt to meet this challenge directly.

NOTES

1. See, for example, studies by the following: David Dillon, "Does the School Have a Right to Its Own Language?" *The English Journal* 69 (April 1980):1460–1474; Warren G. Findley and Mirian M. Bryan, "Ability Grouping: A Review of the Literature," Part 3 (Washington, D.C.: Office of Education, 1970); Melvin L. Kohn, *Class and Conformity: A Study in Values* (Chicago: University of Chicago Press, 1977); Charles Miller, John A. McLaughlin, John Madden, and Norman M. Chansky, "Socioeconomic Class and Teacher Bias," *Psychological Reports* 23 (1968):806–810; Ray C. Rist, "Student Social Class and Teacher Expectations: The Self-Fulfilling Prophecy in Ghetto Education," *Harvard Educational Review* 40 (August 1970):411–451; Morris Rosenberg and Roberta G. Simmons, *Black and White Self-Esteem: The Urban School Child* (Washington, D.C.: American Sociological Association, 1971); and Charles B. Schultz and Roger H. Sherman, "Social Class, Development, and Differences in Reinforcer Effectiveness," *Review of Educational Research* 46 (1976):25–59.

2. Olive Banks, *The Sociology of Education* (London: B. T. Batsfield, 1976), pp. 68, 69.

3. These are the three major areas Bernstein has identified as crucial to our understanding of the socially determined value placed on various types of knowledge. See *Class, Codes and Control,* vol. 3 (London: Routledge and Kegan Paul, 1975), p. 85.

4. A. H. Halsey, A. F. Heath, and J. M. Ridge, *Origins and Destinations* (Oxford: Clarendon Press, 1980), p. 7.

5. Paul Dimaggio, "Cultural Capital and Social Success," *American Sociological Review* 47 (April 1982):189–201.

6. Nell Keddie, "Classroom Knowledge," in *Knowledge and Control,* ed. Michael F. D. Young (London: Collier, 1972), pp. 133–160.

7. Jerome Karabel and A. H. Halsey, eds., *Power and Ideology in Education* (New York: Oxford University Press, 1977), p. 67.

8. Maureen Anne Scully, "Coping with Meritocracy" (Thesis, Harvard College, 1982), pp. 85–101.

9. Henry A. Giroux, *Theory and Resistance in Education* (London: Heinemann Educational Books, 1983), p. 95.

10. See the following: Viktor Gecas, "Contexts of Socialization," in *Social Psychology: Sociological Perspectives,* eds. Morris Rosenberg and Ralph H. Turner

(New York: Basic Books, 1981); Rosenberg and Simmons, *Black and White Self-Esteem*; Morris Rosenberg, *Conceiving the Self* (New York: Basic Books, 1979); Morris Rosenberg, "The Self-Concept: Social Product and Social Force," in *Social Psychology: Sociological Perspectives*; Richard J. Shavelson, Judith J. Hubner, and George C. Stanton, "Self-Concept: Validation of Construct Interpretations," *Review of Educational Research* 46 (Summer 1976):407–411; Arthur L. Stinchcombe, *Rebellion in a High School* (Chicago: Quadrangle Books, 1964).

11. Howard B. London, *The Culture of a Community College* (New York: Praeger, 1978).

12. Robert K. Merton and Alice S. Rossi, "Contributions to the Theory of Reference Group Behavior" in *Social Theory and Social Structure* (New York: Free Press, 1968), pp. 319–322.

7

LEVELED ASPIRATIONS: SOCIAL REPRODUCTION TAKES ITS TOLL

With the ethnographic description from the preceding chapters at our disposal, we now can attempt to analyze the forces that influence the aspirations of these two groups of boys from Clarendon Heights. That many boys in both groups do not even aspire to middle-class jobs is a powerful indication of how class inequality is reproduced in American society. These youths' prospects for socioeconomic advancement are doomed before they even get started; most of the boys do not even get a foothold on the ladder of social mobility. In this chapter, the task before us is to illuminate in as much detail and depth as possible the process of social reproduction as it is lived by the Hallway Hangers and the Brothers.

The regulation of aspirations is perhaps the most significant of all the mechanisms contributing to social reproduction; however, aspirations themselves are largely a function of structural mechanisms that should be considered when possible. Mention already has been made of the effects of tracking and the school's valuation of the cultural capital of the upper classes, both of which influence aspirations but also have independent effects on reproducing class structure. An additional and essential component of social reproduction is the process by which individuals in a stratified social order come to accept their own position and the inequalities of the social order as legitimate.

Whereas force and coercion often have ensured the cohesion of societies and the maintenance of oppressive relationships, ideology is more important in fulfilling this function in contemporary America. In particular, the achievement ideology is a powerful force in the legitimation of inequality and, ultimately, in social reproduction. In short, this ideology maintains that individual merit and achievement are the fair and equitable sources of inequality of American society. If merit is the basis for the distribution of rewards, then members of the lower classes attribute their subordinate position in the social order to personal deficiencies. In this way, inequality is legitimated.[1]

In their theoretical formulations, both Weber and Marx touch on the role of ideology in the maintenance of social cohesion. In Weber's terms, ideology is the "myth" by which the powerful ensure belief in the validity of their comination. "Every highly privileged group develops the myth of its natural superiority. Under conditions of stable distribution of power . . . that myth is accepted by the negatively privileged strata."[2] Although Marx considered economics the major determinant in the perpetuation of class relations, he discusses the function of ideology in preserving exploitative relations in capitalist societies. Ideology, which is proffered to the subordinate classes as an accurate depiction of the social order, is actually a "false consciousness," an apparently true but essentially illusory set of views that disguises and distorts the true workings of the capitalist system. The ruling class, in order to justify its dominance, "is compelled . . . to represent its interest as the common interest of all the members of society. . . . It has to give its ideas the form of universality, and represent them as the only rational, universally valid ones."[3] Thus, by obscuring the truth of conflictual relations and exploitation, ideology serves to make capitalist societies appear legitimate.[4]

In contemporary America, the educational system, by sorting students according to ostensibly meritocratic criteria, plays a crucial role in the legitimation of inequality. Because the school deals in the currency of academic credentials, its role in the reproduction of inequality is obscured. Students believe that they succeed or fail in school on the basis of merit. By internalizing the blame for failure, students lose their self-esteem and then accept their eventual placement in low-status jobs as the natural outcome of their own shortcomings. If individuals are convinced that they are responsible for their low position in society, then criticism of the social order by the subordinate classes is deflected. The process of social reproduction goes on, unscrutinized and unchallenged.

If this legitimation function is working, then members of the lower classes will suffer from low self-esteem, which originally was developed in the school and then carried into later life to reconcile them to their position. In gauging the degree to which lower-class individuals accept the social order and their position in it as legitimate, we must determine whether they attribute their inferior social position to personal inadequacy or to external forces as well.

THE HALLWAY HANGERS: INTERNALIZING PROBABILITIES, RESCUING SELF-ESTEEM

Perhaps the most potent theoretical construct available to aid us in our understanding of the aspirations of the Hallway Hangers is Bourdieu's concept of habitus. Although Bourdieu's model is somewhat deterministic and does not account for cultural innovation and resistance, his view that aspirations reflect an individual's internalization of the objective probabilities for social mobility has much to recommend it. Bourdieu's argument that subjective hopes mirror objective chances, although positing too mechanistic a relationship, is nevertheless a very useful explanatory tool with respect to the Hallway Hangers.

The Hallway Hangers view their prospects for substantial upward mobility as very remote, which accounts for their low occupational aspirations. Drawing on the experiences of their families, and on their own encounters with the job market, the boys' appraisals of the possibility for social upgrading often preclude the formation of any aspirations at all. Moreover, the available evidence indicates that the boys' parents do not intercede significantly in their children's aspiration formation. In general, the parents of the Hallway Hangers have little influence in their sons' lives. Like most parents, they want the best for their children, but if Stoney's mother is any indication, they also are hesitant to encourage excessively high aspirations in their sons for fear of setting them up for disappointment.

Although the families of the Hallway Hangers have a pervasive influence on their aspirations, so have their own work experiences. All the Hallway Hangers have held summertime employment since they have been of working age. Most are searching for full-time work, except Steve. In their struggles to find meaningful, stable employment all have been thwarted. Invariably, once they think they finally have found a decent job, the opportunity falls through. This type of firsthand experience on the job market further deflates any illusions they might have had about the openness of the opportunity structure. When a boy searches in vain for work that pays seventy-five cents more than minimum wage, his estimation of the prospects for significant upward mobility is bound to be low.

In addition to family and work, school has an important, if less direct, influence on aspirations. Because the school devalues the cultural capital of the Hallway Hangers, their chances for academic success are diminished substantially. Although the Hallway Hangers do not see the intricacies of this process taking place, half have remarked that students from "higher" social backgrounds have a better chance to do well in school. The Hallway Hangers have seen their older siblings fail in school; they see their friends fail as well. Even their Clarendon Heights peers who try to succeed in school meet with only modest success; for verification of this the Hallway Hangers need only look to the Brothers. Thus, the Hallway Hangers question their own capacity to perform well in school, a view that informs their assessment of the chances for social mobility.

Of more importance is the Hallway Hangers' belief that performance in school is of only tangential importance in securing a job. They challenge the widely held notion that success in school translates into success on the job market. But if they feel that schooling will not boost them up the ladder of social mobility, what will? In essence, the Hallway Hangers see a ladder with no rungs on it, or at least none they can reach. They believe that the educational system cannot deliver on its promise of upward social mobility for those who perform well in school. Thus, in part, their leveled aspirations reflect their feeling that schooling is incapable of doing much for them.

In concentrating on this point, however, it is easy to miss some of the intraschool processes that affect the aspirations of the Hallway Hangers. The school is distinctive not for what it does but for what it fails to do.

Lincoln School officials are aware of the process of social reproduction (although they would not conceptualize it in these terms). Bruce Davis, a young, enthusiastic, and dedicated guidance counselor in the Occupational Education Program acknowledges social reproduction as a simple fact of life.

BD: These kids [those enrolled in the Oc. Ed. Program] go directly into hard jobs. They're generally from homes where people are laborers. I mean, kids who go to college are from families whose parents went to college. That's how it works, it seems to me. That's where these kids are coming from; they're geared to manual labor jobs, like their brothers, sisters, fathers, uncles, whatever— mothers, like the jobs they have.

Rather than attempting to use the resources of the school to mitigate this process, school officials seem content to let it unfold unhindered. The Oc. Ed. Program, for example, is designed to prepare its students for the rigors of manual work.

BD: We constantly stress to the kids that they have to be responsible, reliable, and dependable, that they can't be a screw-off. Really, we're just trying to make the kids accountable for themselves. Y'know, most of these kids won't go to college. When they leave here, they can't sleep 'til eleven and then get up and go to three classes. They've really got to be disciplined. They're going to be right out there working. In Oc. Ed., that's really what we're all about. We're trying to simulate a work experience, make class just like a job. It's not just their competency that matters; to be a good worker, your willingness to cooperate, your attitude, is so important.

Bowles and Gintis's argument that working-class students are socialized for working-class jobs and that the social relations of school mirror those of the workplace hardly could be better substantiated.

My point here is not that the school, consciously or unconsciously, levels the aspirations of some students but that it accepts and exacerbates already existing differences in aspirations. By requiring the Hallway Hangers, as eighth graders, to choose their educational program, the school solidifies what is often a vaguely felt and ill-defined preference for manual work or a desire simply to be with one's friends into a definite commitment to a future in manual work. The decision is essentially their own, and it makes a good deal of sense considering that experience in a trade ostensibly will be of some advantage on a difficult job market. Slick's decision to enter the Oc. Ed. Program, despite his high level of achievement in grammar school, typifies the quandary of these boys. Very few middle-class students with decent grades would select a vocational program, but Slick felt the need to do so in order to improve his chances of getting work after graduation.

Although the boys chose their various programs, there are grounds for skepticism about the degree to which this was a completely uncoerced choice. James Rosenbaum, in his 1976 study of a working-class high school, found that guidance counselors and teachers applied subtle and not-so-subtle techniques to channel students into particular tracks and keep them there, sometimes against the students' wishes. But the school officials did this in such a manner that both the youngster and his/her parents believed it was a free choice by the student.[5]

Lincoln High School boasts a more liberal educational philosophy than that of Rosenbaum's school, so we hardly can extrapolate his findings to Lincoln High. Nevertheless, in response to a question concerning the process by which students choose their program, Wallace responded, "Oh, that's done for them in grammar school." Sensing that I had picked up on the "for them," she hastily went on to say that it is a process that initially involves a conference between the eighth grade counselor and the student as well as parents. "According to however they performed in grammar school, the counselor will come up with a suggested schedule and send it home for approval. Of course, the parent can disagree and pick other courses."

Resolution of the extent to which this is a decision of self-selection requires detailed ethnographic data on the transition from grammar school to Lincoln High, without which we must stop short of Rosenbaum's conclusion that the school exacerbates and actually creates inequality by its discriminatory tracking procedures. There is no doubt, however, that the school, by requiring that such choices be made at a young age, reinforces existing differences in aspirations.

In trying to understand the impact of family, work, and schooling on the aspirations of the Hallway Hangers, Bourdieu's theory that the habitus engenders aspirations that reflect objective probabilities seems accurate. The process of social reproduction as Bourdieu sees it is captured in the following passage in *Reproduction*:

The structure of the objective chances of social upgrading according to class of origin and, more precisely, the structure of the chances of upgrading through education, conditions agents' dispositions towards education and towards upgrading through education—dispositions which in turn play a determining role in defining the likelihood of entering education, adhering to its norms and succeeding in it, hence the likelihood of social upgrading.[6]

But the concept of the internalization of objective probabilities, because it limits the scope for human agency and creativity, has little explanatory value when we consider the influence of the peer group on the Hallway Hangers. This is a serious deficiency because according to our ethnographic sketch the peer group, especially for the Hallway Hangers, is of primary importance in these boys' lives.

In a country in which success is largely measured by income and occupational status, the Hallway Hangers have a problem. Unemployed, living in public housing, at the very bottom of the socioeconomic spectrum, they are regarded as failures, both by others and, at least to some extent, by themselves, a phenomenon Sennett and Cobb document for working-class people in general in *The Hidden Injuries of Class*.[7] The Hallway Hangers have been enrolled in programs that are designed for "fuck-ups" (as Mike of the Brothers put it), have been placed in the lowest educational tracks, and have received failing grades; all these constitute part of the emotional attack the boys suffer in school. The Hallway Hangers may have little of their self-esteem tied up in school, but, as Scully argues, they cannot help but feel "a judgement of academic inferiority cast upon them, be it by teachers, classmates, or their seemingly objective computerized report card."[8] The subculture of the Hallway Hangers must be understood as an attempt by its members to insulate themselves from these negative judgments and to provide a context in which some semblance of self-respect and dignity can be maintained.

To characterize the subculture of the Hallway Hangers as a defense mechanism against these onslaughts to their self-esteem, however, would be incomplete. Scully argues that most student countercultures have both defensive and independent features[9]; studies by Sennett and Cobb, Stinchcombe, and Willis verify this duality. The Hallway Hangers, like Willis's lads, have their own distinct set of values. These values are indigenous to the working class; they do not arise simply in opposition to the school. The Hallway Hangers' valuation of physical toughness, emotional resiliency, quick-wittedness, masculinity, loyalty, and group solidarity point to a subculture with its own norms, which are passed on from the older to the younger boys. Frankie describes how the subculture of the Hallway Hangers is learned and passed on.

(in a group interview)

FRANKIE: We were all brought up, all we seen is our older brothers and that gettin' into trouble and goin' to jail and all that shit.

Y'know, seeing people—brothers and friends and shit—dying right in front of your face. You seen all the drugs, Jay. Well, this place used to be a thousand times worse than it is now. We grew up, it was all our older brothers doing this. We seen many fucking drugs, all the drinking. They fucking go; that group's gone. The next group came. It's our brothers that are a little older, y'know, twenty-something years old. They started doing crime. And when you're young, you look up to people. You have a person, everybody has a person they look up to. And he's doing this, he's drinking, he's doing that, he's doing drugs, he's ripping off people. Y'know, he's making good fucking money, and it looks like he's doing good, y'know? So bang. Now it's our turn. We're here. What we gonna do when all we seen is fuckin' drugs, alcohol, fighting, this and that, no one going to school?

By providing a realm in which to be bad and tough are the main criteria for respect, the peer group of the Hallway Hangers reverses conventional cultural norms. Like almost all subcultures, however, the Hallway Hangers cannot escape the dominant culture's definitions of success. No matter how strong and insular the group, contact with the dominant culture, especially through school and work, is inevitable. Listening to the Hallway Hangers describe their descent through the school's programs, one detects a sense of shame, despite all their bravado. For Frankie to report that he finally found work, but as a temporary employee with the city's sanitation department as a garbage collector, clearly involved quite a swallowing of pride.

This inability on the part of a subculture to shelter itself completely from the dominant culture's values and norms has been documented widely: Willis's lads are pained by teachers' insults; the children Sennett and Cobb describe as having developed their own "badges of dignity" still have much of their sense of self-worth tied up in academic performance and teacher approval; and, the inside world of black streetcorner men who congregate at Tally's Corner in Elliot Liebow's study "is no more impervious to the values, sentiments and beliefs of the larger society than it is to the blue welfare checks or to the agents of the larger society, such as the policeman, the police informer, the case worker, the landlord."[10]

Despite the fact that the Hallway Hangers' subculture affords its members only partial protection from the negative judgments of the dominant culture, it does provide a setting wherein a person can salvage some self-respect. The Hallway Hangers, who have developed alternative criteria for success, understand their situation in a way that defends their status; they manage to see themselves differently from the way the rest of society sees them. This is not entirely a self-protective psychological inversion; their ways of understanding their situation also are real. The Hallway Hangers are not living a fantasy. The world of the street exists—it is the unfortunate underside of the American economic system, the inevitable shadow accompanying a society that is not as open as it advertises. Moreover, the Hallway Hangers *are* physically hard, emotionally durable, and boldly enterprising. Those of us who are supposed to be succeeding by conventional standards need only venture into their world for the briefest moment to feel as though our badges of success are about as substantive and "real" in that environment as the emperor's new clothes.

The subculture of the Hallway Hangers is at odds with the dominant culture. The path to conventional success leads in one direction; the path to a redefined success lies in another. A boy cannot tread both paths simultaneously; orthodox success demands achievement in school, a feat that only can be accomplished by respecting the authority of teachers, which is inconsistent with the Hallway Hangers' alternative value scheme. All the current members of the Hallway Hangers have chosen, more or less definitively, to tread the path to a redefined success. (It should be remembered, however, that this choice is not an altogether free one; the Hallway Hangers see the path to conventional success as blocked by numerous obstacles.) Nevertheless, some do choose the path to conventional achievement; Billy, who expects to attend college next year, is being studied carefully by the Hallway Hangers as a testament to what they may have passed up.

The decision to break away from the group and pursue conventional success is not just a matter of individual calculation, however. More complicated forces are at work, forces that strain the individualistic orientation of American society. The solidarity of the Hallway Hangers is very strong. We have seen, for example, that the sense of cohesion and bonds of loyalty are such that Slick would not leave Shorty at the scene of a crime, preferring to be arrested himself. These communitarian values act to restrain individual Hallway Hangers from breaking away from the group and trying to "make it" conventionally. Slick, for example, scores very well on standardized tests, attended Latin Academy for a year, and is very articulate. Despite class-based barriers to success, he had a relatively good chance of "making it." But Slick also demonstrates the strongest sense of loyalty to the group. In a group interview, for example, he commented, as the rest of the group nodded their heads in agreement, that "money is secondary to friendship; I think friendship is more important than money." Jinks realizes that this loyalty can constrain individuals from striving for upward social mobility.

(in an individual interview)

JM: Do you have anything else to add about kids' attitudes down here?

JINKS: I'd say everyone more or less has the same attitudes towards school: fuck it. Except the bookworms—people who just don't hang around outside and drink, get high, who sit at home—they're the ones who get the education.

JM: And they just decided for themselves?

JINKS: Yup.

JM: So why don't more people decide that way?

JINKS: Y'know what it is Jay? We all don't break away because we're too tight. Our friends are important to us. Fuck it. If we can't make it together, fuck it. Fuck it all.

One of the forces operating to keep the Hallway Hangers from striking out on their own is the realization that there is little chance of their making it as a group and to leave the others behind is to violate the code of loyalty. Recall how Slick contrasts the Hallway Hangers and the "rich little boys from the suburbs." "How do you think they got rich? By fucking people over. We don't do that to each other. We're too fucking tight. We're a group. We don't think like them. We think for all of us." This group loyalty rests on some very strong communitarian values and vaguely parallels an affirmation of class solidarity over individual interests, a point to which I shall return.

With respect to the influence of the peer group on social reproduction, there are some complicated processes at work that Bourdieu's theory fails to capture. Conceptually, Bourdieu's model is "flat." It is unable to account for the resistance and nonconformity characteristic of the Hallway Hangers' subculture. To some extent, membership in the sub- culture of the Hallway Hangers tends to level one's aspirations. Although influenced by the definitions of the dominant culture, the value scheme of the peer group devalues conventional success; the norm among the Hallway Hangers is low aspirations. This ethos, passed down from older to younger boys, is a powerful force on the individual. In addition to the general climate of the peer group, there is a tendency among the Hallway Hangers to resist raised aspirations because to act on them would involve breaking one's ties and leaving the group, a transgression of the code of loyalty.

It is possible to examine the workings of the process of legitimation as it applies to the Hallway Hangers. We have seen that their self- esteem is relatively resilient to poor academic performance, for little of each boy's sense of self is invested in the school. In addition, the peer group subculture affords the Hallway Hangers additional protection for their self-esteem and alternative ways of generating self-esteem through the value system of the group. Although failure in school is psychologically debilitating for the Hallway Hangers in some ways, their self-esteem is partially buttressed from the assaults of the educational system.

If legitimation were functioning smoothly, the Hallway Hangers, in addition to low self-esteem, would internalize their failure and point only to personal inadequacy as the cause of their plight. But such is not the case; the Hallway Hangers realize that internal and external factors contribute to their low social position. Although they do blame themselves to some degree for their failure, they also recognize external barriers to success.

When the Hallway Hangers talk, one almost can feel the struggle being waged in their minds between the tenets of the achievement ideology and the lessons distilled from their own experiences. This tension produces a deep-seated ambivalence. At times the boys are prone to take full responsibility for their dismal social status, but on other occasions they blame external obstacles to their social advancement. Boo-Boo reproaches himself at the beginning of an interview ("I just screwed up") but later maintains that boys from a middle-class neighborhood have an advantage when it comes to achieving social and economic prosperity. Other boys hold a similarly dichotomous outlook.

CHRIS: I guess I just don't have what it takes.

(in a separate interview)

CHRIS: We don't get a fair shake and shit.

FRANKIE: We're all just fucking burnouts. . . . We never did good anyways. . . . We've just fucked up.

(in the same interview)

FRANKIE: If I had the fucking money to start out with like some of these fucking rich kids, I'd be a millionaire. Fucking right, I would be.

SHORTY: I'd go in there, and I'd try my hardest to do the work, right? I'd get a lot of problems wrong cuz I never had the brains much really, right? That's what's keepin' me back.

(in a different interview)

SHORTY: Hey, you can't get no education around here unless if you're fucking rich, y'know? You can't get no education. . . . And you can't get a job once they find out where you come from. "You come from Clarendon Heights? Oh shit. It's them kids again."

The Hallway Hangers see through parts of the achievement ideology, but at some level they accept the aspersions it casts on lower-class individuals, including themselves. However, although the Hallway Hangers do not escape emotional injury, neither does the social order emerge unscathed. In the eyes of the Hallway Hangers the opportunity structure is not open, a view that prevents them from accepting their position and the inequalities of the social order as completely legitimate.

Although the legitimation of inequality could be working more efficiently with respect to the Hallway Hangers, the whole process is not ready to collapse. Like the lads in Willis's study, these boys' insights into the true workings of the system are only partial, and often vague and ill-defined at that. Moreover, although they are cognizant of external barriers to success, the Hallway Hangers raise no fundamental challenge to the fairness or efficacy of the system as a whole. For the most part, in the absence of any systematic critique of capitalism, the Hallway Hangers simply are plagued by a sense of unfairness and the uneasy conviction that the rules of the contest are biased against them. Thus, there is a discrepancy between their strongly felt conviction that they are getting "the short end of the stick," and their inability to understand fully how this is so.

They conveniently fill this gap with racism. The Hallway Hangers seem to believe that if they are stuck with the short end of the stick, it must be because the "niggers" have the long end. Their feelings of impotence, frustration, and anger are subsumed in their hatred of blacks and in their conviction that their own plight somehow has been exacerbated, if not caused, by the alleged economic and social advancement of black Americans. Recall how Shorty attributed his brother's unemployment to the "Spics and niggers." Frankie and Smitty account for their predicament with one reason.

SMITTY: All the fuckin' niggers are getting the jobs.

FRANKIE: Fuckin' right. That's why we're hanging here now with empty pockets.

Affirmative action affords the Hallway Hangers a handy explanation for their own demise. Slick, despite his perceptiveness, succumbs to the same misunderstanding. Although his decision to quit school was undoubtedly the result of many factors, Slick insists that he dropped out of school solely because of supposed favoritism toward black students at Lincoln High. In a different interview, Slick begins by accusing the school of class-based prejudice but muddles the issue by suddenly bringing blacks into the discussion: "They favor all them fucking rich kids at that school. All the rich people. They fucking baby 'em. They baby all the fucking niggers up there."

This confusion between class bias and alleged reverse racial discrimination is symptomatic of the Hallway Hangers' outlook. By directing their resentment at affirmative action and those who benefit from it, the Hallway Hangers can spare themselves blame, but then the social order also is spared any serious scrutiny. In Willis's terms, racism is a serious "limitation" on the cultural outlook of the Hallway Hangers. Just as the lads' reversal of the usual valuation of mental versus manual labor prevents them from seeing their placement into dead-end, low-paying jobs as a form of class domination, so does the Hallway Hangers' racism obscure reality.

Thus, the Hallway Hangers harbor contradictory and ambivalent beliefs about the legitimacy of their social position. Their identification of class-based barriers to success and their impression that the deck is unfairly stacked against them, insights that could catalyze the development of a radical political consciousness, are derailed by their racism. On the one hand, the Hallway Hangers puncture the individualistic orientation of American society by their adoption of communitarian values to the point where a realization that the entire group cannot "make it" prevents individuals from striving for conventional success—a point of view that runs in the same direction as a class logic. But on the other hand, the Hallway Hangers support some politically conservative values and leaders. The prevalence of this type of dual, contradictory consciousness, embodying both progressive, counterhegemonic insights and reactionary, distorting beliefs, is discussed at length by Antonio Gramsci.[11] More recently, Michael Mann has argued convincingly that ambivalence about social beliefs leads to "pragmatic acceptance" of the social order rather than complete acceptance of it as legitimate.[12]

It is instructive to compare in detail this analysis of the Hallway Hangers with Willis's depiction of how social reproduction takes place for the lads in his study. The Hallway Hangers, as residents of public housing, are from a lower social stratum than the lads, who are from stable working-class families. Moreover, the British working class, with its long history, organized trade unions, and progressive political party, has developed an identity, pride, and class consciousness that are lacking in the United States. Despite these differences, substantial similarities in the way each peer group experiences the process of social reproduction warrant a comparison.

Willis argues that the lads' rejection of the achievement ideology and of the values and norms of the educational system is based on some key insights into the situation of their class under capitalism. However, the crucial element in the process of social reproduction—placement into manual labor jobs—is experienced by the lads as an act of independence and self-election, not a form of oppression. Because of the value placed on machismo in the wider working-class culture, which the lads appropriate for their own, they choose to enter the bottom of the occupational structure. At the root of social reproduction for the lads is the cultural inversion by which manual labor, equated with the social superiority of masculinity, is valued over white-collar work, which is associated with the inferior status of femininity.

Whereas the lads' reject school because it has no bearing on the manual labor jobs they intend to pursue, the Hallway Hangers reject school for different reasons. For the lads, the seeds of leveled aspirations, and hence social reproduction, lie in their cultural affirmation of manual labor. Like the lads, the Hallway Hangers place a heavy premium on masculinity; their emphasis on being cool, tough, streetwise—in a word, bad—indicates the prevalence of machismo in their cultural outlook.

Nevertheless, this emphasis on masculinity seldom is linked with distaste for white-collar work. The subculture of the Hallway Hangers contains no systematic bias toward manual work; their depressed aspirations result from a look into the future that sees stagnation at the bottom of the occupational structure as almost inevitable. The Hallway Hangers' outlook is more pessimistic than that held by the lads; there is no room on the job market for independence, election, or even choice. Thus, the Hallway Hangers reconcile themselves to taking whatever job they can get. Given this resignation, their belief that education can do little for them, and their assessment of the costs of educational success, the Hallway Hangers reject the institution of school. Although they do not experience unemployment or entry into low-level jobs as acts of triumph but rather as depressing facts of lower-class life, neither do the Hallway Hangers incriminate the social order as entirely unjust. Thus, although in both cases the structure of class relations is reproduced, largely through the regulation of aspirations, the processes through which it happens for the lads and the Hallway Hangers vary.

It is difficult to conceptualize the process of social reproduction when it is depicted in general terms. To facilitate our understanding of how the aspirations of the Hallway Hangers are leveled, I now describe the mechanisms associated with social reproduction as they affect Jinks. By looking at his experiences, the processes we have been discussing can be rendered concrete.

According to one of his friends, Jinks was an A student in his freshman year. At first, he worked hard and conformed to the rules of the school, but during his sophomore year, he started to weigh the costs and benefits of attendance and hard work. Every morning, he would socialize with the rest of the boys at Pop's for about fifteen minutes, maybe smoke a joint, and then head to class. "Hey, man, what the fuck? Sit down and smoke another bone. Whaddya wanna go to school for? You like them teachers better than us?" After leaving the group to comments like this, in class his mind would wander back to his friends sitting in Pop's, getting high, relaxing. He would think about his brother who dropped out of school at the age of sixteen and had a union job at the shipyards. He would think about another brother who had graduated the year before and joined the navy, about a third who had dropped out and also enlisted in the navy, and about his oldest brother, who was dead. He would think about the older boys at the Heights, some graduates of high school, some dropouts—all unemployed or in lousy jobs. Gradually, Jinks's attitude toward school started to change.

JINKS: I started hanging around, getting high, just not bother going to school . . . started hanging down Pop's. Cutting, getting high.

JM: What were the reasons behind that? Why'd you start going down to Pop's?

JINKS: Friends, friends. . . . I'd go to my classes and meet them at lunch, but when I was with 'em, I'd say, "The hell with it. I ain't even going." Besides, I didn't really care to try in school. . . . You ain't got a chance of getting a good job, even with a high school diploma. You gotta go on to college, get your Masters and shit like that to get a good paying job that you can live comfortably on. So if you're not planning on going to college, I think it's a waste of time.

By his junior year, Jinks attended school only sporadically, and when he did go to class, he was often drunk or high, a necessity if he was to "listen to the teachers talk their shit."

Faced with the need for income to pay for, among other things, his weekly ounce of marijuana, Jinks began to deal drugs on a small scale, stopping only after a close call with the police. After four months of searching and waiting, Jinks landed a job and began working in the afternoons, attending school for a few hours each day. Convinced that school was doing him little good and faced with the opportunity to work full-time, Jinks quit school, only to be laid off shortly thereafter. Although his parents wanted him to finish school, Jinks downplays their influence on him: "They want me to graduate from high school, but I ain't gonna. They'll be mad at me for a week or two, but that's life."

Now that he is out of school, out of work, and out of money, Jinks does not have much to which he can look forward. Nevertheless, he is not as "down and out" as we might think. He has plenty of time for his friends and accepts his predicament placidly, with neither thorough disrespect for the system nor for himself. The situation is, after all, not much different than he had expected.

THE BROTHERS: INTERNALIZING FAILURE, SHORN OF SELF-ESTEEM

If the mechanisms by which the Hallway Hangers and lads end up in dead-end jobs are somewhat different, the process of social reproduction as it operates with respect to the Brothers presents an even sharper contrast. Applied to the Brothers, Bourdieu's concept of the internalization of objective probabilities does not ring true. Undoubtedly, the Brothers do internalize their chances of "making it," and this calculation certainly moderates their aspirations. Yet, their view of the probabilities for social advancement is informed not only by the objective opportunity structure but also by their parents' hopes for their future and the achievement ideology of the school. In this sense, there is no such thing as the internalization of objective probabilities, for all perceptions of the opportunity structure necessarily are subjective and influenced by a host of intervening factors. The actual habitus of the Brothers is much more complex than Bourdieu would have us believe. Because Bourdieu's theory of social reproduction stresses a correspondence between aspirations and opportunity, it cannot explain the excessive ambitions of the Brothers. Bourdieu underestimates the achievement ideology's capacity to mystify structural constraints and encourage high aspirations. The Hallway Hangers reject the achievement ideology, but the situation for the Brothers is quite different.

Like the Hallway Hangers, the Brothers come from families in which their parents either hold jobs that are at the bottom of the occupational structure or are unable to find work at all. An important difference, however, is that, with the exception of Derek, all the Brothers are either the oldest male sibling in the family or have older brothers and sisters who attend college. Thus, the Brothers are not faced with a picture of nearly uniform failure in school. In addition, the parents of the Brothers actually encourage high aspirations in their children, as a tool to motivate them to achieve in school and perhaps as a projection of thwarted ambitions. Thus, from their families, the Brothers take away a contradictory outlook. On the one hand, they see that hard work on the part of their parents has not gotten them very far, an implicit indictment of the openness of the opportunity structure, but on the other hand, they are encouraged by these same people to have high hopes for the future.

For the Brothers, work is an exclusively summertime affair; only Juan is on the job market full-time. Thus, their experience on the labor market is very limited, and that experience has been sheltered from the rigors and uncertainties of finding work. Most of these boys have been enrolled almost exclusively in federal summer youth employment programs and only have had to fill out an application form to be placed in a summer job. Whereas the more extensive contact of the Hallway Hangers with the world of work tends to level their aspirations, a comparable process has not taken place for the Brothers—at least not yet.

The Brothers' peer group does not tend to level their hopes for the future. Because the Brothers do not comprise a distinctive subculture but rather accept the norms and values of the dominant culture and strive to embody them, their peer group does not provide them with a redefinition of success. The Brothers are achievement oriented, prize accomplishments in school and obedience to the law, and measure success as does the rest of society. The ethos of their group encourages high aspirations and reinforces behavior that contributes to the realization of their goals.

The Brothers unconditionally accept the school's achievement ideology, a step that requires a belief in equality of opportunity and the efficacy of schooling. But at the same time that their aspirations tend to rise because of their faith in these precepts, the Brothers are being prepared psychologically for jobs at the bottom of the occupational structure. In low educational tracks and the recipients of poor grades, the Brothers are only modestly successful in school. They blame themselves for their mediocre academic performances because they are unaware of the discriminatory influences of tracking, the school's partiality toward the cultural capital of the upper classes, the self-fulfilling consequences of teachers' expectations, and other forms of class-based educational selection. Conditioned by the achievement ideology to think that good jobs require high academic attainment, the Brothers may temper their high aspirations, believing not that the institution of school and the job market have failed them, but that they have failed themselves.

For most of the Brothers, this "cooling-out" process, documented by Burton Clark in his study of a community college,[13] will not be completed until they actually graduate from high school and are face to face with the job market. Armed with a high school diploma and a good disciplinary record, the Brothers will have a better chance to land suitable jobs than the Hallway Hangers do, but the Brothers' opportunities still will be quite limited. Juan, the only Brother to have graduated, already has begun to "cool out."

Juan, who left high school with a diploma and a skill (he spent 1,500 hours in school learning culinary arts), has lowered his aspirations significantly after six months of unemployment. Although he previously expressed distaste for a job in auto mechanics because of its association with dirty manual work, Juan now hopes to find work in precisely that area. We can expect many of the Brothers to undergo a similar reorientation after graduation.

From the description of the Brother's experiences in school it seems clear that the legitimation of inequality is working smoothly for them. In general, the Brothers, without the protection of a peer group with a distinctive subculture, suffer from low self-esteem as a result of their academic performances. In addition, they do not acknowledge the existence of external barriers to their success in school and instead blame themselves for their mediocre performance. We can expect that the same will be true for what may turn out to be their low occupational status.

Whereas the Hallway Hangers are analogous to Willis's lads, the Brothers are closer to the ear'oles. Although our picture is complicated by the variable of ethnicity, the Brothers' experiences illuminate the process of social reproduction as it is undergone by conformist lower-class youth, a subject into which Willis does not delve. Reflecting their acceptance of the achievement ideology and the concomitant notion that all those who are capable can get ahead on their own merits, the Brothers have developed significant ambitions. Relative to the depressed aspirations of the Hallway Hangers, the middle-class aspirations of the Brothers attest to their belief that they are involved in a fair competition. If they fail to get ahead, they will probably attribute their social and economic fate to their own incapabilities, to their own lack of merit.

But we cannot be sure. Will the Brothers and the ear'oles become disillusioned with themselves when they are "cooled out," or will their disillusion encompass the social order as well? This issue demands a longitudinal study spanning a number of years, without which no definite pronouncements are possible. I suspect that although some cynicism about the openness of American society will result, the achievement ideology has been internalized so deeply by the Brothers that their subsequent "careers" will be interpreted in its light. Moreover, if one of the Brothers should be lucky enough to "make it," those that do not will be all the more likely to blame themselves. Far from contradicting the social reproduction perspective, the limited social mobility that does take place in liberal democracies plays a crucial role in the legitimation of inequality. A completely closed society cannot maintain a semblance of openness, whereas a society that allows some mobility, however meager, can hold up the self-made man as "proof" that barriers to success are purely personal. This "controlled mobility" encourages working-class self-reproach and goes a long way toward explaining why in the United States working-class students with Super's outlook far outnumber those with Jinks's perspective and why in Britain there are more ear'oles than lads.

When Super switched from the Occupational Education Program to House C in the regular academic program, he was placed in the lowest educational tracks for nearly all his subjects because of his low academic performance in grammar school and the fact that switching into the classes in the middle of the semester would have been difficult for him academically. Now in his sophomore year, Super still is enrolled in the "basic" tracks and maintains a high D average.

Super aspires to professional or middle-class work, which reflects his parents' insistence that Super aim for a white-collar job, the premium his peer group places on conventional success, his minimal contact with the job market, and the achievement ideology of the school. Within the course of a year he variously expressed hopes of becoming a doctor, a businessman, or a computer specialist. Reconciling these aspirations with his academic performance is a difficult exercise for Super. At the same time that he affirms the achievement ideology ("It's easy to do anything as long as you set your mind to it") and his own effort ("I swear, I'll be tryin' real hard in school"), Super admits that his performance is lacking ("I just can't seem to do it"). The only explanation left for him is that his own abilities are not up to par, a conclusion that Super accepts, despite its implications for his sense of self-worth. Every lower-class student who internalizes the achievement ideology but struggles in school finds himself or herself in this dilemma. Moreover, the way is clear for lower-class students again to attribute their failure to personal inadequacies when they find themselves in a low-status job. The feeling is a harsh one, but the American school system and the structure of class relations demand that it be borne by many. That Super and the other Brothers feel it strongly is evidence that the legitimation function of the school and the larger process of social reproduction are at work.

If schooling is the training ground at which students are prepared to participate in the race for the jobs of wealth and prestige, the Brothers are being cheated. Told over and over again that the race is a fair one and led to believe that they are given as much attention during the training as anyone, the Brothers step to the starting line for what they see as an equitable race. When the starter's gun goes off and they stumble over the first few hurdles while others streak ahead, they will in all likelihood blame only themselves and struggle to keep going.

The Hallway Hangers see that the race is unfair. They reject official declarations of equity and drop out of the training sessions, convinced that their results will be unsatisfactory no matter how hard they train. They expect to do poorly, and even those who might stand a chance stay back with their friends when the race starts. Instead of banding together, however, and demanding that a fair race be held, the Hallway Hangers never really question the race's rules and simply accept their plight.

This leaves us with an important question: How can the same race be viewed so differently? Why is it that the entrants who have racial as well as class-based hurdles to overcome are the ones who see no hurdles at all?

THE SOURCES OF VARIATION

Although the distinctive processes of social reproduction that have been detailed previously make internal sense, what accounts for the variance between them? What factors contribute to the fundamental incongruity between the two peer groups in the first place? Why is the influence of the family so different for the two peer groups? Why are their experiences in school so dissimilar?

To answer these questions, we must move to a deeper level of analysis that is centered on the role of the achievement ideology. The Hallway Hangers reject this ideology; the Brothers accept it. It is at this point that their paths diverge and the groups experience the process of social reproduction in different ways.

The achievement ideology runs counter to the grain of all these boys' experiences. Neither the residents of their neighborhood nor the members of their families have "made it." In a housing project plagued by unemployment and crime, we might expect both groups of boys to question the existence of equality of opportunity, yet only the Hallway Hangers do so. Of course, they have their own experiences on the job market to which they can point, but this explanation is only of limited value because in most instances they have dismissed the ideology even before experiencing the job market firsthand. The question remains: Why do the Hallway Hangers dismiss the achievement ideology while the Brothers accept it?

The Hallway Hangers reject the achievement ideology because most of them are white. Whereas poor blacks have racial discrimination to which they can point as a cause of their family's poverty, for the Hallway

Hangers to accept the achievement ideology is to admit that their parents are lazy or stupid or both. Thus, the achievement ideology not only runs counter to the experiences of the Hallway Hangers, but is also a more serious assault on their self-esteem. Acceptance of the ideology on the part of the Brothers does not necessarily involve such harsh implications, for they can point to racial prejudice to explain their parents' defeats. The severe emotional toll that belief in the achievement ideology exacts on poor whites relative to poor blacks explains why the Hallway Hangers dismiss the ideology while the Brothers validate it.[14]

The Brothers believe the achievement ideology to be an accurate depiction of the opportunity structure as it exists in the United States today because they perceive the racial situation to be substantially different for them than it was for their parents. Whereas their parents were barred from lunch counters and disqualified from the competition before it began, the Brothers see themselves in entirely different circumstances. Mokey's mother, for example, in commenting on Mokey's chances of "making it," says, "I feel Mokey has an equal chance to [be successful], regardless of money or color. That's a chance I never had." We saw in Chapter 5 that of all the Brothers only Juan believes that young blacks face any racial barriers to success. Indeed, it is amazing how often the Brothers affirm the openness of the opportunity structure. Presumably encouraged by perceived gains made in the last two decades, the Brothers seem to believe that equality of opportunity exists today as it did not in their parents' time. This view allows them to accept the achievement ideology without simultaneously indicting their parents. Because the Brothers fully expect to "make it" themselves, embracing the achievement ideology involves little assault on their self-esteem.

This belief that the situation for blacks has improved in the United States also explains why the parents of the Brothers encourage high aspirations in their children while the Hallway Hangers' parents do not. Believing the situation that contributed to their own condition to have changed, the Brothers' parents are convinced that their children have a better chance of "making it" and see no danger in encouraging lofty aspirations. The Hallway Hangers' parents, in contrast, believe that the deck is stacked against their children as it was against them and are wary of supporting unrealistically high aspirations.

Quantitative studies on the generation of ambition have produced equivocal results about whether blacks have higher aspirations than whites from the same socioeconomic background. In general, more recent studies indicate higher aspiration levels for blacks, while those utilizing data from the 1960s and early 1970s find that whites maintain higher aspirations than blacks. The only issue on which there is a consensus amongst quantitative practitioners is that the aspiration levels of blacks seem to have risen during the past ten to fifteen years,[15] a finding consistent with the attitudes of the Brothers and their families.

A number of factors can account for the increased aspirations of blacks. Because black youths perceive a change in the opportunity structure their parents faced (a change that may or may not have occurred to the degree perceived), they may feel that affirmative action has reduced the occupational handicap of color and that discrimination in employment has abated. Or it may be that the incontrovertible gains of the civil rights movement (e.g., affirmation of basic political and civil rights for blacks, an end to legal Jim Crow segregation, the emergence of black leaders on the national stage) have imbued many blacks with a general sense of progress and improvement that has affected their occupational aspirations. Or political mobilization itself may have created feelings of efficacy and resistance to being "cooled out" that have led to the higher aspirations. To the extent that the civil rights movement was about aspirations and dreams and a refusal to be reduced to hopelessness, blacks may feel that diminutive aspirations are somehow a form of surrender and a betrayal of past gains.

The divergence between how the Brothers and Hallway Hangers react to the achievement ideology is not entirely racial. As I noted in Chapter 4, many of the Hallway Hangers and their families have lived in low-income housing projects for a long period of time, and some have been on public assistance for as many as three generations. This extended duration of tenancy in public housing cannot help but contribute to a feeling of hopelessness and stagnation on the part of the Hallway Hangers. With family histories dominated by failure, the Hallway Hangers' cynicism about the openness of the opportunity structure and their rejection of the achievement ideology are understandable.

The Brothers' situation is quite different. Their families have lived in public housing, on average, for less than half the time the Hallway Hangers' families have. The Brothers' families also have resided in the Clarendon Heights neighborhood for a substantially shorter period of time. Many of the families see their move to the neighborhood as a step up in social status; some families came from less pleasant projects in the area, others from tenement flats in the black ghetto. Moreover, some of the Brothers' parents (Super's, James's, Mokey's) have moved up from the south, bringing with them a sense of optimism and hope about making a fresh start, feelings that have not yet turned into bitterness. For those families that have come to the United States from the West Indies in the last twelve years (Craig's, Juan's), this buoyancy is even stronger. Like the optimism felt by turn-of-the-century immigrants despite their wretched living conditions and the massive barriers to success that they faced, the Brothers' outlook encompasses a sense of improved life chances. Although at the bottom of the social ladder, the Brothers feel that they are part of a collective upward social trajectory, a belief that is conducive to acceptance of the achievement ideology.

Another factor that bears on the Hallway Hangers' rejection of the achievement ideology and the Brothers' acceptance of it is the way in which these peer groups define themselves in relation to one another. The character of the Brothers' peer group is in some measure a reaction to distinctive attributes of the Hallway Hangers. Thus, we can understand, in part, the Brothers' aversion to drugs and alcohol and their general orientation toward achievement as a response to the Hallway Hangers' excessive drinking, use of drugs, and general rejection of the standards and values of the dominant culture. As Super remarks pointing at a group of the Hallway Hangers loitering in doorway #13, "As long as I don't end up like *that*." Having moved into a predominantly white neighborhood that is generally unfriendly toward blacks and having been taunted and abused by a group of disaffected, mostly white boys, the Brothers' reaction has been to disassociate themselves completely from the Hallway Hangers and to pursue a distinctly different path— one that leads to success as it is conventionally defined.

For these and other reasons, the Brothers are not representative of poor black teenagers generally. One might discover black peer groups with a similar ethos in other lower-class, predominantly white communities, but if one ventures into any black ghetto, one finds an abundance of black youths hanging in doorways who are pessimistic about the future and cynical about the openness of American society. These youths have formed subcultures with values similar to those of the Hallway Hangers and present a marked contrast to the Brothers in outlook and behavior. The sources of these differences are explored in Chapter 8.

To view the general orientation of the Brothers' peer group as a mere reaction to that of the Hallway Hangers would be a vast oversimplification that fails to account for both the complexity of their reaction to the situation in which they find themselves and their powers of social discernment. We have seen that the Hallway Hangers see through the achievement ideology, not so much because of greater insight into the workings of the system but because of the assault this ideology makes on their self-esteem. The Brothers' acceptance of the ideology and their own individualistic orientations toward achievement are not entirely uncritical. The Brothers are not ideological dupes. They make their own partial "penetrations"[16] into their economic condition, and these insights inform their actions.

The Brothers' decision to "go for it," to work hard in school in pursuit of a decent job, makes a good deal of sense in view of the Hallway Hangers' decision to opt out of the competition. With the number of "good" jobs fixed, one's objective chances increase as individuals remove themselves from contention. Thus, the bipolarity between the Hallway Hangers and the Brothers should not surprise us. In deciding whether to purchase a raffle ticket, the wily individual takes note of how many others are buying them, conscious that the less sold, the more sense it makes to purchase one. Lower-class individuals generally do not have a good chance of "making it," but as one social group eschews the contest, others see it in their interest to vie seriously. Where we have a group like the Hallway Hangers, it is only natural that we have a group with the outlook of the Brothers. Willis notes a similar logic in

Learning to Labor: "The ear'oles' conformism . . . takes on a more rational appearance when judged against the self-disqualification of the lads."[17]

The Brothers' orientation toward individual achievement is even more understandable when we consider affirmative action measures. Although a far cry from what is needed to ameliorate racial injustice in the United States, affirmative action for minorities does increase the Brothers' objective chances of securing stable employment. There is, of course, no analogous measure offered to the lower classes as a whole to mitigate class injustice in the United States, so the anger of the white working class about affirmative action should not surprise us. The perception among whites in Clarendon Heights is that blacks now have an advantage on the job market. There may even be a measure of support for this view among blacks. Chris, for example, believes that although the white boys will face unemployment, his fate could be different: "Watch when I go for a job for the city or something: I'll get it. They'll say, 'Minority— you got the job.'" The Brothers' decision to "buy into" the system also seems to be based on the understanding that, all other things being equal, affirmative action can give them an advantage over their white lower-class peers on the labor market. The sharpening of racial division in the lower classes about affirmative action policies, alluded to throughout this study, also has important political ramifications, to be taken up in the next chapter.

There are, then, a number of factors that contribute to the dissimilarity between the Brothers and the Hallway Hangers. The Brothers, who have moved to the northeastern United States within the last generation and recently have moved into public housing, see themselves on a social upswing. This ambience of ascension is intensified by their impression that racial injustice has been curtailed in the last two decades, thereby making the opportunity structure they face more pliant than the one their parents encountered. The Hallway Hangers have no such grounds for optimism. Hailing from families who have resided in the projects for many years, some in Clarendon Heights for three generations, the Hallway Hangers feel that little has changed and consequently are despondent about their own futures. We also might point to variances in the families of the two groups as a source of their divergent outlooks. The Brothers' family members, especially their older siblings, have achieved a slightly higher status in terms of educational and occupational achievement than have the Hallway Hangers' family members.

Although all these factors contribute to the optimism of the Brothers and the pessimism of the Hallway Hangers, they do not in themselves account for the wide disparity between the two groups, nor do they explain the distinctive subculture of the Hallway Hangers. This oppositional culture partially shelters the Hallway Hangers from the abnegations of the dominant society, the negative judgments they sustain as poor members of an ostensibly open society. The Brothers are pained by these appraisals, too, of course, but the achievement ideology represents a more potent assault on the Hallway Hangers because as white youths they can point to no extenuating circumstances to account for their poverty. The subculture of the Hallway Hangers is in part a response to the stigma they feel as poor, white Americans. Finally, the differences between the two groups seem to be amplified by their tendencies to define themselves in relation (i.e., in opposition) to one another.

Where are these two paths likely to lead? In all probability, the Brothers will be better off than the Hallway Hangers. With a high school diploma, a positive attitude, and a disciplined readiness for the rigors of the workplace, the Brothers should be capable of landing steady jobs. An individual or two may work his way into a professional or managerial occupation, and a few might slide into a state of chronic unemployment, but the odds are that most of the Brothers will end up members of the stable working class, generally employed in jobs that are toward the bottom of the occupational ladder but that afford some security.

The Hallway Hangers probably will end up quite differently. Dependent on alcohol or drugs or both, disaffected and rebellious, and without qualifications in a credential-based job market, the Hallway Hangers generally will end up as Slick predicts: "They're not gonna be more than janitors or, y'know, goin' by every day tryin' to get a buck." An alcoholic himself, who becomes more despondent every day that he remains unemployed, Slick may well meet the same fate, despite his exceptional intelligence and articulate nature.

Of course, the Hallway Hangers do not deny that upward social mobility is possible. Their rejection of school was based not on the premise that they could not succeed but on the premise that the prospects for limited social mobility did not warrant the attempt, given the costs involved in the try. This is a calculation they all now have come to question. Having experienced life on the streets without a job, the Hallway Hangers generally indicate that if they had it to do over again, they would apply themselves in school.

JM: Would you do anything different if you could do it over again?

(all in separate interviews)

Boo-Boo: Yeah, lots. Wouldn't screw up in school as bad as I did, wouldn't get high with my friends as much.

Chris: I dunno, man, wouldn't fuck up in school. I guess I shoulda learned to live with their shit. It's just the way I am. Like, if I decide, if I say I'm not going to do something, I don't give a fuck what they do to me. I'm not going to do it. That's just the way I am. I guess that's what's gonna fuck me over in the long run.

Frankie: Yeah, definitely. I wouldn't have fucked up as much. I coulda been a—I fucked it up for myself, maybe. Maybe I woulda tried going to school more. But still, I don't think I woulda come out much better. So, y'know, just fuckin' bein' less rude to people, truthfully.

STEVE: Yeah, I'd make sure I got more credits my freshman year. I only got five fucking credits, man. That's rough to fuckin' jump back on and shit. It's a bitch.

JINKS: I'd probably get more interested in school, but it's too late now.

Almost any price would be worth paying to avoid the pain and misery of hopelessness at such a young age.

NOTES

1. Maureen Anne Scully, "Coping with Meritocracy" (Thesis, Harvard College, 1982), p. 6.
2. Max Weber, *Economy and Society* (Berkeley: University of California Press, 1970), p. 953.
3. Karl Marx and Friedrich Engels, *The German Ideology* (New York: International Publishers, 1947), pp. 65–66.
4. Scully, "Coping with Meritocracy," p. 3.
5. James Rosenbaum, *Making Inequality* (New York: Wylie and Sons, 1976).
6. Pierre Bourdieu and Jean-Claude Passeron, *Reproduction in Education, Society, and Culture* (London: Sage, 1977), p. 156.
7. Richard Sennett and Jonathan Cobb, *The Hidden Injuries of Class* (New York: Vintage Books, 1972).
8. Scully, "Coping with Meritocracy," p. 83.
9. Ibid., p. 85.
10. Elliot Liebow, *Tally's Corner* (Boston: Little, Brown, 1967), p. 209.
11. Antonio Gramsci, *Selections from Prison Notebooks* (London: Lawrence and Wishart, 1971).
12. Michael Mann, "The Social Cohesion of Liberal Democracy," *American Sociological Review* 35 (June 1970):423–439.
13. Burton Clark, "The 'Cooling Out' Function in Higher Education," *American Journal of Sociology* 65 (1960):576–596.
14. This is a difficult point and one that is easily misunderstood. My argument concerns the ramifications of the achievement ideology on self-esteem, not the effects of racial prejudice on self-esteem. The debilitating psychological effects of racism on blacks are tremendous. Because the object of racial intolerance often takes on the attributes bigotry assigns to him or her, black youths are taught to hate themselves. Almost every time Mokey or Juan turn on the television, for example, the programs and advertisements imply that their culture and lives are less important and valuable than those of white Americans. There is no solace in this, no relief from these assaults.

All this does not contradict my contention that acceptance of the achievement ideology would involve greater emotional duress for the Hallway Hangers than it does for the Brothers. Discrimination against blacks is a historical fact that most Americans accept. With this backdrop, one of the traumas of being poor is lessened for blacks. The issue is the emotional toll the acceptance of the achievement ideology takes on poor blacks relative to poor whites. I am not arguing that blacks living in poverty are psychologically better off than their white counterparts. Given the effect of racial prejudice on the psyches of blacks, such is clearly not the case. It is only in considering the effect of the achievement ideology alone that I am making a comparative statement about the emotional suffering of blacks and whites.

15. Kenneth I. Spenner and David L. Featherman, "Achievement Ambitions," *Annual Review of Sociology* 4 (1978):388.

16. The term, of course, is borrowed from Willis, who first directed my attention to the penetrations of the Brothers after reading a draft of the book.

17. Willis, *Learning to Labor* (Aldershot: Gower, 1977), p. 148.

IMPLICATIONS FOR
THEORY, EDUCATION,
AND POLITICS

The theoretical literature comprising reproduction theory was discussed in Chapter 2. Conceptualizing reproduction theory as a spectrum, with one end dominated by economic determinist theories and the other by theories asserting the autonomy of the cultural level, we reviewed the work of Bowles and Gintis on the determinist end of the continuum, progressed through the theories of Bourdieu and Bernstein, and ended up considering Willis and Giroux at the other end of the spectrum. Having examined in detail the specific mechanisms of the process of social reproduction as they occur in one low-income neighborhood, we are now in a position to assess the cogency of the theories outlined in the first chapter and to develop a revised theoretical perspective.

REPRODUCTION THEORY RECONSIDERED

This book's basic finding—that two substantially different paths are followed within the general framework of social reproduction—is a major challenge to economically determinist theories. Two groups of boys from the same social stratum who live in the same housing project and attend the same school nevertheless experience the process of social reproduction in fundamentally different ways. This simple fact alone calls into question many of the theoretical formulations of Bowles and Gintis. If social class is the overriding determinant in social reproduction, what accounts for the variance in the process between the Brothers and Hallway Hangers? Bowles and Gintis, in considering a single school, maintain that social reproduction takes place primarily through educational tracking. Differential socialization through educational tracking prepares working-class students for working-class jobs and middle-class students for middle-class jobs. But the Hallway Hangers and the Brothers, who are from the same social class background and exposed to the curricular structure of the school in the same manner, undergo the process of social reproduction in substantially different manners. The theory of Bowles and Gintis cannot explain this difference.

Bourdieu's notion of habitus, however, can be used to differentiate the Hallway Hangers and the Brothers. The habitus, as defined by Giroux, is "the subjective dispositions which reflect a class-based social grammar of taste, knowledge, and behavior inscribed in . . . each developing person."[1] According to Bourdieu, the habitus is primarily a function of social class. Bourdieu does not give an adequate sense of the internal structure of the habitus, but there is some precedent in his work for incorporating other factors into constructions of the habitus; for example, he differentiates people not only by gender and class, but also by whether they come from Paris or not. Although Bourdieu sometimes gives the impression of a homogeneity of habitus within the boundaries of social class, I understand habitus to be constituted at the level of the family and thus can include, as constitutive of the habitus, factors such as ethnicity, educational histories, peer associations, and demographic characteristics (e.g., geographical mobility, duration of tenancy in public housing, sibling order, and family size) as these shape individual action. Although Bourdieu never really develops the notion along these lines, he does allude to the complexity and interplay of mediations within the habitus. "The habitus acquired in the family underlies the structuring of school experiences, and the habitus transformed by schooling, itself diversified, in turn underlies the structuring of all subsequent experiences (e.g. the reception and assimilation of the messages of the culture industry or work experiences), and so on, from restructuring to restructuring."[2] When understood along the lines I have indicated, the concept of habitus becomes flexible enough to accommodate the interactions among ethnicity, family, schooling, work experiences, and peer associations that have been documented in this book.

Although we may accept the notion of habitus as a useful explanatory tool, we must reject the inevitability of its *function* in Bourdieu's theoretical scheme. According to Bourdieu, the habitus functions discreetly to integrate individuals into a social world geared to the interests of the ruling classes; habitus engenders attitudes and conduct that are compatible with the reproduction of class inequality. The outstanding example of this process is the development by working-class individuals of depressed aspirations that mirror their actual chances for social advancement.

The circular relationship Bourdieu posits between objective opportunities and subjective hopes is incompatible with the findings of this book. The Brothers, whose objective life chances probably were lower originally than those available to the Hallway Hangers because of racial barriers to success, nevertheless nurture higher aspirations than do the Hallway Hangers. By emphasizing structural determinants at the expense of mediating factors that influence subjective renderings of objective probabilities, Bourdieu presumes too mechanistic and simplistic a relationship between aspiration and opportunity. This component of his theory fails to fathom how a number of factors lie between and mediate the influence of social class on individuals; Bourdieu cannot explain, for instance, how ethnicity intervenes in the process of aspiration formation and social reproduction.

Thus, the theoretical formulations of Bowles and Gintis and the deterministic elements of Bourdieu's theory, although elegant and intuitively plausible, are incapable of accounting for the processes of social reproduction as they have been observed and documented in Clarendon Heights. These theories give an excellent account of the hidden structural and ideological determinants that constrain members of the working class and limit the options of Clarendon Heights teenagers. What the Hallway Hangers and the Brothers demonstrate quite clearly, however, is that the way in which individuals and groups respond to structures of domination is open-ended. Although there is no way to avoid class-based constraints, the outcomes are not predefined. Bowles and Gintis and Bourdieu pay too little attention to the active, creative role of individual and group praxis. As Giroux maintains, what is missing from such theories "is not only the issue of resistance, but also any attempt to delineate the complex ways in which working-class subjectivities are constituted."[3]

From Ethnography to Theory

Once we descend into the world of actual human lives, we must take our theoretical bearings to make some sense of the social landscape, but in doing so we invariably find that the theories are incapable of accounting for much of what we see. The lives of the Hallway Hangers and the Brothers cannot be reduced to structural influences or causes; although structural forces weigh upon the individuals involved, it is necessary, in the words of Willis, "to give the social agents involved some meaningful scope for viewing, inhabiting, and constructing their own world in a way which is recognizably human and not theoretically reductive."[4] We must appreciate both the importance and the relative autonomy of the cultural level at which individuals, alone or in concert with others, wrest meaning out of the flux of their lives.

The possibilities open to these boys as lower-class teenagers are limited structurally from the outset. That they internalize the objective probabilities for social advancement to some degree is beyond question. The process by which this takes place, however, is influenced by a whole series of intermediate factors. Because gender is constant in the study discussed in these pages, race is the principal variable affecting the way in which these youths view their situation. Ethnicity introduces new structurally determined constraints on social mobility, but it also serves as a mediation through which the limitations of class are refracted and thus apprehended and understood differently by different racial groups. The Brothers comprehend and react to their situation in a manner entirely different from the response the Hallway Hangers make to a similar situation; ethnicity introduces a new dynamic that makes the Brothers more receptive to the achievement ideology. Their acceptance of this ideology affects their aspirations but also influences, in tandem with parental encouragement, their approach to school and the character of their peer group, factors that in turn bear upon their aspirations.

If we modify the habitus by changing the ethnicity variable and altering a few details of family occupational and educational histories and duration of tenancy in public housing, we would have the Hallway Hangers. As white lower-class youths, the Hallway Hangers view and interpret their situation in a different light, one that induces them to reject the achievement ideology and to develop aspirations and expectations quite apart from those the ideology attempts to generate. The resultant perspective, which is eventually reinforced by the Hallway Hangers' contact with the job market, informs the boys' approach to school and helps us understand the distinctive attributes of this peer group. Thus, although social class is of primary importance, there are intermediate factors at work that, as constitutive of the habitus, shape the subjective responses of the two groups of boys and produce quite different expectations and actions.

Having grown up in an environment where success is not common, the Hallway Hangers see that the connection between effort and reward is not as clearcut as the achievement ideology would have them believe. Because it runs counter to the evidence in their lives and because it represents a forceful assault on their self-esteem, the Hallway Hangers repudiate the achievement ideology. Given that their parents are inclined to see the ideology in the same light, they do not counter their sons' rejection of the American Dream.

A number of important ramifications follow from the Hallway Hangers' denial of the dominant ideology: the establishment of a peer group that provides alternative means of generating self-esteem, the rejection of school and antagonism toward teachers, and, of course, the leveling of aspirations. In schematizing the role of the peer group, it is difficult not to appear tautological, for the group does wield a reciprocal influence on the boys: It attracts those who are apt to reject school and the achievement ideology and those with low aspirations and then deepens these individuals' initial proclivities and further shapes them to fit the group. But at the same time, the peer subculture itself, handed down from older to younger boys, is the product of the particular factors that structure the lives of white teenagers in Clarendon Heights.

In addition to the peer group, the curricular structure of the school solidifies the low aspirations of the Hallway Hangers by channeling them into programs that prepare students for manual labor jobs. Low aspirations, in turn, make the Hallway Hangers more likely to dismiss school as irrelevant. Once on the job market, the Hallway Hangers' inability to secure even mediocre jobs further dampens their occupational hopes. Thus, although each individual ultimately retains autonomy in the subjective interpretation of his situation, the leveled aspirations of the Hallway Hangers are to a large degree a response to the limitations of social class as they are manifest in the Hallway Hangers' social world.

The Brothers' social class origins are only marginally different from those of the Hallway Hangers. Being black, the Brothers also must cope with racially rooted barriers to success that, affirmative action measures notwithstanding, structurally inhibit the probabilities for social advancement, although to a lesser degree than do shared class limitations. What appears to be a comparable objective situation to that of the Hallway Hangers, however, is apprehended in a very different manner by the Brothers.

As black teenagers, the Brothers interpret their families' occupational and educational records in a much different light than do the Hallway Hangers. Judging by the Brothers' constant affirmation of equality of opportunity, the boys believe that racial injustice has been curbed in the United States in the last twenty years. Whereas in their parents' time the link between effort and reward was very tenuous for blacks, the Brothers, in keeping with the achievement ideology, see the connection today as very strong: "If you work hard, it'll pay off in the end" (Craig). Hence, the achievement ideology is more compatible with the Brothers' attitudes than with those of the Hallway Hangers, for whom it cannot succeed against overwhelming contrary evidence. The ideology is not as emotionally painful for the Brothers to accept because past racial discrimination can help account for their families' poverty, whereas the Hallway Hangers, if the ideology stands, are afforded no explanation outside of laziness and stupidity for their parents' failures. The optimism that acceptance of the achievement ideology brings for the Brothers is encouraged and reinforced by their parents. Thus, we see how in the modified habitus ethnicity affects the Brothers' interpretation of their social circumstances and leads to acceptance of the achievement ideology, with all the concomitant results.

Chief among these results is a positive attitude toward education that influences the Brothers' relations with teachers and reaction to the curricular structure of the school, thereby making it less likely for the boys to select a future in manual work via a vocational program. Their validation of the achievement ideology also affects the ethos of their peer group, which in turn influences each individual's orientation toward school as well as his aspirations. Because their contact with the job market has been minimal, the Brothers have yet to undergo experiences that might upset or alter their perspective. Once they graduate from high school, the Brothers probably will need to temper their aspirations as Juan has done. Whether they begin to question the achievement ideology and the openness of American society or whether they reproach themselves for frustrated ambition remains to be seen. From a political perspective this is an intriguing question, but from a sociological angle what is equally fascinating is the way ethnicity mediates the limitations of class, thereby creating a refractive effect that catalyzes the Brothers to construct meaning out of their existence in an entirely different manner from the Hallway Hangers.

A fundamental aspect of habitus (but hidden in this book because of its constancy) is gender. As boys, the Hallway Hangers can inhabit a subculture whose values receive a good deal of validation from the dominant culture. The cultural inversion employed to turn "bad" into good is based on a valuation of machismo taken to the extreme. Being tough, "cool," and defiant all derive from an overstated pride in masculinity, an ideal portrayed by such actors as John Wayne, Clint Eastwood, and Sylvester Stallone. The Hallway Hangers exaggerate and manipulate this ideal, investing it with new dimensions until it is so distorted that John Grace can embody it. Lacking in nearly every category that defines success in America, the Hallway Hangers latch onto and inflate the one quality they still have: their masculinity.

Girls from Clarendon Heights experience and manipulate the structural forces of class, race, and gender in their own ways. Although we have no original empirical material to inform our analysis, a rich ethnographic study, recently undertaken by Jane K. Rosegrant in Clarendon Heights itself, offers us invaluable information on how lower-class girls understand their circumstances and what types of action proceed from these interpretations.

Rosegrant delves into the life histories of five women from Clarendon Heights in an attempt to determine the combined importance of the "distinct, yet intertwined threads of influence"[5] of class and gender on their lives. Although small, her sample cuts across racial lines, encompassing three white women, one black, and one Latina. These women and their daughters are subject to even more structural limitations than are the boys in this book because they have to contend with patriarchy as a mode of domination as well as class and, for some, racial barriers to success. Women in Clarendon Heights face a future that holds out little promise. Resolution of the structural forces acting on girls in Clarendon Heights, however, is radically different than for boys because, among other things, girls can realize a goal that seems to promise them freedom from the forces by which they, like the Hallway Hangers, feel trapped.

> It is at this juncture that the "mothering option" raises its head. As
> teenagers, the women of this study . . . underwent the same
> hardships and lived the same stigma that their brothers felt. Certainly
> they knew their families were poor, that they were living different
> lives than the ones they saw depicted on T.V., and that somehow it

was their parents'—especially their father's—"fault" that they were in this position. They certainly felt bad when they did poorly in school and they did not look forward to the jobs they would hold in their lifetimes—work at least as dull as that for which the boys were headed. However, the girls could react to these pressures and find a respite from them, that the boys could not. Within the mainstream of our society, a clearly defined and lauded path existed which they could follow. Thanks to this "escape route," the girls were not forced to cope with an overwhelming image of themselves, either personal or societal, as failures. No matter how poorly they performed in school, or how dismal their employment outlook might have been, they had a route to respectability. The importance the aspiration to mother had in their lives can not be overestimated. In the midst of their often tumultuous childhoods, it gave them something concrete to cling to. Unlike their fathers, brothers and boyfriends, they were headed for a future they desired, one of which society supposedly approved. They could be mothers, and nothing and no one could keep them from realizing this goal.[6]

Rosegrant's finding is substantiated by the daughters of these women as well. When she asked these adolescent girls to what jobs they aspire, they were all indifferent about their future work roles but were un-equivocal in their desire for children, despite their mothers' advice to the contrary. The response from eleven-year-old Sara is especially instructive: "Me? No, I want to get pregnant when I'm sixteen. Get an apartment, have a baby." One girl whose performance in school is exceptionally good nevertheless states, "I don't wanna go to college; I wanna have four kids."[7] While the Hallway Hangers attempt to escape the forces bearing upon them through the protection of their peer group with its celebration of masculinity, the girls look to parenthood and maternity.

As we might expect, however, the relief that mothering seems to hold out is largely illusory. Although none of the women in Rosegrant's study regretted having children, they all came quickly to the painful realization that being poor and a parent (usually a single one) is fraught with inestimable difficulties. As important as the practical burdens motherhood imposes is the denial these women felt when they failed to receive the respect that had been promised them. "If the Hallway Hangers of MacLeod's study felt betrayed by society as teens coping with school and work, these women come to feel this betrayal as young women coping with motherhood. They had done what they understood they were supposed to do—either willingly or by default—but society seemed to be reneging on its part of the deal."[8]

If motherhood, in spite of its promise, offers no relief from the structural forces impinging on lower-class girls, neither can girls expect consolation from a supportive peer group. Whereas the boys can construct a subculture offering alternative ways of maintaining some self-respect and dignity, the girls have no such avenue open to them. Consider the conclusion Anne Campbell draws from her extensive research on the lives of girls in New York street gangs.

> For these girls, there was no escape in the gang from the problems they faced: their female role could not be circumvented, their instability remained and was magnified, their isolation was covered by a rough veneer. The gang was no alternative life for them. It was a microcosm of the society beyond. Granted, it was one that had a public image of rebellion and excitement and offered a period of distraction (discussions of gang feuds and honor and death). But in the end, gang or no gang, the girls remained alone with their children, still trapped in poverty and in a cultural dictate of womanhood from which there was no escape.[9]

Denied the comraderie and solidarity that "male bonding" affords the boys, girls in Clarendon Heights fulfill the roles that patriarchal society defines for them, particularly the role of "girlfriend," which effectively keeps them divided, dependent, and subordinate. Nonconformist girls may well drop out of the race but without the solace of a closely knit peer group that has modified definitions of success. In such a predicament, it is no wonder that the option of motherhood seems attractive.

Another case that demands our attention is the situation of blacks at the very bottom of the socioeconomic strata who react to their predicament in much the same way as do the Hallway Hangers. What aspects of their habitus produce an outcome so different from that of the Brothers? Across the city in the projects housing mostly black and Latino families, one finds an abundance of black youths "hanging" in doorways, pessimistic about the future and cynical about the American Dream. Because they share with the Brothers the three main structural variables of social class, race, and gender, we must look to other factors making up the habitus to understand the differences between the Brothers and their black peers across the city.

For a start, their family occupational and educational histories are slightly more desolate, and there is often a more extended stay in public housing (two or three generations). Living in a neighborhood where black failure (by conventional criteria) is ubiquitous, these boys are likely to view the civil rights gains of the last twenty years as illusory. For them affirmative action is a token gesture that has little bearing on their lives—when the deck is stacked against you, being dealt one face card hardly guarantees a winning hand. Because they view the conditions that contributed to their parents' demise as largely intact, the ethnicity variable does not have the same refractive effect it has for the Brothers. Without the ambience of improved life chances, the achievement ideology rubs harder against the grain of these boys' experiences, thereby spurring them to reject the dominant ideology, disassociate themselves from school, and organize themselves into peer groups with an ethos much different from that of the Brothers. Because these project youths see the path to conventional achievement as blocked and because they are susceptible to racially rooted negative judgments by the dominant culture, it should come as no surprise that they form protective peer subcultures whose evaluative criteria are much like those by which the Hallway Hangers measure success. To be bad is to be successful, at least in the limited sphere of one's peer group. Despite the class, race, and gender variables these boys share with the Brothers, the internal structure of their habitus is substantially different and gives rise to different expectations and actions.

This schematization of intermediate factors between the structural determinants of social class and individual social actors explains a great deal of the empirical material this ethnographic inquiry has uncovered. This depiction of the social landscape inhabited by lower-class teenagers accommodates both the Hallway Hangers and Brothers as well as other social groups about which we have limited empirical data. We also should be able to locate and make sense of the situation of individuals on this social map.

Individuals in the Social Landscape

Boo-Boo and Derek pose an interesting challenge. Not only do they share the variables of class, race, and gender, but these two boys are also from the same family, yet have radically different outlooks on their futures. Because the boys have different fathers, their early home lives were somewhat varied. The crucial point of divergence, however, was Derek's acquisition of a federal scholarship to attend Barnes Academy after third grade. Enrollment at a prestigious private school not only objectively raised Derek's chances for success by providing him with a superior education and new opportunities—it also meant an entirely different form of socialization than that which Boo-Boo and other boys from the neighborhood were undergoing at the local grammar school. Derek was in white, upper-class educational environs for most of the day and spent most of his free time with his Barnes Academy friends. Thus, the two brothers had radically different peer associations. While Derek was spending his summers sightseeing around Texas, Mexico, and Martha's Vineyard with a rich friend and his family, Boo-Boo was hanging in the project with the Hallway Hangers. Both boys, although hesitant to speak about each other, draw attention to their different peers as an important source of variance between them.

JM: How'd you end up hanging with Frankie and them?

Boo-Boo: When I was in school, they was in school. My brother went to Barnes, started hanging with other kids. When he started hanging down here, Juan and Craig were around.

(in a separate interview)

JM: Why do you think your brother hangs with them [the Hallway Hangers]?

DEREK: I don't know. . . . I only started hanging with Super and Mokey and everybody a couple of years ago. Before that, I hung up by Mirror Lake with the guys from Barnes.

Thus, although the main variables of class, race, gender, and family are the same for Boo-Boo and Derek, the differences in other factors making up the habitus, especially schooling and peer associations, readily account for the existing disparity between the brothers.

Billy, the boy who has won a scholarship to attend college, also presents us with a challenge, for he used to be indistinguishable from the Hallway Hangers. He is still friendly with Jinks, Slick, and Frankie and speaks matter-of-factly about his early years in high school.

BILLY: I was getting high with them [the Hallway Hangers], having fun with them, cutting classes. . . . We all hung together. We all used to go out during lunch, about ten of us, get smashed. I'm serious. We'd come back hardly able to stand up and go to shop [Oc. Ed.]. . . . I used to smoke dope every single day. I swear to God, I don't think I went one day without smoking. Then I just went home, went to sleep, wake up, get high, go to sleep.

Billy's family background is similar to that of the other boys as well. Neither parent graduated from high school or worked regularly. But the death of his father and separation from his mother altered his family in a drastic way and thus instigated a reorientation of other intermediate factors that resulted in an outcome far different than that for most of the Hallway Hangers.

The upheavals in his family situation coupled with the brutal murder of his best friend somehow touched off a spark in Billy to buck the odds and "make something" of himself. "I want to become successful in life. I wanna be someone, y'know? I don't wanna live in a housing development or anything like that." In keeping with his suddenly high aspirations, Billy embraced the achievement ideology at the same time his peers were coming to reject it. "Do I have an equal chance to make it as some richer kid? Yeah, I have an equal chance as anyone does. You can be the smartest person if you want to be, unless you have some disabilities, cuz all it takes is hard work and study."

Having chosen Oc. Ed. in eighth grade because "it was the thing to do back then. All my friends, all people from where I live—that's where everyone was," Billy began to work hard in school. He gradually drifted away from the Hallway Hangers, stopped smoking marijuana, and earned a spot on the high school hockey team as the varsity goalie. This, in turn, led to a whole new set of friends with different values and a different lifestyle, a change about which Frankie comments.

FRANKIE: Yeah, Billy figured what the fuck, man. He said, "Hey now I got a chance to fucking do something," and he did it. Good luck to him, y'know. I think he pulled a good move cuz he used to get high and shit all the time. . . . Now he started playing hockey, y'know, and met a lot of kids on the team, ended up hanging with them. That's good, y'know. Hang with them and these dudes are all the time trying to get good grades. Y'know, Billy said, "What the fuck, I'll check this out."

Jinks and Chris see Billy in the same way.

JM: Do you think any of your friends will go to college?

JINKS: I think one might.

CHRIS: Billy?

JINKS: Yeah, that's about it.

JM: Does he still hang with you guys at all?

CHRIS: No, and that's the only reason [that he might make it to college].

JINKS: He used to hang with us.

CHRIS: He used to fuck up.

JINKS: Like eighth grade, ninth grade. Then he just started going to school, doing all his work, started being by himself.

CHRIS: I think because his father died, mostly. He just said, "I wanna do something good with my life."

Billy won a scholarship and plans to attend a small, liberal arts college next year. He may well "make it" and leave behind his old friends, the Hallway Hangers: "I think I'll come back five years from now and I'll see eight out of ten of them still hanging in doorway #13, bummin' money, doing nuttin'."

Because his life illustrates the interplay among family, school, and peer group, Billy is a perfect example of the importance of mediating variables in the habitus and the complex relationships that exist among the various factors. If one variable is changed, it upsets the balance of the habitus, and the consequences can ripple through the other intermediate forces, changing all the interactions to mold a different outcome. Billy had some distinctive familial experiences that altered his aspirations. Changed aspirations led to new attitudes and behavior (in particular new interactions with peers and school), which led in turn to further alterations in expectation and action. Instead of hanging in doorway #13 next year, Billy expects to be settled on a college campus.

Cultural Autonomy Within Structural Constraints

By taking as our starting point the peer cultures of Clarendon Heights and working upward from ethnography to analysis, we have discovered how a number of factors mediate the influence of social class on the individual actors at the cultural level. As long as Bourdieu's concept of habitus is deepened theoretically to accommodate these factors, it is a valuable descriptive device for understanding the social world of Clarendon Heights. Individuals, with their distinctive assets and character traits, have a good deal of autonomy. But although we can in no way predict with confidence the precise effect a particular change in habitus will have on people, the factors that frame their existence and from which they derive meaning go a long way toward explaining their outlooks and behavior patterns.

I am arguing here for a balance between theories that emphasize structural determinants and those that give prominence to the cultural sphere. Willis's insistence on the autonomy of the cultural level, for example, reaches almost polemical proportions and pushes his analysis too far to one end of the spectrum. Thus, although Willis often mentions the importance of structural forces, his actual account of how the lads end up in manual labor occupations is remarkably free of attention to structurally embedded constraints. The interface between the cultural and structural is critical to our understanding of social reproduction, but the theories of Bowles and Gintis, Bourdieu, and Willis do not explain how the two spheres interact. To capture this relationship, the agency-structure dualism must be bridged by analyzing the interpenetration of human consciousness and structural determinants. Aspirations provide a conceptual link between structure and agency because although they are rooted firmly in individual proclivity (agency), they also are acutely sensitive to perceived societal constraints (structure).

Structural features of class, racial, and gender domination permeate American society, but this book has been concerned especially with class-based constraints embedded in the educational system. The school's valuation of the cultural capital of the upper classes and its depreciation of the cultural capital of the lower classes are the most important mechanisms of social reproduction within the educational system, but the discriminatory effects of tracking and of teachers' expectations also inhibit the academic performance of lower-class students. No matter how students from the lower classes respond, the dynamic of the race for the jobs of wealth and prestige remains unchanged. Although a restricted number of individuals of lower- and working-class origin may overcome the barriers to success, the rules of the race severely limit and constrain these individuals' mobility.

My analysis of the aspirations of the Brothers and Hallway Hangers shows clearly the autonomy individuals possess in their response to this received structure of domination. How lower-class youths react to an objective situation that is weighted heavily against them depends on a number of mediating factors and ultimately is contingent. The Hallway Hangers' leveled aspirations demonstrate the extent to which structural constraints can impinge directly on individual attitudes. Confronting what they regard as a closed opportunity structure, the Hallway Hangers attach very little significance to their own occupational preferences in formulating their aspirations. Thus, we see how structure can reach into human consciousness to encourage dispositions that ensure the reproduction of class inequality. With respect to the Hallway Hangers, Bourdieu's perspective is vindicated.

The higher occupational aspirations of the Brothers, on the other hand, indicate that the connection between objective structure and subjective attitudes is tenuous; ideology can cloud, distort, and conceal the mechanisms of social reproduction. Although structural determinants shape the aspirations of the Hallway Hangers, the Brothers attest to the power of ideology to mold perceptions. Cognizant of no external barriers to success, the Brothers consistently affirm the achievement ideology and the actuality of equality of opportunity. Bourdieu does not seem to see that high aspirations may result from a capitalist society's contradictory need to present an ideology of openness and equal opportunity at the same time that the underlying structure of class relations is maintained. However, the Hallway Hangers prove that ideological hegemony is not a fait accompli; such hegemony often is contested and is realized only partially.

Although individuals can interpret and respond to constraint in different ways, they must still face the effects of institutional forms of class domination. As Giroux reminds us, "While school cultures may take complex and heterogeneous forms, the principle that remains constant is that they are situated within a network of power relations from which they cannot escape."[10] Cultural practices operate within the limits defined by class, gender, and racial barriers. In terms of the immediate perpetuation of class inequality, it matters little how lower-class teenagers respond to the vicissitudes of their situation. No matter how clearly they understand their lives, no matter what cultural innovations they produce, no matter how diligently they devote themselves to school, they cannot escape the constraints of social class. Conformists accept the ideology and act within the system but come up against the barriers of class; only a few break through. Nonconformists balk and do no better; in effect, they withdraw from the system, never test its limits, and generally find themselves in worse shape.

Structuralist theories are of value because they can show quite clearly why the end result turns out to be much the same, but in doing so they often obliterate human agency by ignoring "the complex ways in which people mediate and respond to the interface between their own lived experiences and structures of domination and constraint."[11] Culturalist theories give us a sense of the texture of individual lives but too often fail to contextualize attitudes and behavior as responses to objective structures. Giroux's insistence on a dialectical treatment of subjectivity and structure is correct: "Determination and human agency presuppose each other in situations that represent a setting-of-limits on the resources and opportunities of different classes. Men and women inherit these pre-defined circumstances, but engage them in a 'process of meaning-making which is always active' (Bennett 1981), and leaves their results open-ended."[12]

The results may be contingent, but neither of the outcomes documented in this study is positive. It is an open question whether the Hallway Hangers or the Brothers are worse off. The Brothers' mobility is defined by structural constraints that probably will result in the boys' entry into the stable working class. Because the institutional mechanisms of social reproduction hinder rather than block the Brothers' mobility, one or two of the Brothers may even break into the middle class. However, unaware of the constraints (but subject to their effects), the Brothers are prone to blame themselves for their plight. The Hallway Hangers, in contrast, see through the ideology, perceive the constraints, and realize the futility of high aspirations. They salvage some self-esteem but in the process forfeit any chance for individual social advancement. In a sense, cultural innovations like those of the lads or Hallway Hangers aid the process of social reproduction because nonconformists often relegate themselves to the worst jobs.

From a wider standpoint, however, the Hallway Hangers, who see with a certain crudity the true workings of the system, pose a threat to the stability of social reproduction. But as we have seen, the counterhegemonic elements of the Hallway Hangers' perspective are divested of their political potential; the Hallway Hangers' racism, among other factors, impedes the formation of any sort of critical consciousness.

Although the Hallway Hangers' capacity to see through the dominant ideology is not politically empowering, it does allow them to maintain some semblance of a positive identity. In puncturing the achievement ideology, the Hallway Hangers invert the dominant culture's definitions of achievement. Whereas the conventional American example of success might be J. Paul Getty, self-made millionaire, Frankie holds up as an example John Grace, bartender being tried for attempted murder. By turning the achievement ideology upside down, the Hallway Hangers reject the official, authorized interpretation of their social situation; in so doing, they become free to create their own cultural meanings. Because they see the spoils of economic success as beyond their reach, the Hallway Hangers invert the dominant ideology in a way that gives them access to "success," albeit in forms the dominant culture recognizes as failure.

My finding that the Hallway Hangers reject the official ideology and my speculation that the poorest members of the black community do the same makes a good deal of sense. We would expect those clinging to the very lowest rungs of the socioeconomic ladder to reject the achievement ideology, for although all other segments of society can use the dominant ideology as a means to feel superior to whomever is below them, underclass whites and blacks have no one to look down on. Even those only marginally better off can and do use the achievement ideology as a means of self-validation. As public housing tenants, Clarendon Heights residents routinely are depicted as irresponsible, morally lacking, and indolent by the city's other inhabitants. Consider the light in which an auto mechanic living in a working-class neighborhood across the city sees Clarendon Heights residents: "These people are fucking animals. . . . I know what their habits are like; they won't stop at anything to rip you off. Fucking sponges, leeches, they are. They'll suck the blood out of anyone, anything. They suck it out of my pay check every week. . . . At least I work for my money."

Willis writes that the working class does not have a structurally based vested interest in mystifying itself.[13] But, in the United States at least, the working class is so fragmented that only the very lowest strata have no use for ideology. For the poorest segments of the population, both white and black, the only defense against the dominant ideology is to turn it on its head and attempt to salvage as much dignity as possible via the redefined criteria for success. This is a struggle that will never be completely won, for the judgments of the dominant culture are capable of piercing the thickest individual or collective shells. Willis captures the issue in *Learning to Labor*: "One of the time-honoured principles of cultural and social organization in this country as it is enacted and understood at the subjective level is that of 'them' and 'us.' That the term 'them' survives in 'us' is usually overlooked. . . . Even the most 'us' group has a little of 'them' inside. . . . Ideology is the 'them' in 'us.' "[14]

The poorest black and white people in America, who are fodder for the rest of society's hunger for social superiority, ironically turn on each other to fulfill the same function. The Hallway Hangers continually strive to convince themselves of their superiority over "the niggers." We might expect that underclass blacks vaunt themselves over the "white trash" living across the city. The more effective means of maintaining a measure of dignity and self-respect, however, seems to be the inversion of the dominant ideology, a cultural response to class domination by those at the bottom of American society.

The interaction between the cultural and the structural that I have posited—that class-based institutional mechanisms set limits on mobility, thereby ensuring social reproduction, while cultural innovations can be at once both functional and dysfunctional for social reproduction—fits the ethnographic data. By ignoring the cultural level of analysis, determinist theories cannot account for the distinctive cultural practices and attitudes of lower-class individuals; nor can these theories explain how such practices can contribute to and threaten social reproduction. By considering only the lads in his study, Willis is hard-pressed to illuminate the purely institutional mechanisms that constrain the mobility of lower-class individuals.

By striving to understand the world of the Brothers and the Hallway Hangers on their terms, this book has managed to uncover some important mediating factors that influence individuals at the cultural level. It is to these factors that deterministic theories must pay more attention. In addition, theorists such as Bowles and Gintis and Bourdieu must recognize individuals' capacity for reflexive thought and action—in Willis's words, their potential "not only to think like theorists, but act like activists."[15] Individuals are not passive receivers of structural forces; rather they interpret and respond to those forces in creative ways. In asserting the autonomy of the individual at this cultural level, however, we must not lose sight of structural forms of class domination from which there is no escape. To paraphrase Marx, we must understand that teenage peer groups make their own history, but not under circumstances of their own choosing.[16]

SCHOOLING: EMASCULATION OR CONFIRMATION OF STUDENT IDENTITY?

Although the fieldwork I undertook in Lincoln School was limited, the ethnographic data do shed some light on the failure of the educational system to accommodate youths like the Hallway Hangers and do yield some suggestions for improvement. Educational reform must not be viewed as a substitute for more fundamental political, economic, and social change if the enduring problem of the intergenerational transmission of class-based inequality is to be solved, but there are some specific educational reforms that can be introduced to improve the "educability" of working-class young people. My intent, however, is not to put forth a comprehensive alternative educational policy, a task well beyond the scope of this investigation, but rather to sift through my ethnographic data in search of any material that can inform educational policy and help improve the schools.

My first recommendation is that the achievement ideology must go.[17] It is used to cultivate discipline by highlighting the eventual rewards of educational attainment and is neither particularly effective at drawing a measure of obedience and attentiveness out of students nor conducive to the development of a positive self-image by working-class pupils. The familiar refrain of "behave yourself, study hard, earn good grades, graduate with your class, go on to college, get a good job, and make a lot of money" reinforces the feelings of personal failure and inadequacy working-class students are likely to bear as a matter of course. By shrouding class, race, and gender barriers to success, the achievement ideology promulgates a lie, one that some students come to recognize as such. For those pupils whose own experiences contradict the ideology— and in an urban public high school there are bound to be many—it is often rejected and rightly so. Teachers are left with nothing to motivate their students, and it is no wonder that "acting out," aggressive disobedience, and unruliness predominate. School officials can round up the offending students and label them "slow," "learning impaired," "unmotivated," "troubled," "behavior problems," "high-risk," or "emotionally disturbed" and segregate them, but the problem is much more deeply rooted.

Teachers do not promote the achievement ideology because they want to make working-class students miserable. Nor are they intent on maintaining social order and cohesion in the face of class inequality by contributing to the legitimation function of the school. Most teachers are well-intentioned, hard-working men and women who are striving to do a difficult job as best they can. They parrot the achievement ideology because they think it will motivate students, because it probably does not contradict their own experiences, and because they believe it. Most middle-class Americans do. As Willis writes, "What kind of bourgeoisie is it that does not in some way believe its own legitimations? That would be the denial of themselves."[18] The equality of opportunity line of reasoning may have worked in the middle-class high schools from which most teachers hail, but its utility in an urban school serving low-income neighborhoods is diminished greatly.

If students like the Hallway Hangers are to be motivated to achieve in school, it must not be at the expense of their self-esteem but in support of it. Schools serving low-income neighborhoods must help students build positive identities as working-class, black and white, young men and women. Rather than denying the existence of barriers to success, schools should acknowledge them explicitly while motivating students by teaching them, for example, about local figures (with whom the students can identify) who share the students' socioeconomic origins but overcame the odds. Teachers can strive to include material about which the students, drawing on the skills they have developed in their neighborhoods, are the experts. If the school could believe in the legitimacy and importance of students' feelings, perceptions, and experiences as working-class kids, the students themselves might come to do the same, thereby giving them a positive identity and a measure of self-confidence as a foundation for further application in school.

If such measures were undertaken on a systematic basis, boys like the Hallway Hangers might feel as though they belong in school, that they need not choose between rendering themselves naked and vulnerable by stripping off their street identities or aggressively asserting their street culture in disruptive rebellion. I am certain that one of the reasons the Hallway Hangers speak so warmly about Jimmy Sullivan's class is that in his classroom they are allowed to maintain their street identities. Even more importantly, these identities are vindicated and given legitimacy because the teacher himself embodies many of the attitudes, values, and traits the culture of the Hallway Hangers esteems. The Hallway Hangers see in Jimmy a bit of themselves and in themselves a bit of Jimmy; because of the status and authority invested in him as a teacher, in addition to his independent financial success, Jimmy Sullivan vicariously defends and justifies their self-image.

Teachers need not have a black belt in karate, place a premium on machismo, swear in class, or have working-class roots like Jimmy Sullivan; however, they must be prepared to validate the identities their students have taken on as part of growing up. Although more working-class teachers certainly would be desirable, the social relations of schools could be improved vastly by a serious effort at minimizing condescension and creating an atmosphere in which all students can maintain their self-respect.

The curriculum should meet the needs and concerns of working-class and minority students. Class, race, and gender barriers to success should be explored with particular attention paid to the effects they have on specific individuals. Awareness of class, race, and gender stereotyping should be inculcated and students should be forced to confront their own internalization of these stereotypes and its consequences. In making the curriculum responsive to student needs, the gap between academic skill and maturity must somehow be bridged. No one is going to get Frankie Dougherty to read about the Hardy Boys, but on the other hand his reading ability may not be much above a fifth grade level. Novels and poignant nonfiction works dealing with the concerns of working-class and minority youth could be incorporated into the curriculum. It is ludicrous, for instance, to expect students in the Adjustment Class to learn about social studies from a sixth grade U.S. history textbook. Meanwhile, the thirteen-year-old younger brothers of the Hallway Hangers manage to research prison life through books, movies, slides, lectures, and field trips and to produce a thirty-page anthology of interviews with former inmates, many of whom live in Clarendon Heights. Connecting the curriculum with the interests of pupils like the Hallway Hangers can be done; it only requires a commitment—attitudinal and material—to meeting the needs of working-class students.

In attempting to forge an educational environment in which young people from low-income neighborhoods can feel comfortable, wanted, and productive, we must resist the tendency, all too prevalent among educational reformers, to cling to single-solution, essentialist positions. In setting educational policy we must pay close attention to how policies will affect the factors that shape the lives of lower-class teenagers. Policy recommendations must be placed in context; otherwise, the alleviation of one problem may aggravate another. In the absence of any easy solutions, there is no avoiding the intellectual work and policy experimentation required to solve the educational problems that confront us.

Two examples should suffice to prove this point. Let us look first at the Adjustment Class. By teachers' accounts, the class is a huge success; many teachers are filled with admiration for Jimmy Sullivan's ability to control the kids and actually keep them enrolled in school. In examining the class and speaking with the students themselves, it is clear that they are much happier in the Adjustment Class than in any previous class. This, I have argued, is because they are allowed to maintain their street identities and their identities are validated by the teacher. On this count, the class should be emulated. On other counts, however, it is a dismal failure. Sullivan tells me, "See, there's a premium on macho here. You've probably noticed. We've got a reputation for that. I don't know if they told you, but Carl [his assistant] and I both have black belts in karate. . . . If I didn't have the respect of the toughest kid, I couldn't do it. If Frankie could kick my ass, it would be all over."

If part of one's education should involve the examination and confrontation of sexual stereotyping and ingrained sexism, for instance, Sullivan's class is unlikely to receive high marks. There are no girls in the class, and the uncritical affirmation of machismo confronts the observer in every aspect of the room, from the punching bags, posters of Bruce Lee, and *Soldier of Fortune* magazines to the frankly sexist attitudes of the teacher. The point is that there are no easy solutions. Priorities must be set and prospective policies evaluated on the basis of several criteria. For the Adjustment Class, such considerations would include the desirability of segregating boys who the school, by official definition, considers emotionally disturbed, the amount of time actually spent on learning, and the quality of the curriculum and teaching methods. On balance, I consider the Adjustment Class a failure because, for the most part, the students emerge with very few academic skills.

The King School, an alternative, tuition-free high school program for low-income youths, is another, albeit vastly different, example of the need to understand how policy changes are likely to affect student attitudes and behavior. Established in 1969 when there was a good deal of support for alternative education, the King School aims at empowering students, reviving their faith in themselves as capable, intelligent human beings. Toward this end the school employs a democratic decisionmaking structure that allows for a great deal of student involvement and participation in all areas of the institution—from hiring of staff to determination of credit requirements for graduation. This emphasis on student empowerment is linked with a pedagogy and curriculum that incorporate the two basic recommendations detailed previously: a curriculum that springs from the history and needs of the working-class, ethnically diverse student body and an emphasis on providing students with a clear sense of their working-class identity.[19]

On paper, the King School could not look more attractive. In practice, it has educated a racially and sexually balanced student body of low-income teenagers since its inception and educated them in a very positive and constructive fashion. In terms of the social relations between students and teachers, however, the King School was lacking in one major respect: It had very few working-class staff. Although recognized by the school itself, this deficiency lies behind much of Frankie's dissatisfaction with the school. To secure credibility in the eyes of people like the Hallway Hangers, especially in helping students develop a positive self-image as working-class and minority youth, working-class teachers are crucial. Despite its democratic structure and teaching philosophy, the King School's neglect of one basic component severely compromises its performance in meeting the needs of the students it strives to serve.

The King School is proof that a school's structure, curriculum, and pedagogy can be geared successfully to the needs and experiences of teenagers like the Brothers and Hallway Hangers. Jimmy Sullivan's Adjustment Class is a testament to what can be accomplished when teacher-student interaction is marked by class and cultural affinity rather than by distrust and condescension. Incorporation of the positive aspects of these two models in urban high schools would be a large step forward, but such an action would not dissolve the institution's social reproductive function nor would it address head on the fundamental problem of the transmission of class inequality. Thus, educational reform should not be pursued as an end in itself but as a component of more fundamental change in the social fabric of American society.

THE POLITICAL IMPLICATIONS
OF SOCIAL REPRODUCTION

The picture that has emerged from this ethnography deviates substantially from the myth of America as the land of opportunity in which any child can grow up to be president. American society is not as open as we like to think; the ladder of social mobility is not accessible to all, nor are its rungs easy to grasp. This ethnography has uncovered a group of boys at the bottom of the class structure who feel so trapped in their subordinate position that they do not even aspire to move upward. The other group of boys is intent on improving its lot, but bearing in mind the forces against which the boys must struggle, we may hazard a guess that their journey up the class structure will be a rather short trip. Both the Brothers and the Hallway Hangers are a testament to the prevalence of social reproduction rather than social mobility in American society. For many of those in the lowest reaches of the social structure, the American Dream is but a mirage.

Such a picture is troubling. It bursts many of our illusions about the fairness of the American economic and social system; it also demands a political response that goes well beyond the offerings of contemporary American liberalism. Before we consider what is needed to address the injustices this book has brought to light, let us first review those solutions that are often proffered to deal with the problem of lower-class immobility.

"Better schools" has been the standard rallying cry for social reformers concerned about sustained economic inequality in the United States. If only poor and minority children had equal access to quality education, opportunity for individual mobility would be equalized across social classes and the gap between rich and poor substantially reduced. The problems with this approach are substantial. First, we have seen how schooling actually maintains and legitimizes social inequality. Because the educational system esteems the cultural capital possessed by the upper classes over that of the lower classes, schooling tends to reproduce the structure of inequality. Moreover, educational reform is incapable of effecting change in the structure of inequality in America. The underlying problem—that there are not enough good jobs to go around, that for every well-paid boss there are many ill-paid workers—remains untouched. The roughly pyramidal shape of the class structure, with relatively little room at the top, ensures that even if everyone strives for the top, the great majority are automatically bound (by these structural constraints, if by nothing else) to be disappointed. Liberals in the United States still have difficulty coming to grips with this fact; educational reform cannot serve as a substitute for more fundamental structural change.

Nor will extension of the welfare state alleviate the problems the Brothers and Hallway Hangers face. Improving the material conditions under which they are forced to live—the provision of less expensive and better housing, larger welfare and unemployment checks, access to inexpensive, quality health care—certainly would be a step in the right direction, but it leaves the basic emotional encumbrance of lower-class life untouched. These boys, including the Hallway Hangers, desperately want to be somebody, to make something of their lives. By denying them that opportunity, by undercutting their very aspirations, by reducing them to hopelessness at the ages of sixteen and seventeen, the economic and social system causes untold misery, waste, and despair. American culture subscribes to a single definition of success but systematically precludes large portions of the populace from attaining it and now, it seems, from even aspiring to it. The ideology that permeates American society holds out the rags-to-riches story as a valid option, despite the fact that very, very few people can live it out. If the Brothers and the Hallway Hangers are to have the opportunity to fulfill their potential as human beings, more will have to change in the American political and social landscape than the expansion of the welfare state.

This is a point on which liberalism is vulnerable.[20] Liberal thought and ideology during the last two centuries has affirmed above all the quest for a society in which all individuals are capable of fulfilling their potential as citizens. In the United States, at least, this ideal is far short of being realized, as both the Brothers and the Hallway Hangers attest. Furthermore, those Americans who call themselves liberals seem none too concerned about it. Perhaps the true custodians of liberal principles[21] in the United States are those who advocate more fundamental change in the class structure.

To improve the situation of the Hallway Hangers and the Brothers a social order in which the life chances of those at the bottom are not altogether different from those at the top is needed. A redress of the grievances discussed in these pages requires a more equitable distribution of economic resources, an occupational structure that is shaped less like a pyramid, and equal occupational access for all individuals regardless of social origins—in short, a truly open society in which social inequality and stratification are substantially reduced. John H. Goldthorpe elaborates both the end for which we should strive and the means to get there in *Social Mobility and Class Structure in Modern Britain.*

> The achievement of a genuinely open society would imply, it may be supposed, the decomposition or at all events the serious attenuation of classes in the sense of aggregates of individuals, or families, identifiable in the extent to which they occupy similar locations in the social division of labour over time. However, class structures are ones highly resistant to change: those groupings who enjoy positions of superior advantage and power cannot be expected to yield them up without a struggle, but will rather typically seek to exploit the resources that they can command in order to preserve their superiority. Change is therefore only likely to be brought about through collective action on the part of those in inferior positions, relying on their numbers and above all on solidarity and organization.[22]

In my opinion, Goldthorpe is correct in his diagnosis and in his assessment of what is needed to remedy the problem. If class society is to be fundamentally modified, it must come about predominantly through class conflict. Change may be slow and piecemeal, it may come about inside and outside of established political channels, and it may involve interclass action based on shared values, but its basic dynamic will in all likelihood be determined by class-based economic interests.

This ethnographic account of the Brothers and the Hallway Hangers, if properly scrutinized, yields some useful information on the potential of the American working class to catalyze this type of social change. We see enabling elements in the attitudes of these lower-class teenagers that hold some promise for the realization of a genuinely open society; these attitudes also contain elements that will impede the formation of class consciousness and solidarity among the working class. Not surprisingly, the impediments substantially outweigh the promising signs, but the outlook is not altogether bleak.

The relation of aspirations to the proclivity of individuals to commit themselves to fundamental political change is rather obvious. Individuals who see their chances for upward mobility as remote are more likely

to involve themselves in collective political action than will their counterparts who see considerable opportunity for significant individual
mobility. A number of social theorists have noted this relationship, as
Goldthorpe points out in his review of the literature. Thus, Werner
Sombart, writing at the turn of the century, contends that "given a
decent standard of living and reasonable opportunities for individual
mobility, there is no compelling reason why members of the working
class *anywhere* should follow the historic path that socialism requires
of them: they may choose to pursue goals of a quite different and, to
socialists, uncongenial kind."[23] Robert Michels argues the converse: "The
certainty of being condemned to hired labour throughout natural life
is one of the most important causes that leads to the rise of anti-
capitalist movements in the modern masses."[24] Given the low occupational
aspirations of teenagers in Clarendon Heights, especially the Hallway
Hangers, they may well be prone to commit themselves to collective
rather than individual attempts at advancement.

The Hallway Hangers' adoption of communitarian values also gives
us grounds for optimism concerning their readiness to act on collective
rather than individual aspirations. The Hallway Hangers view their
solidarity, their "brotherhood," as a marked contrast to the individualism
of the upper classes.

SLICK: What it is, it's a brotherhood down here. . . . If he needs
something and I got it, I'll give it to him. Period. That's the way
it works. . . . We're not like them up there—the rich little boys
from the suburbs. . . . Like up in there, it's not as tight.

Of more significance in this regard is the Hallway Hangers' belief
that although individuals may be capable of upward mobility, as a group
their chances are nil. That this realization, among other factors, leads
the Hallway Hangers to eschew their individual possibilities for upward
mobility is a posture fraught with political potential.

JINKS: I'd say everyone more or less has the same attitude towards
school: fuck it. Except the bookworms—people who just don't
hang around outside and drink, get high, who sit at home—
they're the ones who get the education.

JM: And they just decided for themselves?

JINKS: Yup.

JM: So why don't more people decide for themselves?

JINKS: Y'know what it is Jay? We all don't break away because we're
too tight. Our friends are important to us. Fuck it. If we can't
make it together, fuck it. Fuck it all.

Granted that Billy did break away from the group and that if Jinks were offered a $10,000-a-year job with a chance to move to a more affluent neighborhood he would probably accept it, the articulated collective logic of the Hallway Hangers has important political significance. The analytical distinction between this group logic and a class logic must be conceded, but there is no denying that the collectivist cultural outlook of the Hallway Hangers is a seed that could flower into an affirmation of class solidarity.

Also of considerable political import is the Hallway Hangers' rejection and inversion of the dominant ideology. Eighty years ago Sombart remarked on "the pervasiveness in the United States of an individualistic and achievement-oriented ideology which could effectively inhibit a 'class' interpretation of the social structure and of the fate of individuals within it."[25] The same holds true today. That the Hallway Hangers penetrate this ideology, thereby enabling them to perceive in a rudimentary fashion various class-based barriers to success, improves the likelihood that they could become politically active.

These elements in the outlook of the Hallway Hangers provide grounds for optimism in assessing their ability and inclination to organize in order to bring about a genuinely open society. Unfortunately, this ethnographic material also suggests there are a great many more factors that impede collective, class organization and action. The aspirations of the Brothers are relatively high; the majority of them have ambitions for professional or middle-class employment. Aspirations tend to reduce the solidarity and oppositional tendencies of the working class by inspiring individual rather than collective efforts at social advancement. If it is merely the very lowest stratum that has modest aspirations, the threat to the social order is minimal.

Moreover, there are many divisions in the working class, some of which have been discussed herein. The propensity of workers to vaunt themselves over those elements of the working class in lower status occupations is a well-known phenomenon in the United States. In this way workers can feel good about their accomplishments, no matter how modest. For the bulk of the workforce, there are always groups like the Hallway Hangers to whom they can feel superior.

Another obvious force that fragments the working class and surfaces in this study is racism. As long as white, black, and Latino workers are at odds, there is little hope for the emergence of a strong movement devoted to the fundamental alteration of class society. Moreover, as we have seen in relation to the Hallway Hangers, racism contributes to the retardation of class consciousness. The feeling of the Hallway Hangers that they are the victims of class exploitation is undermined by their conviction that affirmative action and blacks are the real problem. What begins as a rudimentary but promising penetration of the Hallway Hangers' condition under capitalism is derailed into a strident racism that contributes to the oppression of other members of the boys' social class and, ultimately, to their own continued subjugation. This process is typical of the Hallway Hangers' social outlook. They feel the odds are stacked against them, but in the absence of any alternative political philosophy or ideology, these insights abide in their consciousness side by side with political values of an often quite conservative tenor.

Obviously, these political implications are tangential to the central concern of this book—the process of social reproduction. Nevertheless, the political potential of the working class—its capacity for and predisposition toward collective and organized action—is a subject of immense importance that cannot be completely divorced from that of social reproduction. I have attempted to show the constraining and the enabling elements that could spur the subjects of this study to work for radical political change. Not surprisingly, the limitations substantially overshadow the enabling elements. This finding is all the more disturbing because as some of the most marginal members of the populace the Hallway Hangers and the Brothers should be the most amenable to radical politicization. Unfortunately, even if they possessed a revolutionary consciousness, they hardly would constitute a significant threat to the established order without the support of other elements of the working class.

If there is any room for political optimism it comes from my theoretical conclusions. Social reproduction is a complex process; there is no standard formula and no standard outcome. Willis comes to a similar conclusion.

[This view of reproduction] is optimistic, however, in showing that there is no inevitability of outcomes. . . . If there are moments when cultural forms make real penetrations of the world then no matter what distortions follow, there is always the possibility of strengthening and working from this base. If there has been a radical genesis of conservative outcomes then at least there exists a *capacity* for opposition. We have the logical possibility of radicalness. . . . Social agents are not passive bearers of ideology, but active appropriators who reproduce existing structures only through struggle, contestation, and a partial penetration of those structures. . . . Too often it is assumed that capitalism implies thoroughly effective domination of the subordinate class. Far from this, capitalism in its modern, liberal form *is* permanent struggle. . . . Capitalism is never secure. It can never be a dynasty.[26]

Instability and mutation are endemic to the process of social reproduction. A small change in the factors constituting the habitus of the Brothers, for example, could result in a rejection of the achievement ideology and an adoption of a political orientation much more conducive to collective rather than individual advancement. If upon graduation the Brothers experience unemployment as Juan has, we can expect them to be more prone to the cynicism the Hallway Hangers exhibit. The tragedy is that the Brothers are more likely to find fault with themselves than with the economic system.

NOTES

1. Henry A. Giroux, *Theory & Resistance in Education* (London: Heinemann Educational Books, 1983), p. 89.

2. Pierre Bourdieu, *Outline of a Theory of Practice* (Cambridge: Cambridge University Press, 1977), p. 87.

3. Giroux, *Theory & Resistance*, p. 85.

4. Paul E. Willis, *Learning to Labor* (Aldershot: Gower, 1977), p. 172.

5. Jane K. Rosegrant, *"Choosing Children"* (Thesis, Harvard College, 1985), p. 120.

6. Ibid., pp. 125–126.

7. Ibid., pp. 133–134.

8. Ibid., p. 127.

9. Anne Campbell, *The Girls in the Gang* (Oxford: Basil Blackwell, 1984), p. 266.

10. Giroux, *Theory & Resistance*, p. 63.

11. Ibid., p. 108.

12. Ibid., p. 164.

13. Willis, *Learning to Labor*, pp. 122–123.

14. Ibid., p. 169.

15. Paul E. Willis, "Cultural Production and Theories of Reproduction," in *Race, Class, and Education*, ed. Len Barton and Stephen Walker (London: Croom Helm, 1983), p. 114.

16. Karl Marx, *The Eighteenth Brumaire of Louis Bonaparte*, in *Selected Works* (New York: International Publishers, 1968), p. 97.

17. Although schools, as part of an ideological state apparatus, are tied to the imperatives of the capitalist state and its ruling interests, these constraints are not so tight as to preclude abrogation of the achievement ideology as a means of securing discipline in school. The legitimation function the achievement ideology plays in the wider society is clear, but this function explains neither how nor why the ideology is propogated in the school and still less guarantees its continued inculcation in a social site as relatively autonomous as the school. Embedded in the classroom practices, curricula, and pedagogical philosophy of the American educational system and subtly inscribed in student consciousness, the achievement ideology would prove very difficult to eliminate. But teachers can surely be more attuned to its negative effects and can cease reciting it to ensure discipline.

18. Willis, *Learning to Labor*, p. 123.

19. Much of this information was gleaned from a pamphlet published by the King School and rendered from memory. The pedagogical principles and educational philosophy of the King School also have influenced my own educational philosophy, a debt I gratefully acknowledge.

20. John H. Goldthorpe, *Social Mobility and Class Structure in Modern Britain* (Oxford: Clarendon Press, 1980), p. 27.

21. Ibid., p. 21.

22. Ibid., pp. 28–29.

23. Ibid., p. 10.

24. Robert Michels, *First Lectures in Political Sociology* (New York: Harper and Row, 1965), p. 82.

25. As quoted in Goldthorpe, *Social Mobility*, p. 10.

26. Willis, *Learning to Labor*, p. 175.

APPENDIX: FIELDWORK

Few sociologists who employ qualitative research methods discuss the mechanics of fieldwork in their published writings. A frank account of the actual process by which research was carried out might disabuse people of the notion that sociological insight comes from logical analysis of a systematically gathered, static body of evidence. If my own experience is at all typical, insight comes from an immersion in the data, a sifting and resifting of the evidence until a pattern makes itself known. My research methods were not applied objectively in a manner devoid of human limitations and values. Of course, I had access to books that describe the various methods used in sociological field research. But many of these statements on research methods, as Whyte argues in the appendix of *Street Corner Society*, "fail to note that the researcher, like his informants, is a social animal. He has a role to play, and he has his own personality needs that must be met in some degree if he is to function successfully."[1] If, as I would argue, the best fieldwork emerges when the sociologist is completely immersed in the community under study, it means that his or her personal life will be inseparably bound up with the research. What follows, then, is a personal account of my relationship with the Clarendon Heights community and the way I came to understand the aspirations of its teenager members.

Walking through Clarendon Heights for the first time in the spring of 1981, I felt uneasy and vulnerable. Entering another world where the rules would all be different, I was naturally apprehensive. I might have been closer in class background to the people of Clarendon Heights than the great bulk of my university classmates were, but neither my lower-middle-class origins nor my attendance at a regional high school in rural New Hampshire made me particularly "at home" in the project. Most importantly, I was a university student, a status that could breed resentment, for it implied an upward social trajectory to which these people do not have ready access. To undertake research under such conditions would have been inconceivable. But that spring sociological research was far from my mind. I was at the project with three other university students to begin the Clarendon Heights Youth Enrichment Program, with which I would be involved for the next four years. The youth program led to my interest in the aspirations of Clarendon Heights young people and also provided me with a role and an acceptance in the community without which the fieldwork would have been close to impossible.

Contrary to the expectations of the city's professional social workers, the youth program turned out to be a great success. We lived in the neighborhood during the summer months and established close relationships with the children in the program, their parents, and other project residents. Initial distance or coldness gradually gave way to trust and personal regard as the program's reputation and the rapport between counselors and community grew. Engaging nine boys aged eleven to thirteen in a varied mix of educational, cultural, and recreational activities, I gained more than acceptance by the project's residents— I also learned a great deal about their day-to-day problems and concerns. As my understanding of the community and sensitivity to the pulse of the neighborhood developed, so did my self-confidence and sense of belonging. Although class and racial differences could never be completely transcended, by September 1982 I counted among my closest friends many Clarendon Heights tenants.

It was during that second summer working in Clarendon Heights that my interest in the kids' aspirations really began to take shape. I was amazed that many of the twelve- and thirteen-year-old boys in my group did not even aspire to middle-class jobs (with the exception of professional athletics), but rather, when they verbalized aspirations at all, indicated a desire to work with sheet metal, in a machine tool factory, or in construction. The world of middle-class work was completely foreign to them, and as the significance of this fact impressed itself on me, I concerned myself more and more with their occupational aspirations. But at such a young age, these boys could not speak with much consistency or sophistication about their occupational hopes. To understand why aspirations were so low among Clarendon Heights youth, I would have to look to these boys' older brothers and sisters, to those in high school.

I say brothers and sisters because my study of aspirations should have included equal consideration of girls. That this study concentrates solely on boys puts it in the company of many other works in the male-dominated field of sociology that exclude half the population from research. But with class and racial barriers to overcome, I felt hard-pressed to understand the situation of the boys and would have been totally incapable of doing justice to the experience of girls because yet another barrier—gender—would have to be confronted. Already thus handicapped, I felt totally incapable of considering adolescent girls in Clarendon Heights, whose situation was so far beyond my own experience.

The boys presented enough problems. I'd had the least contact with Heights teenagers. I knew a few of the Hallway Hangers on a casual basis because Stoney, Steve, Slick, and Boo-Boo had younger siblings enrolled in the youth program. Still, no relationship extended much beyond the "Hey, how's it going?" stage, and although I was never hassled coming or going from doorway #13, I was still very much of an outsider as far as the Hallway Hangers were concerned. My previous involvement in the community, however, had gained me a small degree of acceptance. They knew that I had been around for more than a year, that I worked hard, and that I got along well with many of the tenants, all of which ensured that I would be considered different from the typical university student. Had I been seen in such a light, I'm not sure I ever would have been accepted by the group, for college students were not welcome in doorway #13. My work with the Clarendon Heights Youth Program, however, allowed me to get my foot in the door and paved the way for future acceptance by the Hallway Hangers.

The Brothers were not so difficult. I played a lot of basketball with the kids in my youth group; we had a team of sorts and used to practice a few hours each week during the day. In the evenings, I invariably could be found at the park a block from Clarendon Heights playing a game of pick-up basketball with the younger kids from the project. Many of the Brothers played, too, and I soon got to know them quite well. Some of them also had younger brothers and sisters in the youth program, so they were acquainted with me from the start. In addition, I had remained close to Mike, and my association with him helped me to befriend the others. For the Brothers my status as a college student was grounds for a measure of respect rather than suspicion. Nor did they seem to distance themselves from me because I was white. How they could endure the racist taunts of the Hallway Hangers and not come to resent whites in general is difficult to comprehend. It may be that I was insensitive to any covert racial strain between the Brothers and me, but I never felt its effects.

By November 1982 I had decided to write my undergraduate thesis on the aspirations of teenage boys in Clarendon Heights. I generally spent a few hours each week down at the project seeing the ten boys in my group anyway, but I began to increase my trips to Clarendon Heights in both duration and frequency. I also made more of an effort to speak to the older guys, particularly members of the Hallway Hangers. But I had an exceptionally heavy academic workload that semester; my real fieldwork did not begin until February 1983 when I enrolled in a course in sociological field methods.

The course introduced me to the mechanics of ethnographic fieldwork. From readings, discussion, and an experienced professor, I learned about the techniques of participant observation, oral history analysis, unstructured interviews, and unobtrusive measures. I realized that the real learning would take place through firsthand experience in the field, but discussion of methods and the examination of representative sociological work using qualitative methods served as a valuable introduction.

My initial research forays into Clarendon Heights were awkward and tentative. I wanted to determine the nature of the teenagers' aspirations and the factors that contribute to their formation. Sensing that there was a conflict between the achievement ideology promulgated in school and the experiences of the boys' families, I particularly was interested in how this tension was resolved. But although it was obvious that the Brothers and the Hallway Hangers experienced school in different ways, I had no idea of the extensive disparity in their outlooks. Most of my trips down to Clarendon Heights in February and March were spent as they always had been: in the company of the younger kids in the youth program helping with homework, talking with parents, and generally maintaining contact with the families to which I had grown close. I also was spending some time with the Brothers, casually asking them about their aspirations, their high school programs, and their family backgrounds. This was possible because I had struck up friendships with Mike's closest friends: Super, Derek, and Craig. But with the Hallway Hangers my acceptance was progressing much more slowly. Those that I knew would return my greeting on the street, but I still was subject to the intimidating glares with which those outside the group are greeted when walking past doorway #13. There was also an element of fear involved. I knew of the fights that took place in and around doorway #13, the heavy drinking, the drugs, and the crime. I also knew of the abuse the Brothers suffered at the hands of the Hallway Hangers and realized that, in their eyes, I was to some extent associated with the Brothers. I was fascinated by the activity in doorway #13, but I needed an "in" with the Hallway Hangers if they were to be included in the study.

Basketball provided the opportunity I was looking for. The city's Social Services Department opened up the gym in the grammar school located just across the street from the Heights for a couple of hours on two weekday evenings. The Brothers were the first to take advantage of this opportunity for pick-up basketball, along with Hank White. Hank is a big muscular fellow, slightly older than most of the Hallway Hangers, who commands the respect or fear of everybody in the neighborhood. After his sophomore year in high school, Hank spent eighteen months in a maximum security prison for allegedly taking part in a rape behind the school building. With scars dotting his face, Hank conforms to the image of the stereotypical street "hood," and the manner with which he carries himself hardly dispels that impression. Nevertheless, he was the least racist of the Hallway Hangers, for in prison he had gotten to know and like a few blacks. He enjoyed playing basketball with the Brothers and was on good terms with all of them. We had seen each other around, but it wasn't until we were matched against one another on the basketball court one evening in early March that Hank took any real notice of me. Both of us are six feet tall, but Hank has the edge in strength and basketball ability. It was a good, hard game, and when it was over we walked back to the project together. It turned out he knew I was the student who ran the youth program. In parting, he grinned at me and told me to come back next week, "so I can kick your ass again."

Thus began my friendship with Hank. Only later would I discover that my new acquaintance was a convicted rapist, and by then I was prepared to believe the disavowals of his guilt. His apparent regard for me clearly influenced the light in which the other Hallway Hangers saw me and helped facilitate my acceptance by the group. If my team had won that evening, his friendliness may well have been enmity, and my status among his friends could have been of an entirely negative type. Still, basketball was turning out to be an important vehicle for gaining acceptance into the community.

The next week a number of the other Hallway Hangers turned up at the gym to play ball. Pick-up basketball, around Clarendon Heights at least, only vaguely resembles the game played at the college and professional level. Defense is almost nonexistent, passing is kept to a minimum, and flashy moves are at a premium. We had access to only half the gym, so we played cross-wise on a reduced court, a fortunate setup because none of us was in good shape. In fact, many of the Hallway Hangers would come in to play high or drunk or both. The games were nearly as verbal as they were physical. A constant chatter of good-natured kidding and self-congratulations could be heard from most players: "Gimme that fuckin' ball! I feel hot tonight. Bang! Get out of my face, Slick. I'll put those fucking fifteen footers in all day." Matched up against Hank again, I responded to his joking insults with abuse of my own, being ever so careful not to go too far. The Hallway Hangers present noticed my familiarity with Hank and treated me accordingly. I was making progress, but it was slow and not without its problems. Every step I gained was accompanied by apprehension and doubt. That night on the basketball court a vicious fight broke out between two people on the fringes of the Hallway Hangers. Everybody else seemed to take it in stride, but I was shaken by the bloody spectacle. I was entering a new world, and I wasn't certain I could handle the situations in which I might find myself. It was an exciting time, but it also provided moments of anxiety and consternation.

The next week, while waiting outside the gym with the Brothers, I was asked to play on a team they were putting together. I readily assented. I sensed that they were confused by my developing association with the Hallway Hangers and in a sense felt betrayed. That I could enjoy their company as well as those who openly and maliciously antagonized them was incomprehensible in their eyes. So I was anxious to reestablish my allegiance to the Brothers and saw participation on their team as a good way of doing so. That same evening, however, after the usual pick-up game, I was approached by Mark, one of Frankie's older brothers recently released from prison, who wanted me to play later that night for a Clarendon Heights team against another housing project across the city. I thought that there might be a league of some kind and, as I already was committed to a team, that I should forego the opportunity. But this was simply a one-time game he had arranged, and after checking with the Brothers, I consented.

About nine of us piled into two cars and sped, screeching around corners, three miles to a grammar school gym adjacent to Lipton Park Housing Development. We lost the game, and I played horrendously, but in terms of my project significant advances were made. There is nothing like a common adversary to solidify tenuous associations and dissolve differences. That night I felt in some sense part of the Hallway Hangers and was treated, in turn, simply as a member of the group. Of course, there were still barriers, and I obviously was different from the rest, a fact that was lost on nobody when they dropped me off at the university on the way home. Nevertheless, even while they jokingly derided me for my poor performance as I climbed out of the noisy, run-down Impala, I felt a sense of belonging that hitherto had eluded me.

Only a week later, however, the status I had managed to achieve in both groups was threatened. The Brothers challenged the Hallway Hangers and their older friends to a game of basketball. Although considerably younger and smaller than the white youths, the Brothers were generally more skilled on the court and, with Craig playing, promised to give the Hallway Hangers a good game. Knowing nothing of the situation, I walked into the gym to find the younger kids cleared off their half of the court. Instead of playing floor hockey or kickball, they were seated in the bleachers, which had been pulled out of the wall for the occasion. At one end of the full-length court the Brothers were shooting at a basket; at the other end the Hallway Hangers were warming up. I heard Super blurt out, "Oh yeah, here's Jay," but I also heard a voice from the other end bellow, "It's about fucking time, Jay; we thought we'd be playing without you." Both teams expected me to play for their side, and I had no idea what to do. To choose one team meant to alienate the other. My own inclination was to go with the Brothers. I remembered the contempt with which Juan had spoken of a white friend's neutrality when a fight had broken out at school between the Brothers and a gang of white kids. I had developed close friendships with Juan, Craig, Super, and Derek, and I didn't want to let them down. On the other hand, in terms of the dynamics of the fieldwork, I needed to move closer to the Hallway Hangers. Tying up my shoe laces, I frantically tried to think of a way out of the situation but came up short.

I walked out to the center of the court where a social service worker was waiting to referee the game. He seemed concerned about the possibility of the contest turning into a violent melee and looked none too happy about his own role. Trying to assume a noncommittal air, I sauntered over to the Brothers' side and took a few shots, then walked to the other end and did the same with the Hallway Hangers. The Hallway Hangers had Hank's older brother Robbie playing, a six-foot-four-inch hardened veteran of the army's special forces. I suggested that the Brothers could use me more, that with Robbie playing for the Hallway Hangers the game might be a blowout anyway. The curt response was something to the effect that if I wanted to play with "the niggers," that was my prerogative. Before I could reply, the referee shouted for me to play with the Brothers to even up the sides, and, hoping this intervention would mitigate the damage done, I trotted over to play with the Brothers.

The game was close and very rough, with several near-fights and nasty verbal exchanges sparked off by elbows flying under the backboards. We were much smaller than the Hallway Hangers and somewhat intimidated, but with Craig playing we undoubtedly had the most skillful player on the court. I made one lucky play early on that probably did more to establish my credibility among teenagers in the neighborhood than any other single incident. With Hank coasting in for an easy lay-up, I caught him from behind and somehow managed to block his shot, flinging the ball clear across the gym. The crowd, about fifty or sixty kids from the neighborhood, roared with surprise, for such ignominy very seldom befell Hank. The Brothers whooped with glee, slapping me on the back, and Hank's own teammates bombarded him with wisecracks. I couldn't suppress a grin, and Hank, taking it well, just sheepishly grinned back. Fortunately, the referee had whistled for a foul, which enabled Hank to maintain some "face." We ended up losing the game by one point, not least because I missed a foul shot in the last minute, but although bitterly disappointed, the Brothers had shown a much bigger and older team that they would not back down to them. The significance of events in the gym extended well beyond its walls, which is why such games between the two groups were contested with intensity and vigor.

At game's end, I made a point of walking back to the Heights with the Hallway Hangers, despite the questions it must have raised in the Brothers' minds as to where my loyalties really lay. As far as both groups were concerned, there was no middle ground between them. Each wondered which side I was on; my attempt to sit on the fence, I began to realize, was going to be a difficult balancing job. There would be other instances, like the basketball game, where a choice would have to be made. It was an uncomfortable position, one that plagued me throughout the research, but I derived some comfort from the fact that at least it indicated I was getting on with the fieldwork.

The research, in fact, made some significant advances that night. I hung around with the Hallway Hangers outside doorway #13 while they smoked cigarettes and talked about the game. Frankie began to insult the Brothers in no uncertain terms, glancing at me to gauge my reaction. Sensing he was trying to find out where I stood, I let it all slide, neither agreeing with him nor defending the Brothers. Finally, apparently satisfied, he said that it was a good thing I had played for the Brothers, for it had evened up the teams. In fact, it hadn't made that much of a difference, but Frankie wanted to believe that it was the sole white player on the opposition who had made the game a close one. In any case, it became clear that although my playing for the Brothers had jeopardized my standing with the Hallway Hangers, I was to emerge relatively unscathed. Soon Frankie and the others were laughing about the confusion a white player on the other team had caused, about how they had nearly passed the ball to me several times, and about the look on Hank's face when I had blocked his shot.

When I boarded the bus heading for the university, I was surprised to find Frankie right by me. Heading to see a girlfriend, he took the seat next to me and struck up a conversation. When we passed Lincoln High School, he pointed to a window in the school and noted that inside was his classroom. "What subject?" I asked, in response to which Frankie launched into a description of the Adjustment Class and his teacher Jimmy Sullivan, both of which fascinated me. He told me he hoped to graduate in June, that he'd be the first of his mother's six sons to do so. After describing his brothers' experiences in prison, Frankie related in a candid and poignant tone the vulnerability he felt in his role at the Heights. "I gotta get away. I gotta do somethin'. If I don't, I'm gonna be fucked; I know it. I ain't ready for fucking prison, man." I only had seen Frankie's hard exterior, and this quite unexpected glimpse of his feelings took me by surprise. In time, I became used to some of the toughest individuals confiding in me things they rarely could reveal to their peers. This particular episode with Frankie created a small bond between the two of us that had crucial implications for my fieldwork. My friendship with Hank was important, but he spent relatively little time actually hanging in the neighborhood with the Hallway Hangers. Frankie, on the other hand, was a fixture in doorway #13 and the undisputed leader of the group. I knew from other ethnographies that good rapport with one key member is often sufficient to gain entree to even the most closed group. William Foote Whyte's sponsorship by Doc allowed him access to the Norton Street gang,[2] and Elijah Anderson's relationship with Herman opened crucial doors to the social world of streetcorner men.[3] With Frankie's friendship, my entree into the Hallway Hangers' peer group was assured.

I remember quite distinctly the first time I actually hung in doorway #13. Of course, I'd gone into that particular stairwell countless times, for one of the boys in my youth group lived in the entryway. Even then I felt uncomfortable making my way up the dark, littered stairway through the teenagers sitting sprawled on the steps and leaning against the walls laughing, drinking beer, and smoking marijuana. Walking in with Frankie, however, was entirely different. Everybody looked up when we came in, but when Frankie initiated a conversation with me, they all, as if on cue, continued on as if I weren't there. No one questioned my presence, and I found it not at all difficult to participate in the discussions. Frankie was collecting money to buy a half pound of marijuana, Chris was peddling cocaine, and at one point someone I'd never seen before came in wanting to buy some heroin but was turned away empty-handed. My presence seemed to have no effect; it was business as usual in doorway #13.

I knew then that I had crossed an important boundary. In the weeks that followed I was amazed at how quickly I came to feel accepted by the Hallway Hangers and comfortable hanging with them in Clarendon Heights. Despite the fact that my home was in rural New Hampshire and that I was a college student, neither of which I concealed from the Hallway Hangers, I was young (looking even less than my twenty-one years), and I was white. Those two characteristics and Frankie's friendship apparently were enough to satisfy the Hallway Hangers. Without consciously intending to do so, I began to fit in in other ways. My speech became rough and punctuated more often with obscenities; I began to carry myself with an air of cocky nonchalance and, I fear, machismo; and I found myself walking in a slow, shuffling gait that admitted a slight swagger. These were not, on the conscious level at least, mere affectations but were rather the unstudied products of my increasing involvement with the Hallway Hangers. To a large degree I was unaware of these changes; they were pointed out to me by fellow students involved in the youth program.

The world of Clarendon Heights and the world of the university were at odds with each other in almost every conceivable way. To stand with one foot in each often proved a difficult posture. It was only a ten-minute bus ride from the dark squalid confines of doorway #13 to the richly decorated college dining hall with its high ceiling and ostentatious gold chandeliers. I remember turning up for dinner directly from the Heights and unthinkingly greeting one of my upper-class friends with, "Hey Howard, what the fuck you been up to?" His startled look reminded me of where I was, and I hurriedly added, "I mean, how's your work going?" The dichotomy between the university and Clarendon Heights and the different standards of behavior expected of me in each were not sources of constant angst, but I found it somewhat difficult to adjust to the constant role changes. That I talked, walked, and acted differently on campus than I did in Clarendon Heights did not seem inconsistent, affected, or artificial to me at the time, nor does it now. I behaved in the way that seemed natural to me, but as Whyte points out in describing his fieldwork, what was natural at the project was bound to be different from what was natural on the college campus.[4]

In Clarendon Heights I found myself playing a number of roles, and the conflicts among these caused me the greatest consternation. In the first place, I was Jay MacLeod, human being with personal needs, including that of maintaining a certain level of self-respect. The Hallway Hangers' racism angered me a great deal, and the feeling was especially pronounced because of my proximity to the Brothers. The deep emotional scars left on the victims of racial prejudice were only too apparent. So naturally I often had the inclination to confront the racism of the Hallway Hangers, to tell them, in their terms, to "fuck off." But as a researcher I was striving to understand the boys, not change them. Challenging their racism also would be of no great help in facilitating my acceptance by the Hallway Hangers. Thus, I generally kept my mouth shut, neither questioning their racist views nor defending the Brothers against bigoted remarks, an exception being the conversation that is used to introduce the Brothers in Chapter 3.

If my roles as a person and as an ethnographer sometimes conflicted, then my role as director of the youth program complicated the picture further. What did the mothers of kids in the program think of me hanging in doorway #13 with Frankie and Hank and company? This was especially serious because by that time I was associated very closely with the youth program. I was seen not just as a counselor but as the major force behind its inception and continued existence. To invite disapproval was to invite condemnation of the program. I was particularly sensitive to this issue because the youth program was still my main priority in Clarendon Heights. I tried to minimize my visibility when associating with the Hallway Hangers, a feat not particularly difficult because they preferred to stay out of view of the police. Still, when lingering outside with the Hallway Hangers, especially if they were "partying," I stepped away from the group or otherwise tried to distance myself when a mother approached. Not surprisingly, this was not a very effective maneuver, and the problem was never resolved completely.

Late one Friday night, after a great deal of alcohol and drugs had been consumed and the noise level in the hallway reflected the decreased inhibitions of the group, a mother whom I knew quite well threw open her door and yelled at everyone "to shut the hell up." Noticing me, she shook her head uncomprehendingly and went back to bed more than a little bewildered. To ease the conflict between these two roles as much as possible, I simply kept up contact with the children's parents so they could see for themselves that I was undergoing no drastic character change. Although never confronted by any of the mothers about my association with the Hallway Hangers, I sensed that it was an issue for them and that it was discussed behind my back.

However, I was able to use this role conflict to my advantage in one respect. One of the stickiest issues with which I was confronted was whether or not to join in with the drinking and use of drugs in doorway #13. As the activity in the hallway revolved to a large degree around the consumption of beer, marijuana, and other intoxicants, I could fit in most easily by doing the same. Still, I was inclined to abstain for a number of reasons. First, both are illegal in the hallway because it is public property, and I had no desire to be arrested. I already had seen Stoney arrested in doorway #13 for possession of mescaline, and a number of older youths also had been apprehended for various drug offenses. Second, I needed to be alert and perceptive in order to observe, understand, and unobtrusively participate in the dynamics of the social relations. I had enough trouble participating in the discussions and writing up accurate field notes when I was completely sober. Third, drug and alcohol use would have hurt my credibility with the children in the youth program and with their parents. This last reservation was the only one I could express to the Hallway Hangers, but they understood and accepted it completely. Although I sometimes had a shot of Peppermint Schnapps or whiskey and smoked an occasional joint, I generally abstained from using intoxicants.

Other facets of the Hallway Hangers' subculture raised few problems. I learned to take and deal out playful verbal abuse; although my wit was never as sharp as Slick's or Frankie's, my capping ability certainly improved in time. I also became comfortable with the physical jostling and sparring sessions that took place in doorway #13, although I was more careful than the others to make sure they didn't erupt into serious bouts. My strongest asset was my athletic ability, but it probably was exaggerated by my sobriety, whereas the Hallway Hangers often were impaired in one way or another. In addition to basketball, we used to play football on the hardtop area between the project's buildings. The favorite sport of white youths in the Heights, however, was street hockey, and even individuals well into their twenties got involved in the neighborhood games. Once I rediscovered a long-abandoned affinity for goalie, I strapped on Jinks's old pads and attempted to turn away the shots Shorty, Chris, Stoney, and the others would blast at the homemade goal we set up against doorway #13.

Another element of the Hallway Hangers' subculture with which I had difficulty, however, was the blatant sexism. Involved tales of sexual conquest were relatively rare; the Hallway Hangers generally didn't discuss the intricacies of their sexual lives. Still, it was quite obvious that they saw the woman's role in their relationships as purely instrumental. Women were stripped of all identity except for that bound up with their sexuality, and even that was severely restricted; the Hallway Hangers always spoke about their own experience, never about their partners' experiences. Women were reduced to the level of commodities, and the discussions in doorway #13 sometimes consisted of consumers exchanging information. "Yeah, fuckin' right, Tracy'll go down on you, man. She's got that nice long tongue, too." Because of the discomfort these conversations caused me, I avoided or ignored them whenever possible. This was a serious mistake. An analysis of the gender relations of the Hallway Hangers could have been a valuable addition to the study, but with very few field notes on the subject, I was in no position to put forth any sort of argument. I managed to stomach the racial prejudice of the Hallway Hangers and in striving to understand their racism came to see its cultural, political, and theoretical significance. Put off by their sexism, I missed an opportunity to understand it.

My fieldwork with the Brothers did not pose nearly as many complications. Neither my status as a student nor my white skin seemed to be grounds for their distrust, and with the help of my long-standing relationship with Mike, I had little difficulty gaining acceptance by the group. But with his involvement in school athletics, Mike began to spend less and less time with the Brothers during the week, and I was often the sole white person in a group of eight or nine blacks, an anomalous position that was especially pronounced when we went into black neighborhoods to play basketball. I tried to fit in by subtly affecting some of the culturally distinctive language and behavior of black youths. It wasn't until I greeted a working-class black friend at the university with "Yo Steve, what up?" and received a sharp, searching glance that I finally realized how unauthentic and artificial these mannerisms were. I dropped the pretensions and found that the Brothers were happy to accept me as I was. Although I naturally picked up some of their lingo, I felt more comfortable with the honest posture of an outsider to black culture. My ignorance of soul and funk music became something of a joke in the group, and they found my absolute inability to pick up even the most basic breakdancing moves greatly amusing.

The Brothers were interested in university life, both the educational and social sides; after a discussion of their attitudes toward Lincoln High School I invariably was called upon to relate my own college experiences. On a couple of occasions I invited them to productions sponsored by the university black students' association—plays and movies—and they seemed to enjoy and appreciate these outings. Personal friendships with each of the Brothers were much more easily and naturally established than with the Hallway Hangers and were less subject to the vicissitudes of status delineations within the group. Whereas the respect I was accorded by many of the Hallway Hangers was based initially on my friendship with Frankie, with the Brothers I was able to establish a series of distinct one-to-one relationships. Spending time with the Brothers may have been less exciting than hanging in doorway #13, but it was certainly more relaxing and pleasurable. The only strain between me and the Brothers arose because of my continued association with the Hallway Hangers. Although I was never confronted directly on this issue by the Brothers (as I was by the Hallway Hangers), they began to recount with increased frequency stories of physical and verbal abuse at the hands of the Hallway Hangers. The implication of the stories and their searching glances was clear; although the Brothers never stated it directly, they wanted to know why I was spending so much time with the Hallway Hangers. Fortunately, it wasn't long before they were provided with an answer.

By April, having established a level of trust with both the Brothers and the Hallway Hangers, I felt ready to go beyond the unobtrusive research techniques I had thus far adopted. Hitherto I had been content to elicit as much information from the youths as I could under the guise of curiosity. I knew in which high school program each of the Brothers was enrolled and had an idea of the occupational aspirations of each boy. But for the Hallway Hangers, who were less tolerant of my questions, I had very sketchy data. I needed to explain to both groups the proposed study, my role as researcher, and their role as subjects. This I did in a casual way before initiating a conversation on their aspirations. I simply explained that to graduate from college, I must write a lengthy paper and that instead of doing a lot of research in a library, "I'm gonna write it on you guys down here and what kinds of jobs you want to go into after school and stuff like that." In general, they seemed happy to be the subjects of my research and patiently answered my questions, which became gradually more direct, pointed, and frequent.

Actually, I probably should have explained my project to them much earlier, but I wanted to be considered "okay" before springing on the youths my academic interest in them. I also was reluctant to be forthright about my research intentions because I was afraid some of the Brothers whom I'd befriended would see our relationship as based on academic necessity rather than personal affinity. This wasn't the case, although there was certainly an element of truth in it, which is doubtless why it bothered me. Neither the Brothers nor the Hallway Hangers, however, seemed as sensitive to this issue as I was. Although my researcher status added a new dimension to my relationship with each youth, all seemed willing to accept and distinguish between my academic agenda and my personal regard.

The revelation of my scholarly interest in the boys had one very important positive ramification. It gave me a special position in both groups, a niche that justified my continued presence but set me apart from the others. Whereas previously neither the Brothers nor the Hallway Hangers could understand my association with the other group, my involvement with both became much more explicable once I revealed in full my intentions. As Frankie explained to a fringe member of the Hallway Hangers who confronted me as I emerged from Super's apartment, "No man, see, to do his shit right for his studies he's got to check out the fuckin' niggers, too." Likewise, the Brothers had more tolerance for the time I spent with the Hallway Hangers. Although simultaneous affiliation with both peer groups still caused problems for which there was no solution and with which I found myself constantly burdened, the situation improved significantly.

This position of being at once of and yet apart from the group had other positive implications, especially for my standing with the Hallway Hangers. There are many things that go along with membership in that subculture of which I wanted no part: the violence, the excessive consumption of alcohol and drugs, and the strident racism and sexism. Had I completely integrated myself into the group, I would have been expected to partake of all of the above. Fortunately, the unwritten rules that govern the behavior of the Hallway Hangers did not always apply to me. Had I been vociferously insulted by another member, for instance, I would not be confronted necessarily with the only two options normally open to an individual in that situation: fight or lose a great deal of social standing in the group. For this special status within the group I was thankful.

I was not, however, totally free of the group's status delineations. The fact that I spent a good deal of time with the Hallway Hangers talking, joking, exchanging insults, and playing sports meant that I could not stay entirely outside the group's pecking order, even if my position in it was very fluid. My friendships with Hank and, especially, Frankie must have troubled those who received less attention from them when I was present. I wanted to excel in some of the things that matter to the Hallway Hangers in order to gain their respect, but attempting to do so necessarily threatened the status of others in the group. It was the same situation I faced on the basketball court that first evening with Hank: I wanted to play well, but I didn't want to imperil his status on the court. Hanging in doorway #13, I learned to be acutely aware of status demarcations and the threat I posed to the standing of other individuals. I would try to placate those whose positions suffered at my expense by self-disparagement and by consciously drawing attention to their superiority over me. I'm certain that I was not as sensitive to these situations as I could have been, but I did come to realize the importance of minimizing the degree to which I could be regarded as a threat by other members of the group. The success of my project depended on good relations not just with Frankie and Slick, but with Shorty, Chris, Boo-Boo, Stoney, Steve, and Jinks as well.

Once I told the youths of my sociological interest in them, I set about gathering information more aggressively. I was intent on amassing material on their attitudes toward school and subsequent employment, but I was still very much at the reconnaissance stage; these unstructured interviews were a preliminary ground survey. Still, my conversations with boys from both groups often were quite lengthy and covered a great many topics. Taping the discussions or taking notes, obviously, was out of the question, so I was forced to rely on my memory. After a conversation with one of the boys, I'd hop on the bus and return to my dorm room immediately, preferably without speaking to anyone, and promptly write up the interview. At first, I made summary notes of the interview, remembering as much of what was said as I could and putting it in paragraph format. I was able to recall more, however, when I tried to reconstruct the interview word for word and wrote it up in script form with each question and answer. The more interviews I conducted and recorded, the better my concentration and memory became, until I could recall most of what was said in a thirty-minute discussion. Writing up the interview as soon as possible with no distractions was crucial. I remember having an excellent discussion with Super, Mokey, and Craig on the way to play basketball at the Salvation Army gym. But after playing two hours of ball, conversing on the way back to the Heights, and finally returning to my room to write up the interview, I had forgotten a great deal of it. Writing up interviews was extraordinarily tedious, especially because after conducting a good interview one wants to relax, but the importance of good field notes was impressed upon me by my professor and was indeed borne out by my own experience.

The requirements for my field methods course spurred me to conduct as many unstructured interviews as I could, for by mid-May I had to produce a paper on my project. By that time I had managed to conduct interviews with fourteen boys, eleven of whom would end up in the final study. I had information on all seven of the Brothers, but only on Chris, Boo-Boo, Stoney, and Frankie of the Hallway Hangers. Except in the cases of Mike and Frankie, the material was very thin, often including not much more than their high school programs, their attitudes toward school, and their expressed aspirations or expectations.

To gain a measure of understanding of the high school curriculum I obtained a detailed course catalogue and conducted an interview with Karen Wallace, the school's career counselor. That I was compelled to examine and organize the data I had collected and search it for patterns and findings at that stage of the research was fortunate. Fieldwork is an organic process that should include a nearly continuous analysis and reorganization of the material into patterns and models that in turn guide the fieldwork in new directions. Writing the final paper for the class forced me to consolidate my research, and although a detailed picture of the social landscape did not emerge, I did gain a vantage point from which to formulate a strategy for exploring in greater depth the terrain staked out for study.

That strategy included fieldwork in the Lincoln School: observation in the classroom and semiformal interviews with teachers, guidance counselors, and administrators. I also planned to interview as many of the Hallway Hangers' and Brothers' parents to whom I could gain access as possible, a number I estimated at about one-half the total. Most importantly, I decided to conduct semiformal, in-depth interviews with all of the boys. My research demanded detailed data on each boy's family background and their experiences in and approaches to school and work, information I could elicit most effectively in private discussions relatively free of distraction. I was unable to construct with sufficient depth a portrait of each individual by piecing together the bits and pieces of data I collected on the street, no matter how much time I spent with each group; I needed to sit down and talk with each boy for an hour or so to gather simple data, such as family members' occupational histories, as well as to probe intricate issues like the degree to which each had internalized the achievement ideology. To this end, I drew up an interview guide, a list of questions that I wanted answered in each discussion. I did not always stick to the guide, but having it before me in abbreviated form prevented me from missing crucial questions when the conversation got too intriguing. The guide also jogged my memory when I wrote up the discussion.

Unfortunately, the interview guide lay dormant for nearly two months, and much of the ethnographic strategy never saw the light of day at all. I simply was too busy with the youth program during the spring and summer to concentrate on the research. I failed to do any substantive fieldwork in the high school aside from conducting interviews with Bruce Davis and Jimmy Sullivan, and in Clarendon Heights I only managed to undertake interviews with Derek and Chris. But in September 1983 my work got a big boost.

Instead of returning to a university dormitory, I moved into a recently vacated, rent-controlled apartment in a large tenement building directly across the street from Clarendon Heights. It was a run-down, cockroach-infested dwelling, but it was large, cheap, and gave me a much-needed base where people could find me and I could conduct interviews. This move enhanced my research in vital ways. Spending time with the Brothers and the Hallway Hangers was no longer a commuting hassle but rather a break from studying, a way to relax and enjoy myself. Living in Clarendon Heights, despite my continued status as a full-time student, also gave me a better feeling for the rhythm of the community and further reduced the degree to which I was an outsider, both in their eyes and in mine. Although my residence in the neighborhood was not free of complications, it marked a positive new development in my research and in my relationship with the entire community.

I began interviewing individuals in the apartment in October. The interviews would last approximately an hour, and I found that even if I made extensive notes it was difficult to recall with precision all that had been said. Finally, I decided that the formality of a tape recorder would be no worse than the formality of the interview guide. I tried it a few times, and although it certainly made people self-conscious at the beginning of the interview and probably deterred some of the Hallway Hangers from being as frank as they might have been about their criminal exploits, the benefits seemed to outweigh the disadvantages. Transcribing the tapes, however, was just as tedious as writing up the discussions from memory, for it generally took at least four or five hours and sometimes up to seven.

Both the Brothers and the Hallway Hangers regarded these interviews as a favor to me. The Brothers generally were more accommodating; I had little difficulty cajoling them up to my apartment for the required session. The Hallway Hangers were more elusive. Theirs is a world in which something is very seldom had for nothing, and they saw quite clearly that there was nothing in this project for them. I was the one meeting an academic requirement for a college degree, a principal attainment in my own pursuit of "success." In a year's time I would be studying on a scholarship in Oxford, England; most of the Hallway Hangers would be back in doorway #13, in the armed forces, or in prison. To be fair, I had contributed to the community through the youth program, as the Hallway Hangers were well aware. They didn't see me as "using" them. However, they did sense an imbalance in the relationship, and when I requested an hour of their time to level a barrage of personal questions at them, many of the Hallway Hangers vaguely expected something in return.

It soon became clear, however, that I had very little to give. I couldn't help the Hallway Hangers with their academic work as I did with the Brothers because those who were still in school very seldom did any. I did assist Slick when he was struggling to finish the work required for his G.E.D., and some of the Hallway Hangers would approach me about legal or personal problems with the often mistaken hope that I could be of some help. More often, however, the requests were less innocent.

Like all the people aged twenty or so who spent any time in doorway #13, I was asked to buy beer for the Hallway Hangers. These requests put me in a difficult position. I wanted to be of some use to the Hallway Hangers, but, well aware of the debilitating role of alcohol in their lives, I didn't want to buy them beer. Moreover, although the risk of police detection was not particularly high, other Clarendon Heights tenants easily might discover what I was doing. Nevertheless, I did make a couple of trips to the local package store for the Hallway Hangers. Those two trips attest, I think, to the unease I felt about the one-way nature of my involvement with the Hallway Hangers, to my desire to maintain my standing in the group, and, of course, to their powers of persuasion and manipulation. One of the biggest mistakes one can make in the company of the Hallway Hangers is to appear hesitant or uncertain; after I decided that buying beer for them was ethically dubious and pragmatically stupid, I answered their subsequent requests with an adamant "no" and was frank and honest in dealing with their appeals and protests.

Despite the fact that there continued to be much take and little give in my relationship with the Hallway Hangers, I did manage to get them all up to my apartment for a taped interview that autumn. In the end, sensing how important it was to me, the Hallway Hangers did the interviews as a personal favor. Some of them consented immediately, and we did the interview as soon as we had some common time free. Getting some of the others up to my apartment in front of the tape recorder was a significant achievement. Stoney, for example, is a very private person. Rather than undergo the weekly ordeal of having to talk about his "drug problem" with a counselor at the city's drug clinic, Stoney opted for a three-month stint in the county jail. In trying to gauge the influence his mother has on him, I asked in the actual interview if they had ever discussed his performance in school. "I didn't talk to her that much. I'm not the type of person who opens up and talks to people. That's why it took you so long to get me up here. I go to the drug clinic, and the lady just asks me questions. I hate it. I just ask her back why she wants to ask me this for. I'm not into it. I'm just doing this for a favor to you."

Once up in the apartment, many of the Hallway Hangers actually seemed to enjoy the interview. Boo-Boo and Frankie both stated that it was good to discuss and examine their feelings and thoughts. I was impressed by the honesty and thoughtfulness with which the Hallway Hangers answered my often probing questions. The Brothers were no less candid, but I had expected the Hallway Hangers to be less forthright and honest. Only Shorty refused to take the interview seriously and maintained a level of distance and invulnerability throughout the session.

Chris and Jinks came up to the apartment together. As Chris already had been interviewed, Jinks and I left him in the kitchen and went into the small room I used as a study where we talked for nearly ninety minutes. We emerged to find Chris sitting at the kitchen table smoking a joint. On the table was a mound of marijuana, probably a half pound, which Chris was rolling mechanically into thin joints at an amazing pace. Chris must have seen the look of surprise on my face because he immediately offered up a couple of joints to placate me. Jinks and I had a good laugh but were interrupted by the doorbell. My mirth faded quickly as I figured that with my luck the police were onto Chris and had picked this opportune moment to make the arrest. Fortunately, it was only Craig and Super inviting me to play ball in the park. I declined and quickly shut the door before they could catch a glimpse of Chris and Jinks or a whiff of the joint. I sat in the study and began to transcribe the tape while in the kitchen Chris rolled his joints and Jinks smoked.

I conducted a number of discussions with more than one individual, but one really stands out in importance for the amount of information it produced. On a cold afternoon in December I managed to assemble Frankie, Slick, Shorty, Chris, and Jinks in my apartment. The discussion, which lasted more than an hour and a half, began this way.

FRANKIE: Okay, man, ask us a fucking question, that's the deal.

JM: I wanna know what each of you wants to do, now and . . .

CHRIS: I wanna get laid right now (*laughter*).

JM: Everyone tell me what they wanna be doing in twenty years.

SHORTY: Hey, you can't get no education around here unless if you're fucking rich, y'know? You can't get no education. Twenty years from now Chris'll prob'ly be in some fucking gay joint, whatever (*laughter*). And we'll prob'ly be in prison or dead (*laughter*). You can't get no education around here.

JM: How's that though? Frankie, you were saying the other day that this city has one of the best school systems around (*all laugh except Frankie*).

FRANKIE: Lincoln is the best fucking school system going, but we're all just fucking burnouts. We don't give a fuck.

SHORTY: I ain't a fucking burnout, man.

JINKS: (*sarcastically*) You're all reformed and shit, right?

SHORTY: Shut up, potato head.

I had very little control of the interview and wasn't able to cover all of the ground that I'd hoped to, but the material that emerged as the conversation swept along from subject to subject was very rich and poignant. Disagreements and conflicts between individuals, some of which I actively probed, produced some fervid and well-argued viewpoints that never would have emerged from an individual interview. It took me an entire day to transcribe the discussion, and I never had time to conduct another one, but the yield from this group interview was very impressive. Although the ethnographer must weigh the impact of the dynamics of the discussion on its content, this added task should not deter researchers from cultivating this fertile area more thoroughly than I did.

By November, time constraints were cutting into more than my capacity to conduct group interviews. I had to scrap my plans to do any kind of extensive fieldwork in the school. Although I only had interviewed half the subjects in the study, I already had accumulated more than three hundred pages of field notes and interview transcriptions. I desperately wanted to interview as many of the youths' parents as I could, for I saw that as crucial to the study. In fact, I still see it as crucial to the study, but I simply did not have the time to conduct interviews with more than two mothers—Stoney's and Mokey's. Chapter 3 consequently is incomplete, and I think the study as a whole suffers from the limitations on my research into each boy's family. Another important item on my fieldwork agenda that I never was able to carry out and that would have been quite enjoyable was hanging at Pop's, the little store where the Hallway Hangers and their friends congregated during the school day. These casualties of my research strategy were the unfortunate results of my full-time student status and of the community work with which I continued to be involved in Clarendon Heights.

After I moved into the apartment, I found myself entwined in the lives of many families to a degree I hadn't experienced before. Youngsters in the youth program would stop by to say hello or to ask for help with their schoolwork, as did the Brothers. During this period I became very close friends with Billy, the former member of the Hallway Hangers who had won a scholarship to college as a high school junior the previous spring. Billy was struggling with the academic workload of the Fundamental School, having recently switched from Occupational Education, so I ended up spending about ten hours a week assisting him with homework, advising him about college admissions, and generally just hacking around. I also became a regular tutor to an eighth grader who had been in my youth group the previous three summers. He really was struggling in school, both academically and with respect to discipline, and at his mother's urging I met with his teachers, but to no particular avail. In none of these roles did I consider myself a social worker. I was simply a friend, and I probably got more out of these relationships in terms of personal satisfaction and fulfillment than they got from me. Sometimes the rewards were more tangible: A Haitian family to which I'd grown particularly close used to cook me a delicious West Indian meal about once a week, brought to my apartment wrapped in dish towels by nine-year-old Mark, fourteen-year-old Kerlain, or sixteen-year-old Rhodes.

Despite the fact that I never was viewed as a social worker, except perhaps as a very unorthodox and informal one, I was approached more and more often by people with serious problems. I stopped by to see Freddie Piniella, a tough little twelve-year-old kid whom I'd known for three years. He wasn't home, but his mother was. Mrs. Piniella always had maintained a cool distance from me, but suddenly she began to relate in a subdued, beaten tone her daughter Vicki's predicament. Vicki was a resilient fourteen-year-old girl whose violent temper, exceptionally loud voice, and strong frame made her at once an object of grudging admiration and resentment by her peers. Mrs. Piniella had found out that morning that Vicki was pregnant, well past her first trimester. She would need to have an abortion, but Mrs. Piniella had less than eighty dollars in the bank, and the cost of terminating such a late pregnancy was more than five hundred dollars. Mrs. Piniella, a part-time custodial worker at the university, was on welfare, but the state would under no circumstances, not even rape, fund abortions. I agreed to try finding a hospital or clinic that would carry out the operation at a reduced cost, but none of the places I contacted would do so for a pregnancy beyond the third month. Nor could Planned Parenthood or any other agency direct me to a hospital that would.

I returned the next day to report this news, only to hear from her very depressed mother that Vicki, it turned out, had gonorrhea as well. Eventually a social worker attached to the local health clinic located a hospital that would accept a reduced payment on a monthly basis, and Vicki had the abortion and was treated for venereal disease. I don't know how Vicki managed to cope with the strain of the whole experience, but I spoke with her the next week, and she seemed very composed. Her plight had quite an effect on me and pointed up the dichotomy between Clarendon Heights and the university more starkly than ever. It was an ironic contrast to learn of her predicament and then to hear the consternation my student friends were expressing about their upcoming midterm exams.

One morning in mid-December I was awakened by the door buzzer at four o'clock. It was a very cold Super who had left home two days earlier after being beaten by his father. I found a blanket, and he slept on my couch. Later that morning we tried to decide what to do. Super was adamant in his refusal even to consider going home and trying to reach some sort of reconciliation with his parents. He had come that night from his uncle's apartment on the other side of the city, but reported that his uncle had a severe drinking problem and was prone to violent outbreaks. With nowhere else to go, Super urged me to find a place for him in a home for runaways. So together we embarked on a very circuitous, time-consuming, and frustrating exploration of the social service bureaucracy. No shelter for teenagers would accept Super without a referral from a social worker, but the city's Social Services Department would not assign him one. Instead, they insisted on tracking down his family's social worker, a process that took four days. We finally got the woman's name and phoned her office repeatedly, but she must have been exceedingly busy because we never heard back from her. I called the high school, and Super finally managed to get one of the youth workers attached to the school to secure him a place in a teenage runaway home. By that time, however, all the beds were full, and he was put on a waiting list. Finally, after more than a week with me, Super moved into a youth home for ten days before returning to his family in Clarendon Heights. I always had assumed that the stories I'd heard from residents about the inefficiency and ineptitude of the social services bureaucracy were exaggerated. Now I was not so sure, although the problem clearly lay not with the social workers themselves; the problem was too little funding and too much work. It was, however, especially frustrating to be asked by those who could not deal effectively with Super's situation whether I was aware that it was against the law to harbor a runaway.

During the year I spent conducting research in Clarendon Heights I often was troubled by legal issues. By spending time with the Hallway Hangers in doorway #13 I quite clearly ran the risk of arrest, but this was not especially distressing. Had I been corralled in one of the periodic police raids of the hallway, the charges against me would have been minimal, if any were brought at all. Although being in the presence of those smoking marijuana was illegal, possession of narcotics, especially with intent to sell, is what the police were generally after. Still, I saw people arrested in Clarendon Heights for simply having a beer in their hand, so I had to contend with the possibility of arrest. Had that happened, I certainly would have had a lot of explaining to do: to kids in the youth program and their parents, to the Brothers, to university officials, and to my parents.

A greater cause for concern was my unprotected legal status as a researcher. Whereas lawyers, journalists, doctors, and clergy can withhold information to protect their clients, for academic researchers there is no clearcut right of confidentiality. If any law enforcement official came to know about my study, my field notes could be used as evidence, and I could be put on the witness stand and questioned. In such a situation I would have two options: incriminate my friends or perjure myself. To avoid such a dilemma, my field methods professor urged me to explain to the youths that I preferred not to hear about their criminal exploits or at least not to record their accounts in my notes. But I found the criminal activity of the Hallway Hangers very interesting and also quite relevant to the study. Besides, my legal position was no different from their own. The Hallway Hangers had all the information I did, undoubtedly more, and they had no legal coverage, nor were they particularly worried about it. I was a more likely source for the district attorney because as a university student I was presumably less concerned about indicting my friends than I would be about lying under oath. Not wanting to draw attention to this fact and risk losing the trust of the Hallway Hangers, I made no effort to remain ignorant of potentially incriminating information, although I destroyed or erased all the interview tapes and was exceptionally careful with my field notes.

In fact, one absolutely hallowed rule among the Hallway Hangers and a large proportion of the project's older residents was not to "rat" to the police. As an ethnographer I wasn't interested in passing an ethical judgment on this maxim. I was there to understand as much as I could, and selective noncooperation with the police seemed to make sense as a means of self-protection for a certain segment of the community. When I saw two young men who recently had been released from prison arrested while they sat quietly drinking bottles of beer on the steps of doorway #13 and realized that the "offense" would mean up to six months in prison for them as a violation of parole, I began to appreciate people's reluctance to cooperate with the police.

My own subscription to this maxim was put to a very serious test in mid-October. Paddy, a Green Berets veteran on the fringes of the Hallway Hangers, shot his girlfriend Doreen, and I was the sole witness. Doreen, whom I knew well, wasn't critically wounded; the bullet pierced her arm and lodged in her breast, and after undergoing surgery she recovered rapidly and was out of the hospital in a few days. The details of the incident and subsequent events are too involved to relate here, so I'll concentrate on the issues I had to face as a citizen, as a researcher, and as a member of the Clarendon Heights community.

I was questioned by the police at the scene of the crime first as a suspect and then as a witness. I hadn't actually seen the shooting itself, but I had overheard the preceding altercation from within my apartment and knew what had happened. My first inclination was to relate everything, but I checked myself and repeatedly told the officers only what I'd seen after hearing the shot and running out into the street, thereby leaving out the key incriminating material I had heard. Doreen, it turned out, also refused to incriminate Paddy, but the police were nevertheless quite confident that he had committed the crime. He was arrested, but when Doreen refused to bring criminal charges, it looked as though the case might be dropped. Instead, the state decided to press charges, and I soon received a letter from an assistant district attorney asking me to phone him.

I was faced with a serious problem. Do I tell the whole truth, incriminate Paddy, and see justice done the American way? I had a number of doubts about this course, not all of them pragmatic, such as my physical well-being, my standing in the community, and the future of the study. Practically speaking, to "finger" Paddy would have had disastrous consequences, and I think most people under the circumstances would have balked at full cooperation with the authorities. I also happen to think that withholding information was not only expedient but also morally justifiable. Such an opinion may be pure self-delusion, as most people to whom I've related the incident seem to think, but from my position I couldn't help feeling that way.

As a member of the Clarendon Heights community and more particularly as a trusted associate of the Hallway Hangers, I felt in some ways that it was incumbent upon me to subscribe to their behavioral codes. There were obviously limits to this adherence; other duties or commitments (e.g., to justice) could override this allegiance to the group's rules of conduct, but I definitely felt in some sense drawn to respect the code of silence.

There were, of course, competing impulses. Paddy had shot and could easily have killed Doreen, and no community wants to tolerate that sort of behavior. Yet they were both very high and very drunk, and a violent argument had precipitated the incident. In addition, the shooting was not completely intentional (she was shot through a closed door), and Paddy immediately had repented of his action, rushing her amid hysterical tears to the hospital. Moreover, Doreen herself had lied in order to protect Paddy, and the two of them were back living together within a matter of days. But although I was conscious of these circumstances, they failed to diminish my conviction that Paddy should be punished.

Still, having spent the bulk of the previous summer researching prison life as part of a project undertaken by the kids in my youth group, and having tutored inmates at a state prison, I knew only too well what kind of impact a stint behind bars was likely to have on Paddy. In the end, this proved decisive. I was unwilling to jeopardize all that I had gained in Clarendon Heights in order to put Paddy in prison when he was likely to come out a much more dangerous person.

I decided to say nothing about the argument that preceded the shooting. When the trial finally took place in midwinter after a number of postponements, Paddy was found guilty despite my incomplete testimony, so all my speculation turned out to be academic. Convicted of illegal possession of a firearm, illegal discharge of a firearm, and assault with a deadly weapon, Paddy was sentenced to serve two years in a state prison. I didn't feel good about my role in the proceedings, especially refraining from providing information under oath, but neither did I lose sleep over the incident. Bourgeois morality has diminished relevance in a place like Clarendon Heights where the dictates of practical necessity often leave very little "moral" ground on which to stand.

During the fall of 1983 I felt myself drawn into the community as I had never been before, into its political and social life and into the web of personal, economic, and social problems that plague its residents. At the university, I had a full academic schedule, a work-study job, and a large extracurricular load. It was a very busy time, and I also found it emotionally draining, especially in trying to reconcile the two lives I led: the one on the university campus and the other on the streets of Clarendon Heights.

It was, of course, this study that bridged the two worlds. One of the most challenging (and rewarding) aspects of an ethnographic study is the synthesis the sociologist must create between a perceived intellectual tradition and the data daily emerging from the fieldwork. Without a theoretical framework to make some sense of the overwhelming quantity and variety of empirical material, the researcher would be swimming in a sea of field notes, each new interview tossing him or her in a different direction. By the same token, there is all too much theoretical abstraction with no experiential grounding whatsoever coming from scholars who are locked in their academic offices. This book began with a review of reproduction theory and, after the ethnographic material was laid out, moved on to a reconsideration of the theoretical perspective. That is the way this intellectual enterprise was actually carried out, although the progression was not nearly so linear. Since the beginning of the fieldwork in spring 1983 I had been studying the theoretical literature. The thinking of Bowles and Gintis, Bourdieu, Bernstein, and especially Willis (I didn't read Giroux until long afterward) informed my own thinking at every stage of the research. My empirical data and the theoretical perspective were held in a kind of dialectical tension, and I found myself moving back and forth between the two until my own ideas coalesced.

The emergence of my ideas was a slow, circuitous process; I had expected to have problems analyzing the data, but the earlier stage of simply organizing the empirical material proved more difficult than I had foreseen. By January 1984 I had in excess of five hundred pages of field notes. By March I had to turn this mass of data into a senior honors thesis. I knew the analytical and theoretical sections would prove intellectually taxing, but I didn't realize how difficult it would be to organize my notes into the basically descriptive chapters on the peer group, family, work, and school.

I failed to make theoretical notes throughout the months of research. I had plenty of notes depicting events and conversations, but kept no record of my more abstract sense of the observed phenomena. By November, the ideas that make up the backbone of Chapter 7 were beginning to emerge, albeit in a rough and rudimentary form. I was especially cognizant of these ideas in carrying out the remaining interviews and strove to collect information that would help determine the validity of my fresh theoretical discernments. The entire research period, in fact, involved a nearly constant appraisal and reappraisal of abstract ideas I thought could help me make sense of the data. But, ludicrously, I kept no written record of the development of these ideas. I would mentally cultivate and modify my views in line with the empirical material, but I should have noted after every interview how the new data had forced revisions in or had affirmed my previous thinking. Had I kept such notes, the stage between the end of my fieldwork and the beginning of the actual writing would have been considerably less hectic and would have filled me with much less dread.

I remember spending days reading through my field notes again and again, sifting through the material trying to come up with an organizational framework. I began keeping a record of all new insights, some of which would come to me at the most bizarre times and places, often touched off by a chance incident or a stray comment. In order to get some sort of grasp on the data, I developed a one page index for each youth, on which I recorded information that struck me as particularly relevant or important. Perhaps the most useful organizing tool I employed was a huge chart that contained for each individual information on the following specifications: race, peer group, high school grade level, school program, expressed aspiration, acceptance of achievement ideology, faith in the efficacy of schooling, father in the household, employment of father, employment of mother, educational attainments of parents, duration of tenancy in public housing, duration of tenancy in Clarendon Heights, and whether the subject smokes cigarettes, drinks alcohol, smokes marijuana, or has been arrested. Once the data had been systematically laid out, patterns began to emerge.

Such patterns gave form and further meaning to the lives of these boys and helped me measure the relative significance of the various structural and cultural factors that shape aspirations. Ultimately, however, it was on the basketball court with the Brothers or in doorway #13 with the Hallway Hangers that I gained whatever understanding I eventually achieved.

NOTES

1. William Foote Whyte, *Street Corner Society* (Chicago: University of Chicago Press, 1943), p. 279.
2. Ibid.
3. Elijah Anderson, *A Place on the Corner* (Chicago: University of Chicago Press, 1978).
4. Whyte, *Street Corner Society*, p. 304.

BIBLIOGRAPHY

Anderson, Elijah. *A Place on the Corner.* Chicago: University of Chicago Press, 1978.

Anderson, J., and F. Evans. "Family Socialization and Educational Achievement in Two Cultures: Mexican American and Anglo-American." *Sociometry* 39 (1976):209–222.

Apple, Michael W. *Education and Power.* Boston: Routledge and Kegan Paul, 1982.

Apple, Michael W. *Ideology and Curriculum.* Boston: Routledge and Kegan Paul, 1979.

Atkinson, Paul. *Language, Structure and Reproduction.* London: Methuen, 1985.

Banks, Olive. *The Sociology of Education.* London: B. T. Batsfield, 1976.

Bennett, T. *Popular Culture: History and Theory.* London: Open University Press, 1981.

Bernstein, Basil. *Class, Codes and Control.* London: Routledge and Kegan Paul, 1975.

Bernstein, Basil. "Social Class, Language, and Socialization." In *Power and Ideology in Education.* Ed. Jerome Karabel and A. H. Halsey. New York: Oxford University Press, 1977.

Bourdieu, Pierre. "Cultural Reproduction and Social Reproduction." In *Power and Ideology in Education.* Ed. Jerome Karabel and A. H. Halsey. New York: Oxford University Press, 1977.

Bourdieu, Pierre. *Outline of a Theory of Practice.* Cambridge: Cambridge University Press, 1977.

Bourdieu, Pierre, and Jean-Claude Passeron. *Reproduction in Education, Society, and Culture.* London: Sage, 1977.

Bowles, Samuel, and Herbert Gintis. *Schooling in Capitalist America.* New York: Basic Books, 1976.

Burris, Val. Rev. of *Learning to Labor,* by Paul Willis. *Harvard Educational Review* 50 (November 1980):523–526.

Campbell, Anne. *The Girls in the Gang.* Oxford: Basil Blackwell, 1984.

Centre for Contemporary Cultural Studies. *The Empire Strikes Back.* London: Hutchinson, 1982.

Chinoy, Ely. *Automobile Workers and the American Dream.* Boston: Beacon Press, 1955.

Clark, Burton. "The 'Cooling-Out' Function in Higher Education." *American Journal of Sociology* 65 (1960):576–596.

Corrigan, Paul. *Schooling the Smash Street Kids.* London: Macmillan, 1979.

Dillon, David. "Does the School Have a Right to Its Own Language?" *The English Journal* 69 (April 1980):13–17.

Dimaggio, Paul. "Cultural Capital and Social Success." *American Sociological Review* 47 (April 1982):189–201.

Durkheim, Emile. *The Division of Labor in Society.* New York: Free Press, 1953.

Erikson, Erik H. *Gandhi's Truth.* New York: Norton, 1969.

Erikson, Kai T. *Everything in Its Path.* New York: Simon and Schuster, 1976.

Findley, Warren G., and Mirian M. Bryan. *Ability Grouping: A Review of the Literature,* part 3. Washington, D.C.: Office of Education, 1970.

Gecas, Viktor. "Contexts of Socialization." In *Social Psychology: Sociological Perspectives.* Ed. Morris Rosenberg and Ralph H. Turner. New York: Basic Books, 1981.

Giroux, Henry A. "Theories of Reproduction and Resistance in the New Sociology of Education." *Harvard Educational Review* 53 (August 1983):257–293.

Giroux, Henry A. *Theory & Resistance in Education.* London: Heinemann Educational Books, 1983.

Goldthorpe, John H. *Social Mobility and Class Structure in Modern Britain.* Oxford: Clarendon Press, 1980.

Gordon, Liz. "Paul Willis—Education, Cultural Production and Social Reproduction." *British Journal of Sociology of Education* 5 (1984):105–115.

Gramsci, Antonio. *Selections from Prison Notebooks.* London: Lawrence and Wishart, 1971.

Halsey, A. H., A. F. Heath, and J. M. Ridge. *Origins and Destinations.* Oxford: Clarendon Press, 1980.

Haraven, Tamara K., and Randolph Langenbach. *Amoskeag.* New York: Pantheon, 1978.

Howell, Joseph T. *Hard Living on Clay Street.* New York: Anchor Books, 1973.

Karabel, Jerome, and A. H. Halsey, eds. *Power and Ideology in Education.* New York: Oxford University Press, 1977.

Keddie, Nell. "Classroom Knowledge." In *Knowledge and Control.* Ed. Michael F. D. Young. London: Macmillan, 1972.

Kerkchoff, A. C. *Ambition and Attainment.* Washington, D.C.: American Sociological Association, 1974.

Kerkchoff, A. C., and R. T. Campbell. "Black-White Differences in the Educational Attainment Process." *Sociology of Education* 50 (January 1977):15–27.

Kohn, Melvin L. *Class and Conformity: A Study in Values.* Chicago: University of Chicago Press, 1977.

Kornblum, William. *Blue Collar Community.* Chicago: University of Chicago Press, 1974.

Liebow, Elliot. *Tally's Corner.* Boston: Little, Brown, 1967.

London, Howard B. *The Culture of a Community College.* New York: Praeger, 1978.

Mann, Michael. "The Social Cohesion of Liberal Democracy." *American Sociological Review* 35 (June 1970):423–439.

Marx, Karl. *Capital.* Harmondsworth: Penguin, 1976.

Marx, Karl. *The Eighteenth Brumaire of Louis Napoleon.* In *Selected Works.* New York: International Publishers, 1968.

Marx, Karl, and Friedrich Engels. *The German Ideology.* New York: International Publishers, 1947.

Merton, Robert K. *Social Theory and Social Structure.* New York: Free Press, 1968.

Michels, Robert. *First Lectures in Political Sociology.* New York: Harper and Row, 1965.

Miller, Charles, John A. McLaughlin, John Madden, and Norman M. Chansky. "Socioeconomic Class and Teacher Bias." *Psychological Reports* 23 (1968):806–810.

Neal, Donald. "A Theory of the Origin of Ethnic Stratification." *Social Problems* 16 (Fall 1968):157–172.

Persell, Caroline Hodges. *Education and Inequality.* New York: Free Press, 1977.

Rist, Ray C. "Student Social Class and Teacher Expectations: The Self-Fulfilling Prophecy in Ghetto Education." *Harvard Educational Review* 40 (August 1970):411–451.

Rosegrant, Jane K. "Choosing Children." Thesis, Harvard College, 1985.

Rosenbaum, James E. *Making Inequality.* New York: Wylie and Sons, 1976.

Rosenberg, Morris. *Conceiving the Self.* New York: Basic Books, 1979.

Rosenberg, Morris. "The Self-Concept: Social Product and Social Force." In *Social Psychology: Sociological Perspectives.* Ed. Morris Rosenberg and Ralph H. Turner. New York: Basic Books, 1981.

Rosenberg, Morris, and Roberta G. Simmons. *Black and White Self-Esteem: The Urban School Child.* Washington, D.C.: American Sociological Association, 1971.

Roy, David F. "The Role of the Researcher in the Study of Social Conflict." *Human Organization* 24 (Fall 1965):262–271.

Rubin, Lillian. *Worlds of Pain.* New York: Basic Books, 1976.

Schatzman, Leonard, and Anselm L. Strauss. *Field Research.* Englewood Cliffs, N.J.: Prentice-Hall, 1973.

Schultz, Charles B., and Roger H. Sherman. "Social Class, Development and Differences in Reinforcer Effectiveness." *Review of Education Research* 46 (1976):25–59.

Scully, Maureen Anne. "Coping with Meritocracy." Thesis, Harvard College, 1982.

Sennett, Richard, and Jonathan Cobb. *The Hidden Injuries of Class.* New York: Vintage Books, 1972.

Shavelson, Richard J., Judith J. Hubner, and George C. Stanton. "Self-Concept: Validation of Construct Interpretations." *Review of Educational Research* 46 (Summer 1976):407–411.

Spenner, Kenneth I., and David L. Featherman. "Achievement Ambitions." *Annual Review of Sociology* 4 (1978):373–420.

Stinchcombe, Arthur L. *Rebellion in a High School.* Chicago: Quadrangle Books, 1964.

Suttles, Gerald. *The Social Order of the Slum.* Chicago: University of Chicago Press, 1968.

Swartz, David. "Pierre Bourdieu: The Cultural Transmission of Social Inequality." *Harvard Educational Review* 47 (1977):545–555.

Tawney, R. H. *Equality.* London: Allen and Unwin, 1938.

Weber, Max. *Economy and Society.* Berkeley: University of California Press, 1970.

Wellman, David T. *Portraits of White Racism.* Cambridge: Cambridge University Press, 1977.

Whyte, William Foote. *Street Corner Society.* Chicago: University of Chicago Press, 1943.

Willis, Paul E. "Cultural Production and Theories of Reproduction." In *Race, Class, and Education*. Ed. Len Barton and Stephen Walker. London: Croom Helm, 1983.

Willis, Paul E. "Cultural Production Is Different from Cultural Reproduction Is Different from Social Reproduction Is Different from Reproduction." *Interchange* 12 (1981):48–67.

Willis, Paul E. *Learning to Labor*. Aldershot: Gower, 1977.

Index